North U.

Weather
for
Sailors

Written by: Bill Biewenga
Edited by: Ken Campbell of Commanders' Weather
Produced in Association with Bill Gladstone and Lou Roberts, Jr.

North U.
Weather for Sailors
1st edition
Written by: Bill Biewenga
Edited by: Ken Campbell of Commanders' Weather
Produced in Association with Bill Gladstone and Lou Roberts, Jr.

ISBN 0-9724361-9-7

Additional copies available through:
North U.
29 High Field Lane
Madison CT 06443-2516 USA
800-347-2457
203-245-0727
www.northu.com

Printed in USA

Contents

Acknowledgements

For a long time I've believed that we're all by-products of our teachers. People come into our lives, present us with some new ideas or viewpoints, and we adopt and adapt them to fit our own perspective and experiences. I've heard it said that Einstein claimed to have only had two original ideas in his lifetime. I suspect we can each claim somewhat fewer. Nevertheless, I believe that we all have our own unique experiences and observations and, in their own way, they can add to the march of human progress.

In August of 1985 I took a boat single-handed from Plymouth, England to Newport, RI in an attempted speed record and as a qualifier for the 1986 Single-handed Round the World Race. At that time, I had already participated in the 1981-'82 Whitbread Round the World Race and had completed numerous trans-Atlantic passages. I knew little or nothing about how weather worked, however. During that passage of 23 days, I managed to be on the wrong side of nearly every wind shift in some of the worst weather I've encountered in the North Atlantic. Being alone, I had ample time to reflect on my need to become educated on the topic.

Now, almost 20 years and a few hundred thousand sea miles later, I don't often end up on the wrong side of a wind shift. I'm still pursuing that education on weather and how it affects us while we're sailing. In the interim I've been blessed with more than a few teachers and people who have helped me along the way – some of them among the best in the world.

First and foremost among them, I have to say that long before Bob Rice and I co-founded Weather Window in 1993, he had provided a huge amount of help to me in understanding weather and how it worked. In those early days, I may have helped him understand a bit about how sailboats operated. He definitely opened my eyes to the possibility that we don't need to be mere pawns in the middle of the ocean, moving at the whim of a mindless weather pattern. We could place ourselves in positions where the weather would actually work to our advantage! Later, Ken Campbell and George Caras added to my continuing education, years before they started their company, Commanders' Weather. Even now, they and the other meteorologists at Commanders' Weather help with an exchange of ideas as we all try to improve our understanding of how to best approach a particular situation. Not the least of the help that has been forthcoming has been Ken Campbell's efforts at editing this book. He and Frank Bohlen, an oceanographer at the University of Connecticut, have kindly reviewed this volume.

Many people have made a positive impact, however, and quite a few organizations have added to our information base. Meteorologists at the Ocean Prediction Center, especially Joe Sienkowitz and Lee Chesneau, have gladly shared their knowledge for the benefit of all of us. The maps presented here are in most cases created by the OPC. Rick Viggiano of Pro-Tech Marine has kindly provided weather satellite pictures received on his WeatherTrac receiver as well as images of Deckman for Windows sailing performance software. I've been lucky enough to cross paths with a number of meteorologists over the years who have quietly added to the ideas I've collected either from them personally or from their writings. They include – but are not limited to – "Clouds" Badham and David Houghton. Each in their own way adds to the information base that is available to us as sailors. Information for this book has been gleaned over many years and from many sources, including Bowditch's "American Practical Navigator," NOAA, NASA, the National Weather Service, and the Jet Propulsion Laboratory.

Assisting with both inspiration as well as organizational abilities, Lou Roberts and Bill

Gladstone have helped to keep this book on track, as we collectively try to convey information that is intended to help you perform your own analysis. Throughout the book, I've tried to inject my own personal perspectives learned on the water. The information contained on these pages has been put to the test thanks in large measure to the owners and teams on the boats with whom I've sailed over the years. Their faith and confidence led to confirmation that "this weather stuff" really does work to provide a competitive edge and safer, more efficient sailing. I'm grateful for having had the opportunity to work with so many talented people and

organizations. This book would be less without their many contributions. Whatever is correct in this book is due in large measure to the people above. Any mistakes I can probably take credit for myself.

The march of human progress neither started nor does it stop with me. Hopefully, you will take this information and build on it, creating your own perspectives and successes along the way. I'll look forward to helping in whatever ways I can.

Bill Biewenga

Prologue

If you enjoy any activity on the water, then you know that weather greatly impacts your passion. Weather has as many effects as there are pursuits. Sailboat racers seek an edge in picking sides of a short windward-leeward course. Offshore racers seek maximum favorable winds. Passage making sailboats seek winds aft of the beam and smooth seas. Power boaters seek smooth seas, and ideally a lack of headwinds. Windsurfers crave side shore winds with an unimpeded shore break. Weather impacts everyone who sets out on the water.

My interest in weather began at an early age. Every advantage that could be gained on sailboat racecourses was sought. At first, a VHF, TV, or newspaper weather report would suffice. Then I started calling Coast Guard Stations to have discussions about the weather reports, seeking more than the brief information provided through mass channels. As my racing became a professional avocation in the early 1990's, a core group of weather forecasting pioneers began to offer tailor-made forecasts on demand. Bob Rice at Weather Window and Ken Campbell at Commanders' Weather regularly provided custom daily faxes for top teams seeking that added edge on competitive courses. Sailors from Lasers to J-24's to IMS campaigns became hooked on these detailed daily forecasts that showed trends by the hour.

The sophistication of weather forecasting blossomed with the explosion of the Internet. Suddenly, real time radar and buoy reports became available, and dozens of sites offered detailed information. The information is available worldwide. If you're out of contact with the Internet, Single Side Band radios and inexpensive satellite systems like Iridium have placed weather information within reach of everyone, particularly voyagers. The impact is immense and daunting. How does one learn weather and learn to apply all of this information?

Back when I set out to learn weather, a few books spelled out the basics, but lacked practical application. About a half dozen of us were enthusiastic to learn, but were at a dead end. Bill Biewenga parked his sea-boots ashore for a few weeks, and determined that he'd teach us weather neophytes a thing or two. The students included solo racer JP Mouligne, renowned author of *Adrift* Steve Callahan, solo racer Bob Adams, and myself. Bill's sessions were enthralling. Our weather club enabled us to discuss and learn the application of weather to our passion. JP went on to win the Around Alone, and the rest of us learned a great deal about staying safe and using weather to our advantage.

To make sure I fully grasped my education, I've hired Bill on several occasions to sail with me on passages. As my weather 'Yoda,' I've watched in real time his teachings. There is no finer teacher. With almost 400,000 miles of ocean sailing, and four Whitbreads (Volvos) under his belt, I believe Bill has seen nearly everything. On our fourth passage together, I told Bill to simply look over my shoulder and only comment if I got something wrong. A 6500-mile passage from Cape Town to Antigua went smoothly. I felt I had graduated...finally.

You, the reader, are extremely fortunate to have happened upon this book. In it are the hard won lessons and learnings of one of the best navigators and weather forecasters on the water. I wish Bill had written this book sooner, as I know it would have sped up my learning curve. Embrace it and utilize it. Weather is there to be used to your advantage.

Peter Johnstone

Peter Johnstone is a Collegiate All-American dinghy sailor, and holds over 16 National Sailing Titles. As an innovator and businessman, he co-created the first retractable bowsprits and asymmetric spinnakers, over-hauled the Sunfish-Laser businesses, set up Edgewater Powerboats, and launched the Olympic 49er class sailboat worldwide. His latest business venture is GUNBOAT, which specializes in high tech luxury cruising catamarans. Peter and his family just spent a year cruising aboard their GUNBOAT 62', 'Tribe'. While based ashore, Peter zooms around on his 18HT (high tech 18') cat with son Nick, and follows his children's junior sailing activities.

Chapter 1
Introduction

Weather surrounds us and affects us virtually all of the time. It is a multidimensional, constantly changing variable. If we can understand how and when that change will take place, we can attempt to put ourselves in a favorable place to take advantage of those changes. At the very least, we should be able to put ourselves in a position to minimize weather's adverse effects.

Why do we care?

As sailors, we may want to win our competitions if we are involved in racing. We certainly want to reduce or minimize our risk to the crew and the boat. And ideally we would prefer to have a pleasant sail or passage. Depending on whether we are cruising on a coastal passage, racing dinghies, or trying to race boats across oceans, our priorities and how we use weather information may change, but many of the elements will remain. We are interested in safety, efficiency and comfort.

Sailing objective

In order to understand and prioritize our goals, we first need to start with a "sailing objective." What are we trying to achieve? Are we competitive long distance racers, racing for 3 or more days? Are we racing around the buoys? Are we cruising for short or long distances? Or are we trying to move a boat efficiently on a delivery?

More competitive long distance racer (multi-day)

As a competitive long distance racer who understands the weather patterns and how they will change, I may be willing to take an unfavored tack that doesn't efficiently move me toward the finish line in the short term, but takes me instead toward a very favorable weather pattern that ultimately will move me much more quickly toward my end goal. Depending on the distance of the race, I may be willing to take initial setbacks for hours or even days, knowing that I will move into a more favorable weather pattern, and my initial investment will eventually pay off over the course of the race.

Offshore If I am racing long distances and the race is primarily offshore, such as a Newport to Bermuda Race, I may not be constrained by a coastline most of the time. My choices may be more flexible because I don't have to be concerned with running out of sea room. I may not have to worry about getting to the beach before an expected wind shift comes through, forcing an unfavored gibing angle.

There can be inherent problems with being offshore during a long distance race, however. If extremely adverse weather is expected, I

CHAPTER HIGHLIGHTS

- **Why do we care?**

- **Sailing objective**

- **Using weather to accomplish your mission**

- **How do we get there?**

Each type of sailing uses weather in different ways. Long distance racers understand that weather will change over the duration of their race and will set themselves up to take advantage of those expected changes.

Inshore racers use weather information to improve their competitive edge.

Day racers use weather information to understand how the wind can be expected to shift as well as how the wind and sea state will interact with each other.

may not have the choice to put into a safe port and wait out the storm.

Coastal For long distance racing that is primarily coastal, such as in a Key West to Baltimore Race, I may have the option of putting into port if the weather is expected to be extremely severe or I suffer damage. The coastline limits some of my choices, however. For example, I can't run off indefinitely in a storm if I'm in danger of running up on the beach or confronting sharper wave patterns as the water becomes shallower.

Understanding the weather and how it will change can be critically important.

More competitive round-the-buoy racer

Competitive 'round-the-buoy' racers need to be constantly in tune with the wind shifts. Do the winds shift to the right or left as you approach the beach or weather mark? How will the wind change over the length of the day? Will that change occur as a weather pattern moves into the area, or will the change be the result of a sea breeze? Understanding what causes those changes and whether or not they will actually occur will provide a huge help in winning your day races. Throughout the course of the race, you will have an understanding of which side of the course is favored and why.

Safer, more enjoyable day sailing experience

Sailors who are cruising for the day or afternoon may have their primary focus on having a good time with a minimum number of problems. Safety and comfort may be your primary considerations. If you're taking your family on an outing, you may prefer to avoid heavy weather or rain. Even if a bit of breeze is less of a concern, you may not want to risk equipment failure. Alternatively, you may not care to go sailing on a day when there is little or no wind.

As day sailing cruisers, we can often choose the conditions in which we sail. By understanding how the weather will change throughout the day, we can be better prepared to get the kinds of conditions that will serve our own purposes. And we can avoid the conditions we don't want.

Safer, more enjoyable distance cruising

Distance cruisers should be particularly attuned to the weather and how it is expected to change. Often, as distance cruisers we may be sailing shorthanded or with crew who have a limited amount of experience in heavy weather. We may be quite a distance away from a safe port or in areas with which we are not totally familiar.

Offshore Cruising great distances offshore, we may have limited resources to handle heavy conditions or prolonged light weather. If unforeseen problems arise, we may be too far from port to effectively sail or motor there. Understanding how the weather will change can help us prepare by making for port or by preparing to deal with the sailing conditions we will expect.

Coastal Coastal cruising allows us to make some decisions to put in if ports are close at hand. But in relatively remote regions such as

Greenland or parts of Canada or Alaska, safe havens may be days away. If the weather gets heavy, we may also be faced with steeper seas in the relatively shallow coastal areas.

Understanding our options and how the expected weather change will affect those options can be crucial to experiencing a safer, more enjoyable cruise.

Maximize efficiency on a long distance delivery

Boat deliveries combine aspects of both long distance racing and long distance cruising.

On one hand, the passage needs to be kept efficient since there is often a time factor. Either the crew is paid by the day or the owner of the boat would like his vessel in a certain place at a certain time.

On the other hand, safety and maintaining the equipment are both high-priority criteria. Getting the boat to its destination in a timely manner, but putting the crew at risk and breaking equipment are undesirable if not unacceptable results.

Understanding how the weather can act to safely speed the passage along while minimizing risk is crucial to keeping the delivery efficient as well as reducing the possibility of injury or damage.

Whether racing, cruising or delivering a boat, all sailors are interested in safety, improving their efficiency and enjoying the sport. Understanding how to apply weather information to our own objective will help us each achieve our own set of goals.

Using weather to accomplish your mission

Once you have identified your sailing objective and the assets and liabilities you have at your disposal, you need to apply the concepts of climatology, meteorology and oceanography to the task in order to tilt the odds of success in your favor.

Applying concepts of climatology, meteorology, and oceanography

Climatology will help you to understand the average weather conditions in a particular area. You can set waypoints for a passage from California to Hawaii six months before departure if you understand the normal conditions.

The waypoints will probably need to be moved just prior to and during the passage due to the actual conditions you expect in near real time. *Meteorology* will tell you what is about to happen or is currently happening. With a 96 hour surface forecast you'll have a better idea of where you want to be in four days than you would have if you just possessed climatological averages.

Further modifying the meteorological information, you will want to be aware of currents and tides and how those *oceanographic* features affect the route you're considering and the weather you expect to encounter.

Gathering relevant meteorological data

In order to understand how the weather will affect your sailing, you will need to collect the relevant analyses and forecast material. These may include the current surface analysis chart for your area, the 24 hour, 48 hour, and 96 hour surface forecast maps as well as the 500 mb analysis chart. Additional information such as text forecasts and satellite imagery will help to confirm and add other information to the charts.

On those occasions when we're caught in heavy weather, understanding how weather evolves over time will help us to understand how to best deal with the situation, either getting into more suitable conditions or making for port.

Interpreting gathered data

After we have gathered the relevant weather data, we will begin to analyze and interpret the information. We will do that several different ways in order to achieve a more thorough understanding of the information as well as to accomplish several different things. By comparing and contrasting the information in different ways, we can also learn how to get a better idea of how accurate the information may be.

Taking appropriate action to accomplish your sailing objective

With the weather information understood, we will be able to take the appropriate course of action to accomplish our desired objective, whether that is improving our racing skills, having a safer, more enjoyable cruise or moving a boat more efficiently on a delivery.

How do we get there?

This is how we will gain an advantage from the weather.

❶ We will begin to understand the fundamental concepts of weather and forecasting – moving from large scale (global) principles to small scale local variations (Chapter 2 - Global Climatology, Chapter 3 - Synoptic Scale Meteorology, Chapter 4 - Local Conditions). These two chapters constitute the theoretical foundation needed before we can apply the practical effects of weather to your sailing objective.

❷ We will acquire an understanding of how those concepts are relevant to weather conditions (Chapter 5 - How Global Climatology, Synoptic Scale Meteorology and Local Conditions Relate to Each Other). We begin to transition to more practical knowledge in this chapter.

❸ We will learn how and where to gather, interpret, analyze, and evaluate weather-related data (Chapter 6 - Gathering Data).

❹ We will learn how to apply that knowledge to our decision-making process (Chapter 7 - Decision Criteria).

❺ Finally, we will take a look at the services that professional weather routers provide (Chapter 8 - The Role of "Weather Routers").

Chapter 2
Global Climatology

If we ask the question, "What creates weather?" there can be quite a few quick answers. Atmospheric pressure. The jet stream. The spinning of the earth. But the underlying principal cause is the sun. The sun's rays create heat. The heat hits the earth in an uneven way, and that temperature differential creates differences in pressure. The initial cause is heat, so we'll begin our discussion there.

Temperature differential

On a global scale, temperature differences are caused by how the earth revolves around the sun as well as how the earth spins on its axis.

Earth rotation

We can look at the earth, spinning on its axis, tilted 23.5 degrees on the plane in which it rotates around the sun. As the earth rotates, London comes into daylight. Later New York, San Francisco, Hawaii, Auckland, Sydney, and so forth come into daylight.

Earth orbit

During the vernal equinox, the equator is the part of the earth closest to the sun. As the earth orbits the sun, and northern hemisphere winter approaches, the sun tracks directly overhead of latitudes south of the equator. On or about December 22nd the sun is directly over the Tropic of Capricorn. As the earth continues to revolve around the sun, on March 22nd the sun is directly over the equator again, marking the vernal equinox. And on or about June 22nd the sun is directly over the Tropic of Cancer. It marks not only the longest day in the northern hemisphere (the shortest day in the southern hemisphere), it also marks the furthest north that the sun is directly overhead on earth. The sun hasn't changed its position. Rather, the earth has changed its orientation to the sun. That change in orientation as the earth orbits the sun gives us the seasons. The change in orientation to the sun as the earth spins on its axis gives us day and night. When orbital changes are done in combination with the earth spinning on its axis, the earth's surface and its atmosphere is heated in a way that is constantly changing. The temperature differential provides us with weather.

Pressure

Here is what happens on a large, broad scale. Think back to the vernal equinox when the sun is directly over the equator. The sun beats down, heating up the surface of the earth. The hotter, less dense

Looking at the Earth rotating, we can see that landmasses spin from left to right.

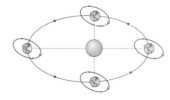

The Earth orbits the sun while rotating on its axis.

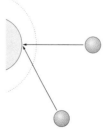

As the seasons change, the angle of the sun to the Earth's atmosphere and surface also changes.

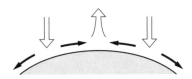

As the sun's rays warm the surface of the earth, air rises, causing a lower pressure. Air converges at the lower elevation. As the air cools at upper levels, it sinks, causing a higher pressure. Air rushes away from the higher pressure, causing divergence.

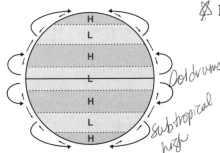

Weather is caused by the sun beating down on equatorial regions, causing air to rise, migrate toward the poles and sink. The diverging air is again warmed, rises and migrates towards the poles. These Hadley Cells result in regions of predominant high and low pressure around the globe in both Northern and Southern Hemispheres.

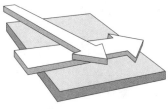

Air moves in 3 dimensions. It moves up and down as well as in a horizontal direction. And air at different altitudes as well as on the surface moves at different speeds and in different directions.

air in the equatorial regions begins to rise. As it rises, there is less pressure on the surface of the earth. Rising air creates lower pressure. This is a concept that will occur many times throughout the study of weather.

As the air rises higher in altitude, it begins to migrate toward the poles, away from the warm equator. Due to cooling, the air begins to sink, creating areas of higher pressure that surround the globe as well as the subtropical jet stream that circles the globe. Cooler, denser air sinks, forming higher pressure. Around the earth, in both the northern and southern hemisphere, these regions of higher pressure are known as "sub-tropical high pressure systems." They exist generally between 25 degrees and 35 degrees north and south latitudes. In the northern hemisphere they have been nicknamed "horse latitudes" and are characterized by generally lighter winds.

High pressure

High pressure is characterized by:

❶ Cold air

❷ Sinking air, large area of clear skies

❸ Diverging air – Air wants to get away from the higher pressure. We can think of air trying to rush out of a balloon blown up to capacity.

❹ Strongest winds are away from the center of the high pressure and where the pressure differential is greatest over a given distance.

❺ Lightest winds are near the center of the high pressure and where pressure differential is minimal over a given distance.

Low pressure

Low pressure is characterized by:

❶ Mix of warm and cold air

❷ Rising air and large area of clouds – at least broken clouds

❸ Converging air – Air wants to migrate towards the lower pressure.

❹ Strongest winds are near the center of the low pressure.

❺ Wind speeds generally diminish as you move away from the low pressure.

Air movement

It's important to realize that in the atmosphere air moves in three dimensions. It moves vertically – up and down – as well as in a horizontal direction. A "surface weather map" tells us what the weather is going to do along one plane – the surface of the earth – and how the weather will move horizontally. An "upper atmosphere weather map" tells us what the weather is doing aloft, perhaps between 15,000 and 20,000 feet above sea level. Just as the weather often differs from one point on the earth's surface to another, the air movement varies as we go up in the atmosphere.

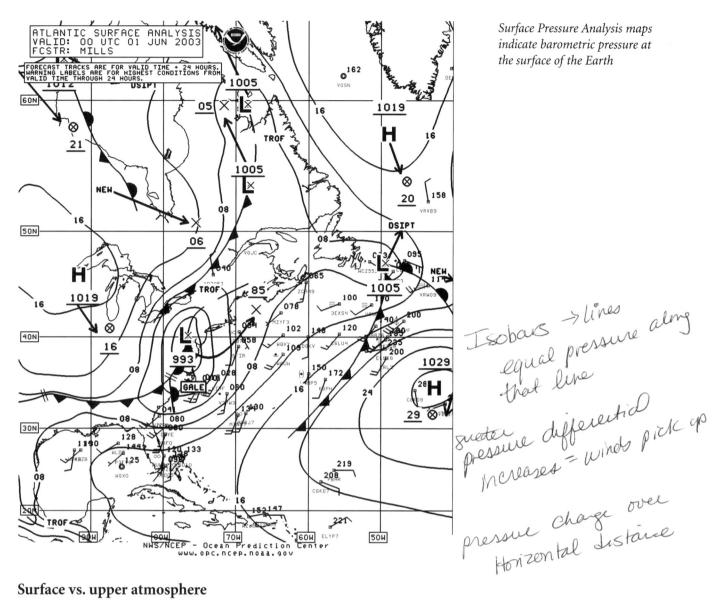

Surface Pressure Analysis maps indicate barometric pressure at the surface of the Earth

Isobars → lines equal pressure along that line

greater pressure differential increases = winds pick up

pressure change over Horizontal distance

Surface vs. upper atmosphere

A surface pressure map tells us what the barometric pressure is at various locations on the surface of the earth. The pressure is measured in mb (millibars), hPa (hectopascals) or inches of mercury. For most marine weather maps we use mb.

We can think about surface pressure as a force that is exerted on the face of the earth. In a high pressure area, there is more force exerted downward than there is in a low pressure area. But that force is still measured on the face of the earth. The isobars on a surface weather map will tell us how pressure changes over horizontal distance. The numbers represent millibars.

Upper atmosphere charts use a different convention. The numbers that are indicated on a 500 mb analysis, for example, are actually height contours. The numbers on the chart/map tell us the height at which weather balloons reach 500 mb of pressure. The number that is indicated on the chart, "564" for example, actually represents 5640 meters above sea level. It's like reading a topographical map, showing peaks and valleys representing the constant pressure of 500 mb.

500 mb Analysis, upper atmosphere charts indicate height contours at which the pressure is a given reading.

Upper Atmosphere chart measure heights not pressure 4x day baloon goes up

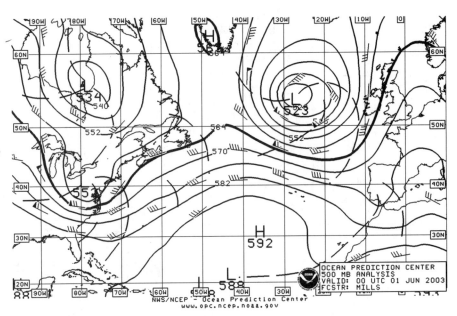

This information helps us understand how height and pressure vary relative to one another. It helps to give us a three dimensional view of the earth's weather.

The weather at the surface is not the same as the weather in the upper atmosphere. However, as we'll see later, the weather of the upper atmosphere helps to direct and influence the weather that develops at the surface. For this reason, the 500 mb charts are important forecasting tools.

Jet stream

The speed, direction and development of the surface weather systems are greatly influenced by the jet stream. To locate the jet stream, take a 500 mb weather chart and, during the late fall, winter, and early spring, color between the 546 and 552 mb contours. During the late spring, summer and early fall color between the 564 and 570 mb contours.

The core of strongest winds, which reach from 75 knots to 150 knots, will be between 15,000 and 20,000 feet. The jet stream, located along the maximum horizontal temperature contrast, directs the movement and development of highs and lows at the surface. The actual jet stream may be located further up in the troposphere (the earth's lowest layer of atmosphere) between 200 mb and 300 mb. The jet stream moves warm air north and cold air south, producing, transporting, and affecting the energy package that causes the development of extra-tropical low pressure systems.

Keep in mind that the lines on a 500 mb chart are actual height contours. You will notice that generally the numbers are lower as you go further to the north (closer to the pole). When a loop dips down toward the south (toward the equator) in the Northern Hemisphere, an upper atmosphere trough is indicated. Conversely, when a loop in the colored lines dips toward the north (toward the pole), an upper atmosphere ridge is indicated.

The jet stream is a current of air that circles the globe with the strongest currents between 15,000 and 20,000 feet. During the late spring, summer, and early fall, the jet stream is often located near the 564 contour.

Why is this important? They help locate surface high and low-pressure systems. Surface low pressure systems are found on the east side of the troughs. Surface high pressure is found under or on the east side of the ridges. Generally, the narrower the band between the lines that are colored, the faster the system will move and the greater the potential energy it has. The wider the band, the slower the system will move and the less potential energy it has.

The surface weather systems will generally move at between 25% and 50% of the wind speed indicated on the 500 mb charts. The surface wind speeds will be approximately 40% of the wind speeds indicated on the upper atmosphere charts. These, of course, are mere approximations, and a great deal will depend on which quadrant of the surface system one is located and on microclimate local conditions.

You can think of this upper atmosphere stream as a sort of "hose" of air. If you constrict the diameter of the hose, the stream moves faster. If the hose diameter is wider, the stream moves more slowly. In the case of the jet stream, the surface systems are kind of dragged along by that flow, even though the surface systems are at a lower altitude and the actual jet stream is located at a higher altitude.

Amplitude

Another upper atmosphere factor that affects the speed and strength of a surface weather system is the "amplitude" of the 500 mb troughs and ridges. You can think of the amplitude like a sine curve. Flat, parallel contours represent a low amplitude system and a high frequency wave pattern indicates a high amplitude weather pattern.

Low amplitude weather patterns indicate fast moving, weak weather patterns.

High amplitude weather patterns indicate slow moving, strong weather patterns.

How that particular amplitude is structured can also have an effect on the speed and strength of a system. A positive tilt upper level trough can imply a fast moving, weak surface low pressure system, while a negative tilt 500 mb trough will indicate a slower moving but stronger surface low pressure system.

Coriolis

Another factor that affects the movement of air is the Coriolis Effect. This force has been generally misunderstood and isn't everything it's cracked up to be. It isn't the force that causes water to rotate down a drain in one direction. What's important to remember about the Coriolis Effect is over time the Coriolis force causes a moving body, in our case the wind, to turn to the right in the Northern Hemisphere or to the left in the Southern Hemisphere. What's important is that the earth must have enough time to move for the forces to have an effect. The wind shifts in direction to the right about 4 degrees per hour. A toilet flushes too quickly for the earth to have any effect on the direction the water goes down the bowl. Instead, how the water enters the bowl determines which way it circulates.

Low amplitude - relatively straight & generally associated with fast moving but weak surface features

High Amplitude - often associated with slow moving - strong weather systems.

The amplitude is the range of fluctuation. An upper level, low amplitude jet stream is one that is relatively straight and is generally associated with fast moving but weak surface weather features. High amplitude jet stream aloft is often associated with slow moving, strong weather systems at the surface.

The Coriolis Effect causes a parcel of air moving from higher to lower pressure to move to the right in the Northern Hemisphere and to move to the left in the Southern Hemisphere.

   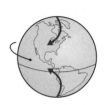

The technical explanation of the Coriolis Effect is as follows. The Coriolis force acts because a moving body on a rotating disk conserves its initial tangential velocity when it moves and changes its distance to the axis of rotation. On a global level, the rotating disk is the earth and the distance to the axis of rotation is about 3,500 nm at the equator. The earth's tangential velocity at the equator is about 900 knots. A second point, say at 45 degrees North latitude, has less distance to go and only has to travel at 650 kts, or 250 kts slower. If you stood at the equator and sent a parcel of air toward a point due North at 45 N, after one hour you and the parcel would move 900 nm to the right while your aiming point would only have moved 650 nm. Eventually, you would miss it to the right. Likewise, if you stood at 45 N and aimed towards the equator, after one hour you and the parcel would have moved only 650 nm while your aiming point would move 900 nm. Again, you would miss it to the right. The earth must have enough time to move for the wind to start turning due to the Coriolis force, however. It is not something that is significant over a few moments.

Another way to conceptualize the Coriolis Effect is to think of a globe (Earth) spinning on its axis. Superimpose a hypothetical "ruler" just above the surface of the globe. As the globe spins on its axis under the ruler, draw a line on the surface of the globe along the edge of the ruler from the North Pole to the equator. You will see that the line curves in a clockwise direction. From the perspective of the North Pole, it curves to the right.

If we think back to the effects of pressure, we realize that air moves from high pressure toward lower pressure. The state of the atmosphere is seeking equilibrium but, because of a variety of factors (the sun heating the earth, the daily spinning of the earth, the earth's orbit around the sun, and so forth), the air pressure never equalizes around the planet. But the air still seeks to move from higher pressure toward lower pressure. As it does so, the air tends to spin in a clockwise (to the right) direction around the high pressure system in the Northern Hemisphere.

Returning to our example of the globe spinning under the hypothetical ruler, if we were to draw a line from the South Pole to the equator, we would see that the line curves to the left or in a counter-clockwise direction in the Southern Hemisphere. As air moves from high pressure to lower pressure in the Southern Hemisphere, the Coriolis Effect bends that direction in a counter-clockwise direction.

Hence, air flows around a high pressure system in a counter-clockwise direction in the Southern Hemisphere.

Again, the only thing that is important to remember is that over time a moving body turns to the right in the Northern Hemisphere and left in the Southern Hemisphere. Air, going from high pressure toward low pressure, bends to the right in the Northern Hemisphere and to the left in the Southern Hemisphere. Later, when we look into interpreting weather charts, we will see that this is essentially the same thing as saying that air flows in a counter-clockwise direction around a Northern Hemisphere low pressure system and in a clock-wise direction around a Southern Hemisphere low pressure system.

Friction

Friction slows the movement of air. The coefficient of friction – the amount of friction or its total effect – varies over different surfaces, just like a greasy surface is smoother than a dry, rough surface. Friction is greater over land, for an example, than it is over water. Friction, always present to some degree, slows the movement of air and affects trajectories or the direction of flow.

Since air is trying to move from high pressure toward lower pressure and Coriolis Effect in the Northern Hemisphere is trying to bend that direction to the right, friction, in its effort to slow that movement, acts in the opposite direction. Friction causes the air to move to the left in the Northern Hemisphere and toward the right in the Southern Hemisphere.

The effects of friction can be seen on the large global scale. As wind circulates around a surface low pressure system, the influence of friction causes the air to turn in from the isobars toward the low by 15 or 20 degrees rather than blowing directly in line with the isobars. That is essentially the same as saying that it turns away from the high-pressure center by about 15 or 20 degrees. Higher in the atmosphere, where the effect of friction is lower on a 500 mb chart, you will notice that wind directions travel in much the same direction as the contours. Even if the air at different altitudes is blowing in somewhat different directions, air streams flowing across other air streams have a lower coefficient of friction than air flowing over either water or land.

In addition to understanding air flow on a global or synoptic scale, these will also be important concepts as we get into studying sea breezes and how they affect us on a local level.

Wind shear

Wind, of course, does not always blow in the same direction or at the same speed. In some areas, the change of wind speed and/or wind direction is more abrupt. The boundary between the quick change in wind speed or direction as we move horizontally or vertically results in significant shear within and between the air masses. One such area of significant shear is near the jet stream.

If you were in a high altitude balloon trying to cross an ocean, you might want to get into the jet stream in order to take advantage of the airflow in the jet stream. However, getting into that airflow can be

Why does this happen? Clockwise around No. Hemisphere High

As air descends, creating a high pressure area, it diverges from the center, rotating to the right in the Northern Hemisphere due to the Coriolis Effect. As air rises, creating a low pressure system in the Northern Hemisphere, converging air rotates left - opposite to that of the high. Friction on the surface of the earth tends to bend the air left, toward the low and away from the high.

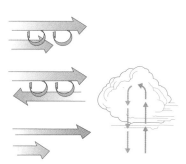

 Wind shear creates turbulence along the boundary layer. It can take place between air currents traveling at different rates, in different directions in both horizontal and vertical directions. Shear also is caused by distinctly different air masses such as warm air aloft over a cold air mass along the surface of the water.

quite tricky. Just below the jet stream, wind speeds may be 40 or 50 knots. Inside the jet stream, the flow may be closer to 100 knots, and the direction may have a similarly radical shift. As the balloon tries to enter the jet stream, the top of the balloon may be quickly pushed in one direction while the gondola tries to move in another. If the transition isn't fast enough, the top of the balloon could be sheared off, causing a catastrophic failure.

Because of the rapidly changing wind conditions at different altitudes, wind eddies along the shear line can be manifested as turbulence.

Wind shear also takes place at lower altitudes. Another prime area for wind shear is when relatively warm air moves over cold, calm air near the ground or ocean surface. The cooler, denser air sets up a boundary layer, and the air flow differs between the layers. We often see those conditions in the spring when water temperatures are cold and in the morning before the sun has had the opportunity to warm the air at the lower levels.

Wind shear can take place in the vertical plane as well as the horizontal. As wind rises in a cloud, it can cool at higher altitudes, causing the cooler air to sink. If the cloud is developing and the air forms a convective flow, the different airflows can set up a shear line.

If we are sailing through a cloud's wind shear and into a downburst, the changes in wind speed and direction can be extremely sudden and dramatic.

Seasonal variations

Air changes its movements through the seasons. The earth orbits around the sun, tilted on an angle of about 23.5 degrees relative to the orbital plane. The sun goes from being directly over the equator at the fall equinox, to being over the Tropic of Capricorn at the winter solstice, to being over the equator again at the spring equinox and over the Tropic of Cancer during the Northern Hemisphere's summer solstice.

With the change in position of the sun relative to the earth's surface, the location of highest heating also changes. As the area of highest heating moves south or north, the whole global weather pattern shifts south or north. During the Northern Hemisphere winter, as the sun tracks further to the south, the subtropical high pressure system is displaced further to the south. The jet stream moves to the south, and the track for the migratory low pressure systems moves to the south. The reverse is true in the Southern Hemisphere.

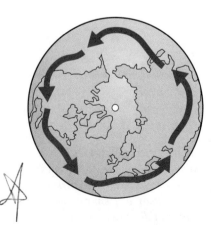

As seasons change, the jet stream and other weather systems move further to the south in the winter and further to the north in the summer.

The cooler temperatures during the winter also lead to generally higher pressure readings for the surface high and low pressure systems.

Oceanography

There is an undeniable and complex interrelationship between oceanography and climatology. On the large scale, trade winds and prevailing winds drive the formation of ocean currents. Currents, such as the Gulf Stream, go on to affect the climatology of Northern Europe.

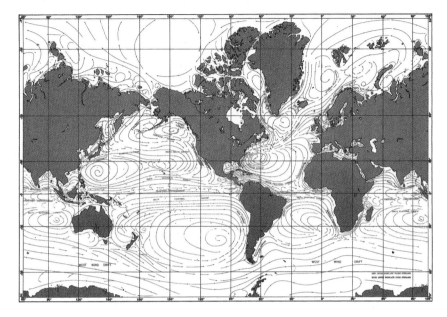

In the large scale, ocean currents are primarily caused by trade winds and the prevailing winds.

In the case of the Gulf Stream, the Northeast Trades of the North Atlantic push warm water toward the Caribbean. As the water continues to warm, it sort of "squirts" up between eastern Florida and the Bahamas reaching flow speeds of up to 5 knots. The volume and speed of the Gulf Stream is such that it continues across the northern part of the North Atlantic and eventually bifurcates into two main branches, one going north past Ireland and the other going south past Portugal.

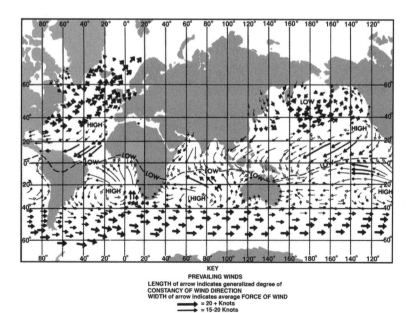

Generalized winds of the world for January and February show stronger winds in the Northern Hemisphere among other distinctions. The length of the arrow indicates wind direction consistency, and wind strength is indicated by the thickness of the arrow.

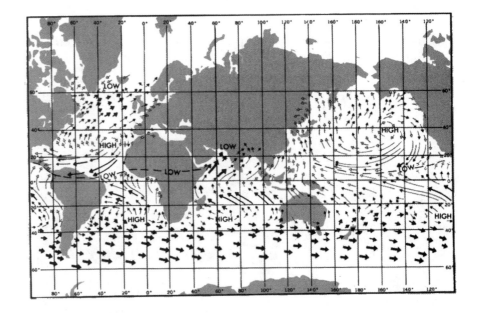

Generalized winds of the world for July and August show how winds change on average from winter months. Compare the winds of the world to the location and direction of the currents of the world.

It is said that there is more water in the Gulf Stream than in all the fresh water lakes, rivers and streams of the world. In one weather briefing it was also said that the Gulf Stream has the water force of 3,000 Mississippi Rivers. The amount of water in the Gulf Stream and its warm temperature have a significant effect on moderating the temperatures of Northern Europe.

Oceanographic features also vary by year. El Niño is one such example of an oceanographic feature that varies from one year to another. It is due to a cyclical weather pattern in which the western Pacific trade winds fail.

El Niño occurs about every 3 to 5 years. It varies in proportion to the failure of the trade winds. The greater the failure of the trade winds, the stronger the effects of El Niño. Warm water normally pools in the western Pacific, pushed there by the trades. When the trade winds fail to develop sufficiently, the warm surface water tends to "slosh" back toward the east and is more uniform across the Pacific.

Because the western Pacific waters are cooler than normal during an El Niño year, the overall air pressures in those areas tend to be higher. Remember that cooler temperatures yield higher pressures. And since the water temperatures of the eastern Pacific are warmer, the pressures in the eastern Pacific tend to be lower.

During the 1997 – '98 El Niño, the largest ocean temperature departure from the norm ever recorded was measured. There was record rainfall in Peru and drought in Brazil – just the opposite of the norm. The record high pressure in Indonesia accompanied an abnormally dry summer. Hurricanes in the eastern Pacific were more frequent than usual, and they were more violent. Meanwhile, there was virtually no hurricane activity in the North Atlantic. There was record rainfall in California, and record high temperatures from N. Dakota to New England. Then, during the summer of '98, the weather was hot and dry in the northeastern U.S. and more hurricanes occurred.

Why do I care?

As sailors, we may seem rather removed from the "big picture" concepts of global climatology. We're not. We are affected both directly and indirectly. Understanding the large scale and the underlying principles of weather will help us to improve our performance as well as increase our safety.

If there are record rainfalls in the Sierra Mountains of California, it will affect the currents of San Francisco Bay. If there is drought in Georgia, the currents off Savannah will be changed from a normal year.

Whether you are a dinghy sailor getting ready for an Olympic campaign or a cruiser preparing for a passage across an ocean, understanding the global patterns and norms will help you understand how the synoptic scale weather and local conditions change those patterns.

As an example, during one work-up period 6 months prior to a Trans Pac Race, a climatological study was undertaken to determine how wind speeds and directions would be affected during a post-La Niña summer. Looking at the anomalous features, resources were more effectively allocated toward sail development and keel configuration.

It may seem obvious that sailors on long passages need to have an understanding of climatology. Whether racing or cruising, understanding the big picture helps us all, each in our own way.

Even buoy racers benefit from understanding what normally occurs in a region and how one set of conditions either reflects that norm or deviates from it.

In another example, during a year long study of currents prior to the Olympic sailing events held off Savannah, GA, it was determined how critical inland rainfall was in determining current over and around sandbars lying near the race course. It's necessary to understand the norms and the information on which they are based before looking into the deviations from the norm.

Additionally, many of the principles involved with large scale weather features occur again and again in smaller scale and in different ways. As example, warm, less dense air rises, causing lower pressure. Cold, dense air sinks, causing higher pressure. That is a principle that forms part of the basis for global weather patterns.

On a smaller scale, knowing that cold air is more dense than warm air, we can begin to understand that significantly colder air will exert more force on our sails, sheets and rigs for a given wind speed than warm air. Colder air is denser than warm air. It has more mass for a given volume than warm air. Think "rubber or plastic bullets vs. spent uranium projectiles going through the side of an armored vehicle." Yes, gear blows out, chafes and breaks at a lower wind speed in the cold Southern Ocean than it does in the tropics. Understanding the principles on the global level will help us understand it on the synoptic and local levels.

Transition from global climatology to synoptic scale meteorology

When we understand the basic concepts of global climatology, it is easier for us to understand how synoptic scale meteorology affects us. We begin to understand how we can avoid or take advantage of the positioning of the various climatological features. If we're trying to avoid a low pressure system, we begin to have an understanding of where to find a high pressure system.

Chapter 3
Synoptic Scale Meteorology

Synoptic scale meteorology is the size and duration of most of our weather forecasts. It may go out into the future as far as 8 or 10 days, and it may cover continental sized areas. The size and duration may vary but, essentially, it is what can be reasonably predicted. Generally, we can get pretty good information from a 4 or 5 day forecast.

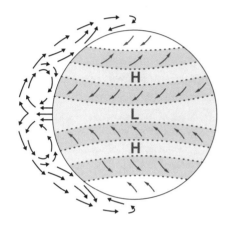

We learned that warm air rises over the tropics, migrates towards the poles, sinks, diverges, warms, rises and again migrates towards the poles to create Hadley Cells, high and low pressure regions, and winds that are different both at the surface and aloft. In synoptic scale meteorology we will look at how those high and low pressure regions interact with each other.

As we get closer to the time that the forecast is expected to take effect, we can expect that the reliability of the forecast will increase. As we narrow the geographic size of the forecast, we can assume that it will also probably be more relevant to our own situation.

HIGH AND LOW PRESSURE SYSTEMS

Weather varies in the horizontal plane. As an example, the weather in Iowa is different from the weather in Ohio at any given time. High and low pressure systems in the horizontal plane affect one another, but they are not necessarily the same.

In a somewhat different way, weather over the vertical dimension also differs. There are upper atmosphere as well as surface high and low pressure systems. Wind speeds and directions as well as temperatures and relative pressure locations are different on the surface than they are at upper atmosphere levels. They are interrelated and affect each other, but they are not necessarily the same.

Upper atmosphere

The upper atmosphere charts serve as a guide and a way to confirm surface forecasts. The jet stream, troughs and ridges will indicate which way the surface systems will travel and how they may develop as discussed earlier.

Upper atmosphere maps often refer to the 500 mb level. The lines represent the height at which a barometer carried aloft by a balloon would record the altitude. Hence, the lines are height contours. The 564 contour refers to 5640 meters above sea level and is the one that is generally associated with the jet stream during the late spring, summer and early fall.

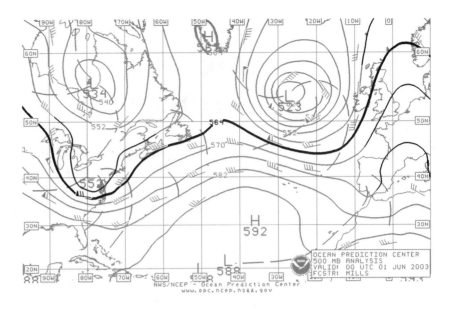

One very general rule of thumb is that surface lows may travel 300 to 600 nm north of the 5640 500mb contour line. Some caution is urged, however, when using rules of thumb. Cut off lows – explained below - can provide one of the exceptions to that rule.

Upper level lows help us to understand the intensity and movements of lower level lows but they are not necessarily on top of the lower level surface low pressure systems. The ridges – coming up from the highs – and the troughs – dipping down from the polar regions – will move and undulate generally from west to east.

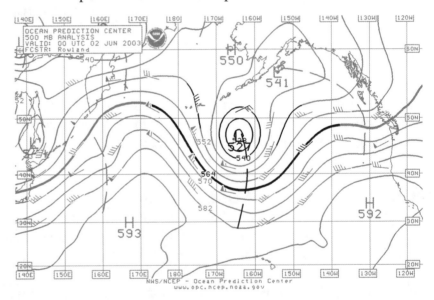

Movement of high and low pressure systems

The upper atmosphere height contours will undulate across the chart over time. They change their shape, proximity to one another and intensity. Troughs may dip lower toward the equator or recede back toward the pole. Ridges may extend upwards toward the pole as they get stronger, or they may recede.

As the upper atmosphere changes its shape and strength, it will affect the weather below it even though the upper atmosphere lows and highs are not stacked on top of the surface lows and highs. *Blocking ridge* An upper atmosphere blocking ridge can extend toward the pole and disrupt the westerly flow of shorter wave patterns. The shorter waves may be deflected in the Northern

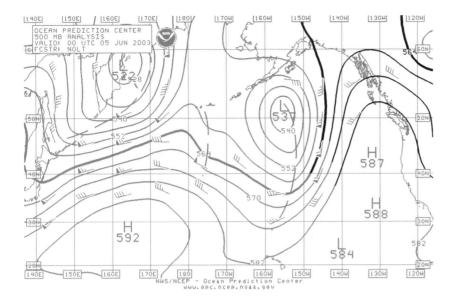

An upper atmosphere blocking ridge can be an example of a high amplitude wave in the jet stream. It will serve to slow down or stop a surface low pressure system approaching from the west, guiding it toward the pole.

Hemisphere in a northerly or northeasterly direction. In the Southern Hemisphere, the shorter wave patterns would be directed in a southerly or southeasterly direction.

The blocking ridges in the upper atmosphere tend to slow the progress of surface lows and direct them toward the poles in many cases.

Occasionally, however, if the blocking ridge is amplified enough, shorter waves may try to dip toward the south in the Northern Hemisphere, diving under the blocking ridge and splitting the westerly flow in the upper atmosphere.

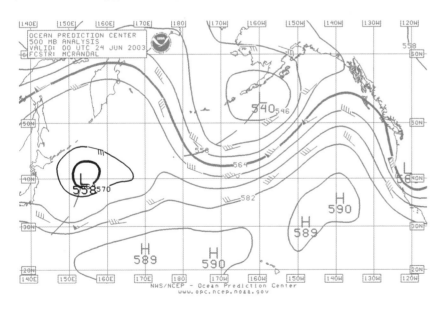

A cutoff low can remain in one general location for an extended period of time because it often lacks the guiding force of the jet stream. Surface lows may also be present, creating an extended period of time during which the weather is generally rainy. They most often occur during the spring or fall as the jet stream is moving north or south with the seasons.

Cutoff lows If the upper atmosphere is sufficiently amplified, an upper level low pressure system may develop on the southern boundary (in the Northern Hemisphere) of the westerlies. If the main body of the jet stream recedes back to the north, it can leave the low cutoff from the westerly flow, creating an upper atmosphere "cutoff low."

Cutoff lows can create havoc on surface weather systems. The systems tend to persist for days or even weeks. Winds can tend to be stronger than usual and from atypical directions.

Cutoff lows tend to form during the spring and fall seasons when jet stream flows are in transition, moving toward the south in the winter and back to the north during the summer.

During one trans-Atlantic passage during April, an upper atmosphere cutoff low had been formed over the Azores. For a couple of weeks, a surface low pressure system persisted in the vicinity of the Azores, creating rainy weather and re-directing the Northeast Trades to a more northerly and northwesterly wind direction as we tried to sail far to the southwest of the Azores.

Surface

Surface weather patterns are dragged, pushed or directed by the upper atmosphere winds and systems. Since we live on the earth's surface, that is the weather we are most directly concerned with. But, it is the upper atmosphere weather that will help us to understand what is happening or going to happen.

Using upper atmosphere information to track surface high and low

Since the upper atmosphere affects the movements and developments of the lower atmosphere systems and vice versa, we can learn quite a bit about how surface systems will move by studying the configuration and changes taking place in the upper atmosphere.

Surface lows will always be found on the eastern side of upper level troughs. Surface highs will always be found either south (in the Northern Hemisphere) or to the east of upper level ridgelines. You won't find a surface low pressure system on the western side of an upper level trough.

Those systems will move at varying rates and become more or less severe. Some hints about the development of surface lows can be

500 mb Analysis, Valid 00 UTC, 01 June, 2003. Note the shape and location of the trough coming down from the north and extending over the eastern Great Lakes. The jet stream located near the 564 contour will help guide surface low.

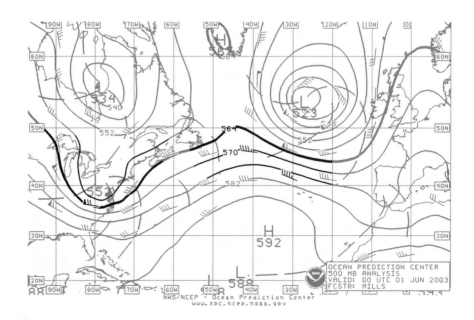

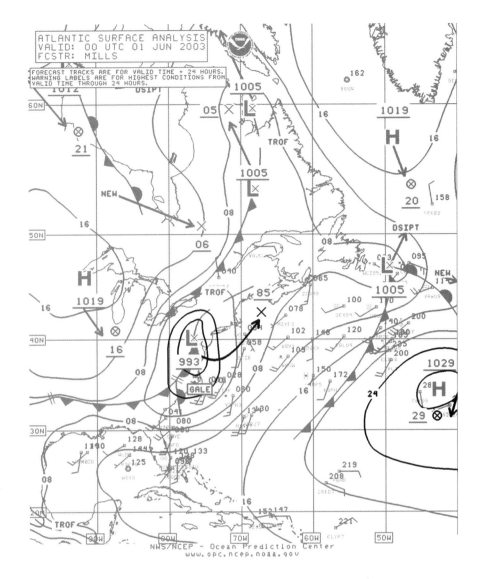

Atlantic Surface Analysis, Valid 00 UTC, 01 June 03. Note that the Surface Analysis for the Western North Atlantic for the same time frame indicates that there is a surface low pressure system at the bottom right of the trough indicated on the preceding 500 MB Analysis map. The arrow on the Surface Analysis chart indicates where the low will go over the next 24 hours, and it will be guided there by the jet stream indicated by the 564 contour line in the preceding 500 MB Analysis map. Note also how the surface high pressure system relates to the upper level high pressure system. They are in similar but not the same position.

gleaned from the tilt of the trough. Positive tilt upper level troughs (those that slant easterly as they point toward the pole) will generally be conducive to fast moving, weak surface low pressure systems. Negative tilt troughs will generally be associated with slow moving, strong surface low pressure systems.

The storm track for surface systems is generally located between 300 and 600 nm north of the 5640 upper level 500 mb line in the Northern Hemisphere.

Surface low pressure systems move at about 1/3 to 1/2 of the wind speed indicated at the upper level. And the surface wind speeds will be about 40% of the wind speeds aloft.

If you look at the contours of the upper level charts, some of them will be closer together than others. The contours that are closer together imply that the wind speeds are higher. A greater pressure difference over a given distance or the same pressure reading over a correspondingly smaller distance translates roughly to the same result: more wind. There is less wind indicated aloft when the contour lines are further apart. Since the surface systems are moving at a relative percentage of the winds aloft, the more closely packed the contours on the upper atmosphere charts, the faster the surface systems will generally be moving.

Storm development

Storms come in a couple of different varieties: extra tropical and tropical. The extra tropical storms are generally the ones that we find north of the subtropical high pressure systems, and usually they have associated fronts. The tropical storms are usually the ones we find in tropical regions. Those are not their major or deciding characteristics, however. They each have their own distinctive characteristics and development patterns.

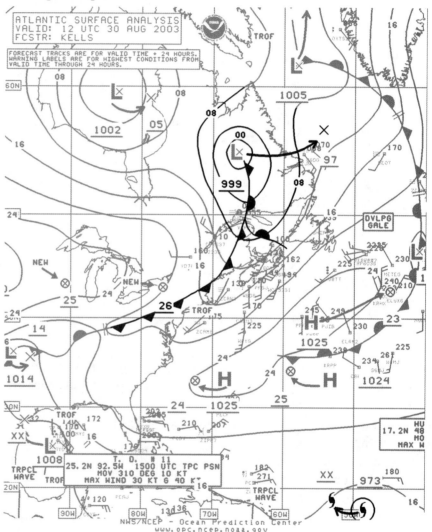

Atlantic Surface Analysis with an extra-tropical low pressure system indicated on the upper part of the chart and a tropical low pressure system – a hurricane in this case – indicated in the lower right hand corner forming in the tropics. Note the size difference.

Extra-tropical low pressure systems

Extra tropical low pressure systems are usually the migratory systems that are often created north of the sub-tropical high system in the Northern Hemisphere or south of the sub-tropical high of the Southern Hemisphere.

Characteristics An extra tropical low pressure system requires a strong temperature contrast at the surface of the earth. On a local level, remember that during the winter there is a stronger temperature gradient along the warm Gulf Stream than during the summer.

Additionally, an extra tropical low requires a strong, high amplitude jet stream above the surface, transporting cold air rapidly south (in the Northern Hemisphere) and warm air rapidly to the north. In the Southern Hemisphere, the southern jet stream would carry cold air to the north (towards the equator in the Southern Hemisphere) and warm air to the south (towards the pole).

A large package of energy is also required at 15-20,000 feet to encourage mixing.

Extra tropical lows are less common during the summer. They are weaker and colder during those warmer months, and they are located further to the north as the jet stream is also located further to the north during the Northern Hemisphere summer months.

Dissect extra-tropical low into quadrants A stereotypical extra tropical low pressure system can be drawn into quadrants, each with its own particular set of wind directions, cloud cover, and typical conditions. By understanding these stereotypes we can gain a partial understanding of where we are located in a system if we experience a particular set of conditions.

Initially, extra-tropical low pressure systems can start out as secondary lows along an existing front. Cold, dense air is on the northern side of the Northern Hemisphere warm front and warm, relatively moist air on the southern side. There is a large temperature gradient between

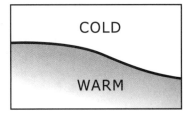

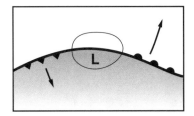

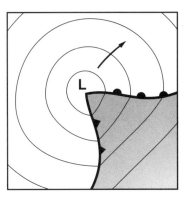

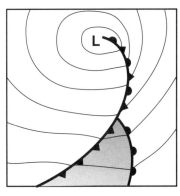

This is how extra-tropicals form, develop and decay over time. The top illustration shows 2 distinctly different air masses, often created when cold air is introduced by the jet stream. If upper atmospheric conditions are conducive, the boundary area will begin to rotate, with the cold air moving toward the warm and the warm toward the cold. As complete rotation continues to evolve, the cold air mass will begin to overrun the warm.

Stereotypical extra-tropical low pressure systems can be roughly divided into quadrants, each with their own characteristics. They are associated with fronts because extra-tropical lows are a mixture of cold and warm air masses.

As low pressure systems occlude and decay over time, the area of greatest wind is often further away from the center of the system. In younger low pressure systems, the greatest winds are often closer to the centers.

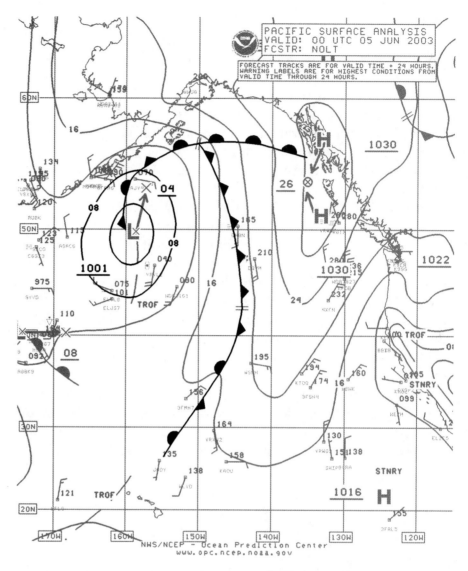

Remotely sensed images, such as the illustration at right of a QuikSCAT image, would show that the wind speeds are lower near the center and greater at the edges in the above occluded low pressure system.

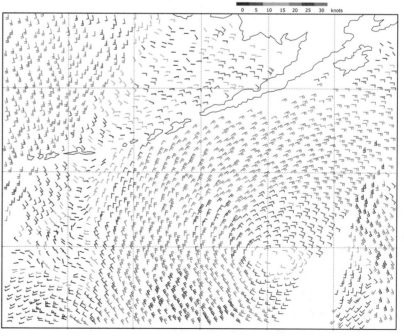

the two air masses. As clouds gather and counter-clockwise circulation begins, the cold air is brought south (in the Northern Hemisphere) and the warm air is brought north (in the Northern Hemisphere), toward the northeast.

As the system matures and circulation grows, the air masses attempt to displace each other along their respective fronts. The extra-tropical system continues to develop in size and perhaps deepen in pressure. As it ages and begins to break down as an occluded low pressure system, the temperature gradient diminishes and wind speeds drop closer to the center of the low.

Tropical lows & storms

Tropical low pressure systems are considerably different from extra-tropical systems. Their characteristics not only differ, the requirements necessary to create a tropical low pressure system are also different from extra-tropicals.

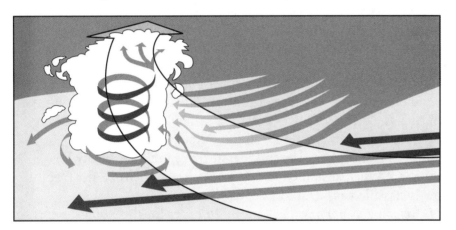

Tropical low pressure systems require warm moist air, an unstable air column that allows the warm air to rise, swirling in a counter-clockwise direction in the Northern Hemisphere. For them to fully develop, upper level wind shear should be absent. Wind speeds aloft should be relatively minimal.

Characteristics For tropical low pressure systems to fully develop, they require a deep layer of warm ocean with temperatures over 80 degrees Fahrenheit. Colder temperatures will create an environment in which tropicals begin to fall apart. They need a heat source and water vapor at their base.

Tropical lows also require converging surface winds. The winds will begin to swirl in a counter-clockwise direction in the Northern Hemisphere.

They require an unstable atmosphere. Air must be able to rise and fall as the air heats up at the surface and cools as it gets higher in the atmosphere. The warm and humid atmosphere must go up to at least 15-20,000 feet. And there must be no wind shear in order that the convective forces at work over the vertical in the unstable atmosphere can act unimpeded.

Wind shear at higher altitudes would serve to limit the development of tropical systems by "ripping them apart" when they get high enough to encounter the wind shear. The presence of something like the jet stream would serve to limit or stop the formation of a tropical system. And there should be high pressure at 25-30,000 feet. The presence of all of these factors will serve to build huge thunderstorms and increase the intensity of the tropical system.

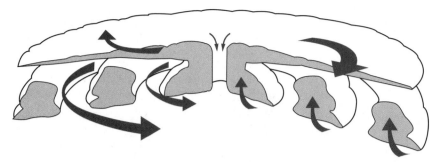

As tropical lows evolve into hurricanes or typhoons, convective action takes the warm air aloft as the system spins in a counter-clockwise (Northern Hemisphere) direction. Wind speeds are at their peak along the eye wall. Aloft, most of the air circulates while some smaller amounts pour back down inside the eye of the hurricane.

Development of tropical low pressure systems During the initial stages of a tropical low pressure system, there will be a disturbed area with clusters of thunderstorms. In the Atlantic, as an example, the clusters could be along a tropical wave that originates in northwest Africa or along an old cold front that can occur anywhere from Cape Hatteras to the Bahamas into the Gulf of Mexico. There will also be the presence of an associated upper level low. When in conjunction with the thunderstorms, the upper level low could take place anywhere west of 40 degrees W and from the Gulf Stream south.

Development into a tropical depression As the tropical low pressure system develops into a tropical depression, the thunderstorms organize, and an area of low pressure forms. The thunderstorms converge towards the center of lower pressure. In the Northern Hemisphere, the thunderstorms spiral in a counter-clockwise direction. In the Southern Hemisphere, the thunderstorms spiral in a clockwise direction. When sustained winds are less than 35 MPH, the tropical low is classified as a tropical depression.

Development into a tropical storm In order for the tropical depression to continue to develop and become a tropical storm, the inflow of thunderstorms and warm humid air must increase. The pressure continues to fall, and sustained wind speeds must exceed 35 MPH. At that point, in the North Atlantic, a tropical storm is named.

Although naming protocols vary in other parts of the world, in the N. Atlantic and both the Eastern and Central North Pacific, each storm is named alphabetically beginning with "A" for the first storm of the new calendar year. In the Western North Pacific, the alphabet is not restarted at the beginning of the new year. Rather, the alphabetical process proceeds through "Z" and restarts at "A" without regard to calendar years. Additionally, some parts of the world refer to storms as "tropical cyclones."

Development into a hurricane With cloud and warm, humid air inflows continuing to build, center pressure continues to drop. An "eye" is likely to form at the center of the low pressure system. Tropical systems become classified as hurricanes when sustained winds reach 74 MPH.

How tropicals diminish in strength Because there are various elements that go into building the strength of a tropical depression, storm or hurricane, if any of these critical elements are removed, the systems can lose some or all of their strength.

As winds exceed 74 mph, tropicals are classified as hurricanes in the North Atlantic and Eastern Pacific. Over warm water they generally travel at relatively low speeds, but as they reach land or colder water, they can greatly increase the speed at which they travel while diminishing in overall strength.

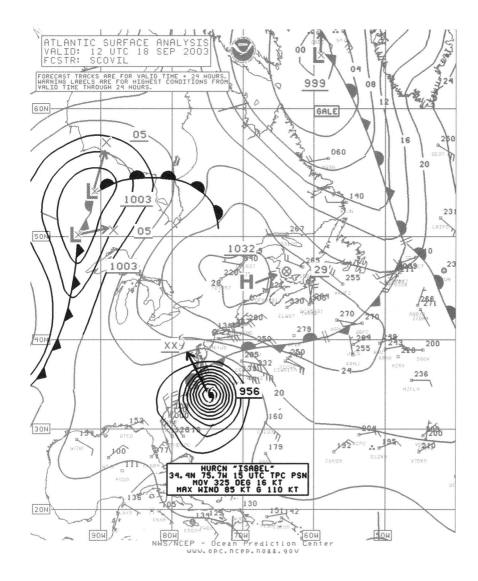

ATLANTIC SURFACE ANALYSIS
VALID: 12 UTC 18 SEP 2003
FCSTR: SCOVIL

FORECAST TRACKS ARE FOR VALID TIME + 24 HOURS.
WARNING LABELS ARE FOR HIGHEST CONDITIONS FROM
VALID TIME THROUGH 24 HOURS.

HURCN "ISABEL"
34.4N 75.7W 15 UTC TPC PSN
MOV 325 DEG 16 KT
MAX WIND 85 KT G 110 KT

NWS/NCEP - Ocean Prediction Center
www.opc.ncep.noaa.gov

Tropical lows, such as Hurricane Isabelle, do not have fronts as extra-tropicals do. Even large hurricanes such as Isabelle are small when compared to extra-tropicals. As tropicals move over land or into colder waters, they can join with extra-tropicals, bringing their warm moist air to join with the mixture of warm and cold air found in extra-tropicals.

As a hurricane goes over land, as an example, it loses its primary source of energy – the warm ocean. Warm air is often replaced by cooler air. Additionally, the increased friction over the surface of land slows the inflow of energy into the convective system. Dry air is introduced, instead of the more moist air of the ocean, so fewer clouds are created. And strong wind shear will tear the vertical structure of the storm apart.

Tropicals can move into cooler regions and join with extra-tropical systems As hurricanes get into colder water they lose a great deal of their concentrated strength. But they can also tend to gain speed over the ground as the systems move forward. In the North Atlantic, as an example, wind speeds may diminish, but the systems can speed up as they pass south of New England and recurve toward Europe. Hurricanes that had been traveling at 5 to 10 knots with over 75 to 150 knot winds may now have wind speeds less than 60 knots but travel at 30 knots or more. As a result, it becomes increasingly important for the mariner to frequently monitor the progress and direction of tropicals that have adopted extra-tropical qualities.

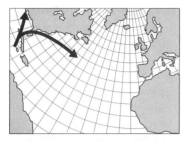

Early season hurricanes in June primarily are spawned in the Caribbean or Gulf of Mexico.

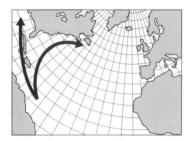

In July, hurricanes begin to form a bit further east and south of the Caribbean.

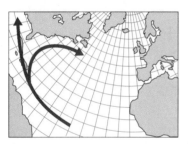

As the water continues to get warmer in the Northern Hemisphere tropics, August hurricanes start their formation earlier in the cycle as weather approaches from the African coast.

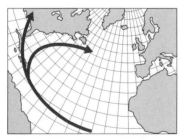

September is the most prolific month for hurricane formation in the North Atlantic. Water temperatures have reached a peak, and formation generally starts further to the east than in other months.

Hurricane Tracks in the North Atlantic Although tropical storms have been recorded in the North Atlantic in every month of the year, and hurricanes have only been absent during the month of April, the primary months for tropicals are during the late summer. That is when the water is the warmest and wind shear at its minimum.

Where hurricanes tend to form in the North Atlantic and how they tend to track, however, vary somewhat with the month. These are general trends, however, and not at all forecast routes. Each tropical will take on its own characteristics of development and track.

Hurricane tracks in the North Atlantic: June Considered early in the North Atlantic hurricane season, June tropical storms and hurricanes frequently form in the Caribbean Sea or Gulf of Mexico. Their tracks generally take them into the Gulf States or across Florida and up the North American East Coast as they recurve towards Europe.

Hurricane tracks in the North Atlantic: July Still somewhat early for the North Atlantic hurricane season, July tropical storms more frequently begin their formation a bit further to the east than the June storms. Tracks often take the tropicals into the Gulf States or northerly along the North American East Coast before they recurve toward Europe.

Hurricane tracks in the North Atlantic: August With the peak of hurricane season approaching and the water temperatures of the tropical North Atlantic continuing to rise, August tropical storms and hurricanes form further to the east. They can form as far east as 40 degrees W. latitude or more. With the eastern formation, the hurricanes have more time to recurve back toward Europe without making landfall in North America.

Hurricane tracks in the North Atlantic: September September is the peak month for hurricane formation in the North Atlantic. Water temperatures are among the warmest of the year. There is relatively little wind shear present compared to other times of year, and clouds are plentiful.

The hurricanes often begin as tropical waves undulating their way off the northwestern coast of Africa. Formation can take place as far east as 30 degrees W. latitude, giving the tropicals a great deal of distance to develop and/or begin a recurve toward Europe prior to reaching the Islands of the Caribbean or North American continent.

Hurricane tracks in the North Atlantic: October As temperatures begin to cool the water in the tropical North Atlantic, hurricanes and tropical storms tend to again form somewhat further to the west or in the southern parts of the Caribbean. This is not meant to imply that

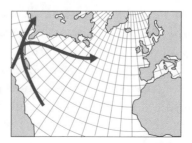

As the water begins to cool somewhat in the tropical North Atlantic, October hurricanes tend to form further to the west than in September.

they are less dangerous or potentially less destructive. Merely it is meant to say that climatologically, their main areas of formation and frequency are changing.

Hurricane tracks in the North Atlantic: November Early November is often considered the "end" of hurricane season. Skippers departing North Atlantic bound for the Caribbean often feel that the danger of tropicals or hurricanes is past. It isn't. Remember that the only month in recorded history that doesn't have a hurricane in the North Atlantic is April – and that month has had a tropical storm recorded as recently as 2003!

With North Atlantic water temperatures continuing to drop in November, storm formation occurs more often in the Caribbean.

Late season hurricanes tend to have somewhat erratic paths. Or, perhaps, another way of looking at it is that, with relatively little data from past late season tropical storms, their paths tend to be somewhat difficult to predict. The hurricane that formed near Jamaica and went "backwards" into the trade winds several years ago, going over the British Virgin Islands, St. Maarten's, and Antigua from the west towards the east, was a late season hurricane. Their tracks are difficult to predict and they should be given a wide berth.

Tropical cyclones in oceans other than the North Atlantic In areas of the world's oceans other than the North Atlantic, hurricanes often exist under a different name. Hurricanes of the Eastern Pacific are named alphabetically starting at the beginning of the year with "A" as in the North Atlantic. In the Western North Pacific names continue through the alphabet without starting at "A" with the start of a new year. Thus the first hurricane – actually called a "typhoon" – of the year in the Western North Pacific could easily begin with any letter of the alphabet.

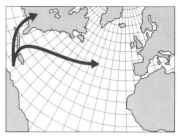

Although November is often considered the end of hurricane season, other months can also see late forming hurricanes. The area of formation is generally moved west from earlier months as the water continues to cool in the tropical mid-Atlantic.

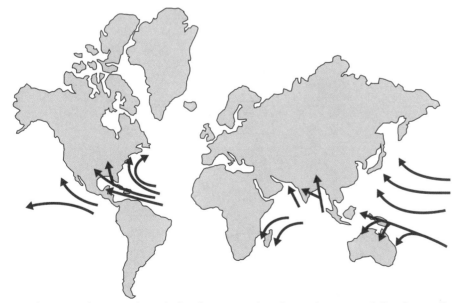

Hurricanes, typhoons and tropical cyclones occur in other regions around the planet, of course. In all cases, their development relies on warm water as an energy source, wave-like patterns in the pressure gradient to encourage circulation, moisture, and relatively little wind shear aloft.

Hurricanes do not occur in the South Atlantic under any name, but they do in most of the other oceans of the world.

Eastern North Pacific Unlike the North Atlantic Ocean, the North Pacific Ocean typically has two distinct high pressure systems due to its large size. Climatologically, the Eastern North Pacific has its high pressure system located between 35 and 45 degrees N/130 to 150 degrees W. The Western North Pacific's high pressure system is generally located between 30 and 45 degrees N/150 to 170 degrees E.

Hurricanes of the Eastern North Pacific usually form off the western coast of Central America. They move north westerly towards the Mexican Baja Peninsula. They also move westerly toward the Hawaiian Islands and can continue on up between the two high-pressure systems.

Western North Pacific Commonly referred to as "Typhoons," the tropicals of the Western North Pacific generally originate in the warm tropical waters of the Western Pacific, curving up toward the Philippines, S.E. Asia and as far north as Japan.

Super-typhoons are terms applied to systems with a center pressure below 920 mb.

The western Pacific can create numerous typhoons. In extreme cases, Super-Typhoons can take place with center pressures below 920 mb.

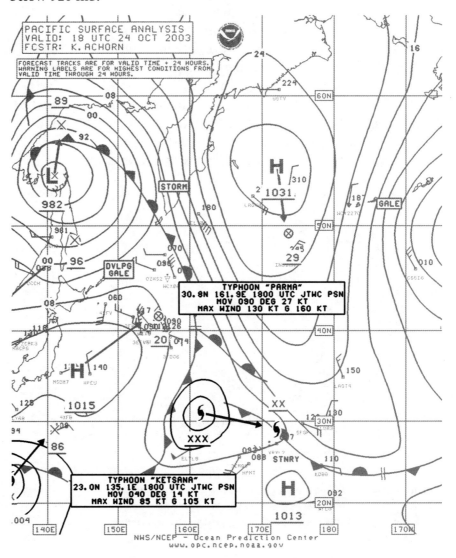

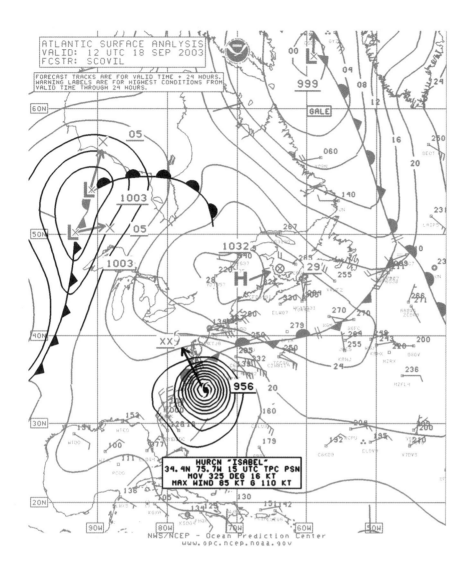

Size matters. As sailors, we may be able to dodge around an oncoming hurricane if we have advanced knowledge of its track. Extra-tropicals, however, may be so large that there is no way we can maneuver around them. Hurricanes, however, have so much wind due to the huge pressure gradient that being caught in them can lead to disaster. And with the rapid shift in wind direction, the sea state can be equally horrific.

South Pacific Like the North Pacific, the South Pacific has two separate high pressure systems. The Eastern South Pacific High is generally located between 30 and 45 degrees S/90 to 120 degrees W. And the Western South Pacific High is generally located between 30 and 45 degrees S/160 to 170 degrees E.

Tropical cyclones in the South Pacific track westerly often starting out in or near the Coral Sea and moving towards Fiji, New Caledonia, and as far south as the Tasman Sea and New Zealand as well as in between the South Pacific Highs.

As in the Northern Hemisphere, tropical cyclones occasionally curve into an area of an extra-tropical storm and merge, losing their tropical characteristics but adding moisture and force to the extra-tropicals.

South Indian Ocean The Southern Indian Ocean has two separate high pressure systems. The eastern system is generally located between 30 and 45 degrees S/90 to 110 degrees East. And the western system is generally located between 30 and 45 degrees S/50 to 70 degrees E.

In the South Indian Ocean, tropical cyclones curve west southwesterly, toward Madagascar and southwestern Africa as well as between the two high pressure systems.

Indian Ocean In the Northern Indian Ocean, there is no strong or persistent high pressure system. The track for tropical cyclones takes them along the eastern and northeastern Indian subcontinent's Bay of Bengal as well as along the western coast's Arabian Sea.

Differences between tropical storms and extra-tropical storm systems

Tropical and extra-tropical storms are different by nature. The characteristics that kick them off, sustain them or lead to them diminishing in strength are all different. Because of their differences, we can treat them differently as well. With severe tropical cyclones or hurricanes, our only hope may be to route around them. With large extra-tropicals, the size of the system may eliminate that option. Here are some of the basic differences.

Tropicals Tropical storms (or tropical cyclones) are warm storms. They feed on warm air and energy from warm water. They intensify because of warm, moist air. The warmer and moister the air, the more the storm intensifies, assuming that upper atmosphere wind shear is not an inhibiting factor.

Tropicals generally are 100 nm to 400 nm wide. The strongest winds are closest to the center of the system. They can have a very distinct eye. And they do not have fronts associated with them.

Extra-tropicals Extra-tropical systems are a mixture of warm and cold air. They intensify because of the mixture of warm, moist air with cold, dry air. The greater the temperature contrast, the stronger the storm. As a result, there can be occasions when a warm, moist tropical storm recurves to the north and mixes with an extra-tropical system containing cold, dry air. The added warm, moist air from the tropical system introduces a greater temperature contrast to the new combined system and the whole entity has extra-tropical characteristics.

Extra-tropical systems are often 500 to 1,000 nm across. The strongest winds are generally located away from the center of the storm, especially as an extra-tropical system gets into a more advanced development stage.

Barometric pressure changes tell a story Barometric pressure readings taken at the earth's surface tell a story about the nature of a particular system. Barometric pressure refers to the pressure the atmosphere exerts on a particular point. The pressure can be measured in inches of mercury, millibars (mb) or hectopascals (hPa). One mb equals one hPa.

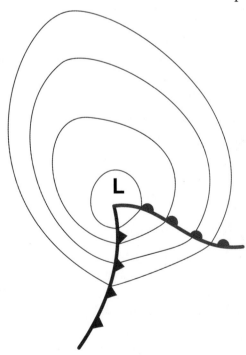

Each isobar around a surface low pressure system represents equal pressure. As the pressure changes faster over a given distance, the greater the pressure differential. The result is that the closer the isobars are, the greater the wind speed. The shape of the isobars tells us the approximate wind direction.

As depressions or storms approach, the barometric pressure drops. The rate at which it drops tells us how steep the pressure gradient is. The larger the pressure differential over a given distance, the greater the amount of wind there will be.

It's a bit like putting air in a balloon. If there is no more air "packed" into a balloon than in a room, there is no reason for the balloon to shoot around the room. On the other hand, if there is a lot of air blown into a balloon – and the pressure gradient is therefore greater between the air in the balloon and the air in the room – the balloon will have a great deal of air rushing out of it.

A barograph measures barometric pressure over time. As time advances, the pressure is recorded, giving us an idea of how fast the pressure is dropping as a system approaches or passes us. Larger storms, traveling at the same rate, of course take longer to approach and move away. The slope of the track on a barograph tells us how fast the pressure is changing. The steeper the slope, the faster the pressure drop, and generally the greater the wind speed.

From the two comparative barograph readings (both taken about 40 nm from the centers of the two storms), we can see that the "Super Storm" was not only a larger storm than Hurricane Bob, it was also longer lasting and had a deeper center pressure. We can deduce that wind speeds may have been somewhat similar between the two systems from the slope of the barograph's lines for each system.

Storms from a sailor's perspective

I suppose that on one hand it may seem like it doesn't matter much what kind of a storm you're in if it's blowing 50 knots. Actually, though, it does matter.

The resultant wind will often create the same kind of characteristics regardless of whether the system is tropical or extra-tropical. The Beaufort Scale describes how the weather actually looks in a marine environment.

If you're in mid ocean, knowing that the storm approaching is tropical, you know that it will weaken over cold water, although there is a good possibility that the overall speed of the system will increase. You know that it is relatively small in size, and you may be able to get away from the worst of it by putting some distance between you and the tropical. You also know that there aren't any fronts to add to the complications.

If you're in an enclosed waterway, such as Chesapeake Bay, you know that as the tropical storm goes over land it will probably weaken also. The heat energy from the warm water will be eliminated and the increased friction of the land's surface will slow the movement of warm air into the system. The tropical will probably still have a great deal of rainfall associated with it because it has picked up a great deal of warm, moist air. Winds may still be substantial, but there is a good probability that the system will weaken over land unless it combines with an extra-tropical system.

Tropical storms are a bit like the proverbial "needle in the haystack."

They're small, but if you happen to sit on it, it will have all of your attention.

Extra-tropicals are different. While the tropical may affect a relatively small amount of coastline at any one time – say a few hundred miles – an extra-tropical can pummel half of the East Coast of the U.S. or much of the British and French coastlines if the system is in that part of the world.

Extra-tropicals don't tend to lose strength over land in the same way that tropicals do. And because they contain cold, dry air, they behave differently over warm currents, especially in the wintertime. The greater temperature contrast can cause a relatively bad extra-tropical storm to become horrific on the Gulf Stream in the late fall or winter.

Winds

One way to categorize conditions is by sea state, as in the Beaufort Scale. Another way to categorize the severity of a storm is by wind speed.

Wind is caused by changes in temperature that lead to changes in pressure and density of the air mass. This physical phenomenon takes place on the global scale as air moves around high and low pressure systems. It also occurs down to the mesoscale and even local scales. Changes in wind speed and direction don't just occur along the horizontal plane as a front approaches, as an example.

Winds can come from aloft as well as along the horizontal plane
Wind conditions change over the vertical, as well. For example, as higher altitude northwesterly winds come down over the southern Connecticut coastline, they may descend as they get over the waters of Long Island Sound, creating sudden gusts in what had been previously a calm day at the surface. Ascending or descending air is said to be vertically unstable.

A wind blowing from the shoreline to offshore will frequently be very puffy. These puffs, or increases in wind speed, occur when the stronger wind speeds aloft, 500-2,000 ft above the earth's surface, flow down to the surface. These puffs are most frequently seen near warm shorelines and over warm waters, such as the Gulf Stream or East Australian Current.

Strong winds Strong winds are created by large differences in pressure or temperature occurring over relatively short distances. On a surface pressure map, they're indicated by closely spaced isobars. The pressure changes a great deal over a relatively small distance. The jet stream is usually the strongest along the greatest temperature gradient.

Strong winds approaching from the horizontal Strong winds approaching on the horizontal plane include approaching cold fronts or areas in which strong low pressure systems push up against strong high pressure systems. In one case we may have cold air mixing with warm air, and in the other case we may have large pressure differentials, often directly associated with temperature changes as well.

Strong winds approaching from the vertical We may also have strong winds literally descending upon us. Towering cumulus clouds can set up their own convective systems in which warm, moist air rises, cools

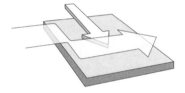

Winds not only can approach us from the horizontal, they can also come from aloft.

Winds that come from aloft are often puffy and inconsistent, potentially leading to some surprises.

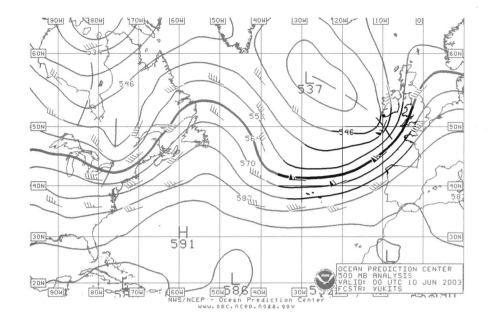

The jet stream is often located along the greatest temperature contrast. As temperature changes, so does the pressure. As the pressure increases at a given altitude, the location of the 500 mb reading gets higher in altitude.

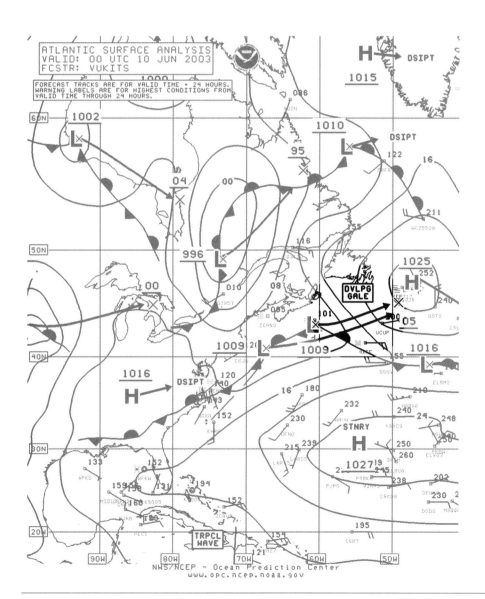

As upper level charts show a high amplitude jet stream as above with tightly packed contour lines, surface charts can show low pressure systems coming up against high pressure systems, creating tightly packed isobars and pressure gradient. The result is a great deal of wind at the surface.

Chapter 3: Synoptic Scale Meteorology **35**

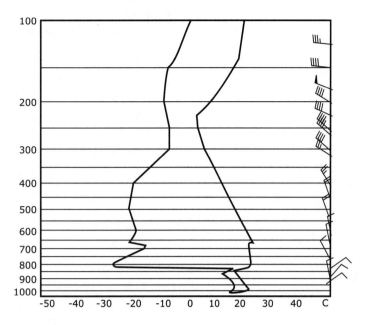

Skew-T diagram with pressure on the left Y-axis as the reading moves aloft. Wind speed and direction is indicated on the right as the readings move aloft. The horizontal X-axis is temperature. Note the radical temperature shift at 800 MB of pressure and the rapid wind shift at that altitude.

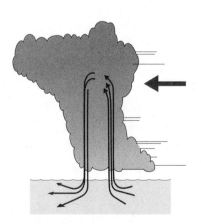

Even on the microclimate scale, high winds can approach us from aloft as warm rising air in a cloud is rapidly cooled and the colder, denser air suddenly rushes down and out at the surface.

at higher altitudes and sinks as cold, dense air. If the cloud is high enough, and the convective system strong enough, downbursts can occur at the base of the cloud. Often a quick drop in the barometric pressure will precede these types of squalls or squall lines.

An example of strong winds approaching in both the horizontal and the vertical planes is a cold front approaching the Gulf Stream in the early winter. The front may have 35 knots of wind associated with it as it travels over cold slope water of the North Atlantic. As the cold front gets over the warm water of the Gulf Stream, the cold, dense air associated with the cold front suddenly begins to sink from higher altitudes over the relatively warm, less dense air associated with the Gulf Stream. In this case, the combined effect of strong wind in the front and dropping air from aloft can create 50 knots of surface wind or more along the north wall of the Gulf Stream.

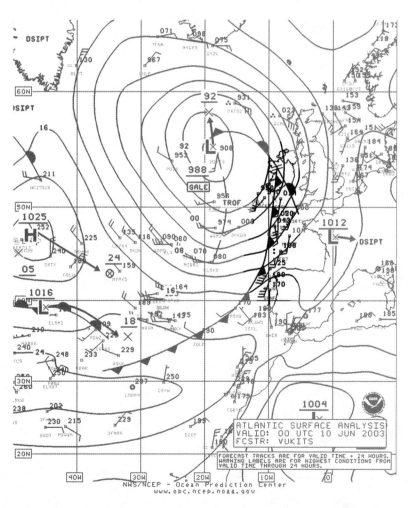

Conditions aloft can favor the creation of large-scale winds at the surface.

Light winds Light winds imply that there is relatively little pressure differential and/or very stable air. Light winds exist in a number of places and under a variety of conditions.

Light winds approaching in the horizontal plane Most of us realize that near the middle of a high pressure system there is relatively little or even no wind. In a large high pressure system, the area of little or no wind can extend for quite a distance – up to hundreds of miles.

Light winds also occur along the surface ridgelines associated with highs and other areas where there is little pressure differential over great distances. During one regatta on Lake Michigan, weather maps indicated only 1 isobar between Chicago and the Canadian border. That implied that there was only 4 mb of pressure differential for hundreds of miles. Needless to say, the water was like glass with winds calm. Although most U.S. weather maps adhere to a convention of 4 mb of pressure difference per isobar, not all foreign maps use the same gradient.

We're also aware that in the middle of hurricanes – inside of the eye – there is often a relatively calm area. In fact, relative calm is also experienced in the middle of quite a few low pressure systems. If the low is coming straight toward you and the middle of the system over-

Marine inversion layers can be identified by the light wind and low level hazy conditions of the sky. Inversions often take place in the presence of cold water, when temperatures aloft are relatively warm. See graph on previous page.

There are numerous regions of light winds including the center of high pressure systems, along ridgelines, between two adjacent low pressure systems – called "cols" – and along stationary fronts. Even the centers of older dying low pressure systems can have relatively light winds.

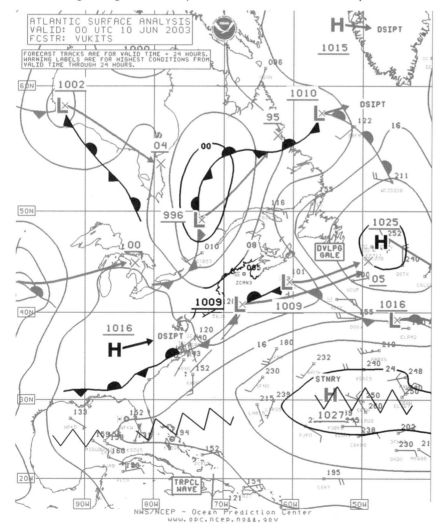

runs your position, you will often experience the calm in the middle of the system, followed by a sharp wind shift – approximately 180 degrees from what it had been prior to the calm – and a sudden increase in the wind. Those characteristics, while considerably less pronounced, are somewhat similar to those that happen with a hurricane.

Areas between adjacent low pressure systems can also be very calm. Referred to as "cols," the saddle-like ridgelines that exist between lows can provide unexpected calms in the middle of two back-to-back storms with their resulting confused seas.

On a much smaller scale, clouds passing overhead can also provide light air under their centers. Like mini-low pressure systems, the clouds set up their own circulation, leaving a zone of relative calm in the middle.

Light winds caused by conditions overhead – in the vertical plane
Light winds can be present even when ships' observations may indicate otherwise.

Marine inversion layers and/or wind shear can set up when there are exceptionally hot days, cold water and/or stable air overhead. General conditions may include hot, hazy days up to the inversion layer, perhaps 500 feet aloft.

Alternatively, a heavy marine layer with significant wind shear can set up in the presence of very cold water. Even in mid-North Atlantic, with 15 to 20 knots of wind being recorded at the masthead, there can be a completely glassy sea surface with no wind down on the deck. Ships, taking their observations from the bridge, may record 15 to 20 kts of relatively warm wind, while down where we sail, there's barely wind to maintain steerage.

While wind may exist only a few hundred feet away in both of these circumstances – a few hundred feet overhead – conditions can persist until something acts to change the situation. Usually, the catalyst for change is either sufficient warming by the sun to make the air temperatures in the two bands more homogeneous, or more wind aloft that will mechanically force the two bands to mix together.

Wind direction tells the story when combined with pressure Wind is caused by pressure gradients or "differences" in atmospheric pressure. The pressure gradients cause air to flow from an area of high pressure to one of relatively lower pressure and to be turned around a weather pattern by the Coriolis force, a deflection of the wind caused by the earth's rotation under the air mass. In the Northern Hemisphere, wind will rotate around a high pressure system in a clockwise direction, and in the Southern Hemisphere it will rotate in a counter-clockwise

Northern hemisphere

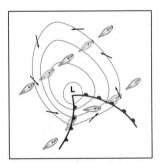

Southern hemisphere

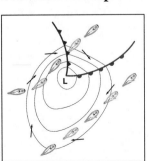
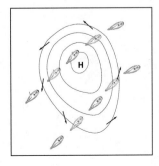

Wind speed and direction change as a boat is placed in different parts of a weather system. The proximity of the isobars tells us about the wind speed, and the shape of the system tells us about the wind direction

direction while toeing out about 15 degrees away from the center of the High and towards a Low. Conversely, wind in the Northern Hemisphere will rotate around a low pressure system in a counter-clockwise direction and in a clockwise direction in a Southern Hemisphere Low.

Since a barometer measures the amount of pressure, we can track the comings and goings of the various weather patterns by watching the rise and fall of the pressure readings. Like a depth sounder for the atmosphere, if we know that we're along the 1020 mb isobar, we can see how the weather system is progressing over our position. A baro-graph provides a running graph of that rise and fall in pressure, while a barometer simply measures the current reading. Gradient wind speed is generally a function of how great the pressure differential is, or, stated another way, how fast the barometric pressure rises or falls over a given distance. Looking on a weather fax map, the rate of change will be indicated by the relative proximity of the isobars on the map. The closer together the isobars, the greater the pressure differential and the greater the expected wind speed.

As the wind swirls around the gradient weather patterns, the direction of the gradient wind (that wind produced by the pressure differential) will indicate the shape of the weather pattern. Simply stated, the pressure will give us good clues if a system is approaching or leaving, and the wind direction will provide hints about its shape and where we're located within the system.

When in the Northern Hemisphere, as a High passes to the south of your position moving from west to east, the wind will back from northerly to NW'ly to W'ly to SW'ly.

If the weather system is a Northern Hemisphere low pressure system, passing to the south of your position and moving from west to east, the wind sequence will generally back from southerly to SE'ly to E'ly to NE'ly as the barometric pressure drops and bottoms out with the winds generally out of the east. The rotation will be reversed for Southern Hemisphere low pressure systems.

Fronts

Fronts are usually associated with low pressure systems. They are always associated with distinctly different air masses. When we think of fronts, we often think about approaching clouds. There may be rain associated with the front, and there may be gusting wind.

There are, in fact, several different types of fronts, each with their own typical structure and characteristics. Understanding those characteristics will help us to prepare for their approach.

Typical characteristics

Fronts are surface weather features. If we look at a surface pressure map, various types of lines representing the kind of front often indicate the location of the front. There are cold fronts, warm fronts, occluded fronts and stationary fronts.

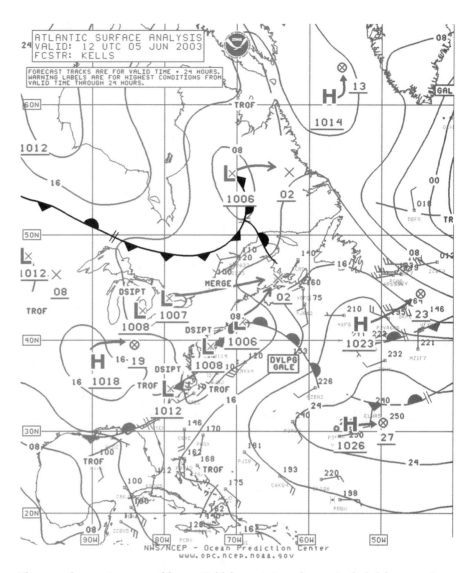

There are four major types of fronts: Cold fronts, Warm fronts, Occluded fronts and Stationary fronts. They each have their own characteristics.

Another way to recognize where fronts may be located is to look at a surface pressure map that doesn't show the lines for a front. Realize that the elongations in the isobars emanating from a low pressure system indicate a drop and subsequent rise in pressure as you move across the chart that may be due to the presence of a front or a trough.

Fronts are often associated with a relatively distinct pressure drop. But the structure and characteristics of the various fronts are quite different. The defining characteristics of the various types of fronts are governed by the relationships between the air masses forming the front.

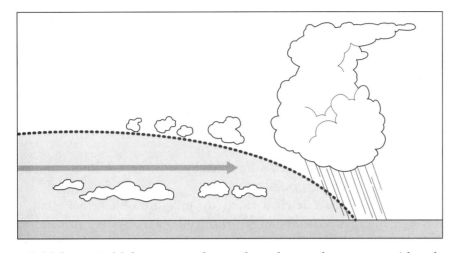

In a cold front a mass of cold, dense air moves to displace a mass of relatively warmer, less dense air. As a result, clouds often form along the leading edge and can grow into towering cumulus clouds due to increased convection.

Cold front Cold fronts are often – though not always – considered the windier of the fronts with the greatest wind shifts. They also tend on average to move somewhat faster than other types of fronts.

If we look at a cross-sectional view of a cold front, we see cold, dense air moving from the left toward the right as it displaces the warmer air preceding it. Since the cold air is more dense, it tends to occupy lower altitudes than the warm air it is displacing and acts a bit like a wedge as it moves forward.

The warm, moist air preceding the cold front thrusts upward and cools as it reaches higher altitudes. As the moist air cools it condenses, forming clouds and squall lines. As the squall lines grow and develop, the cloud tops can reach up into the jet stream, which pushes the whole cloud mass along at a faster rate, further in front of the cold front.

Although the skies preceding a cold front are generally clear to partly cloudy, the squall lines can be up to 100 miles in front of the actual cold front.

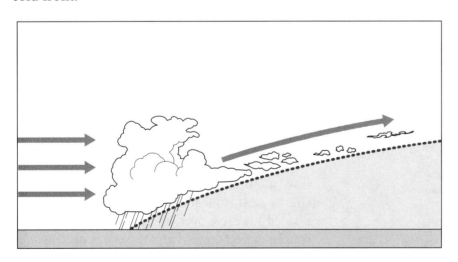

In a warm front, a mass of relatively less dense warm air moves to displace a mass of more dense cold air. As a result, some of the warm air rises above the cold air as well as displacing the entire cold air mass below. Cloud formations are different and rain can be more sustained than in a cold front.

Warm front Warm fronts typically precede cold fronts in a "classic" low pressure system. As the low pressure system swirls around, warm, moist air pushes against and displaces the more dense and dryer cold air mass.

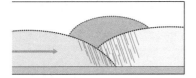

In an occluded front, a cold front has overrun a warm front. The air mass from the earlier cold front has "squeezed" the warm aloft. Although cold air meets cold air, there is still movement in the frontal system and steady rain from the warm, moist air aloft.

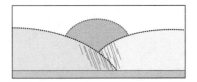

In a stationary front, air masses are similar to that of an occluded front, but neither cold air mass is trying to overrun the other.

Looking at a cross-sectional view of a warm front, we see warm air approaching from the left, displacing the cooler, more dense air represented on the right. The moist air, rising to cooler, higher altitudes and mixing with the cold air creates precipitation. The closer to the warm front that you are located, generally, the more constant or heavier the precipitation. Also, the overcast lowers with fog and drizzle possible just prior to the warm front's passage. There will be considerable right shear on the larger rigs.

Following the warm front, skies often become partly cloudy as the sun begins to shine through.

Occluded front In a newly formed low pressure system there may only be two types of fronts, warm and cold. As the system continues to develop and the low pressure system advances and swirls, the slower warm front can be overrun by the faster-moving cold front. As the fronts combine when the cold front tries to overrun the warm front, the interaction creates a new type of front, an occluded front.

As the low pressure system occludes, it is beginning its stage of decline. Wind speeds tend to drop in the area of the occlusion. Sea state may be confused because of the recent and sudden wind shifts. Generally, higher sustained wind speeds are found further away from the center of the low pressure system that is occluding.

Stationary front Similar to an occluded front, a fourth type of front is the stationary front. In the stationary front, there is no movement of the air masses. Neither cold nor warm air is in the process of over-running the other. The result is general cloudiness, but relatively little wind compared to a more active cold front.

Low pressure system in quadrants and their typical characteristics

Even though there are countless variations, we can break down a "typical" low pressure system into four rough quadrants. Numbering them from left to right and from top to bottom, Quadrant 1 of a low would be northwest of the center of the system. A warm front lies along the line dividing Quadrant 2 and 4 and a cold front lies roughly along the line dividing Quadrant 3 and 4 in our "idealized" low pressure system. We can look at each of the quadrants and deduce what kinds of typical sky, clouds and other characteristics they would each have. If we are in a boat in the upper right of the chart and this idealized Low Pressure system is headed towards, over, and past us, here is what we can expect to find and the types of clouds that will give us the warning of what is in store.

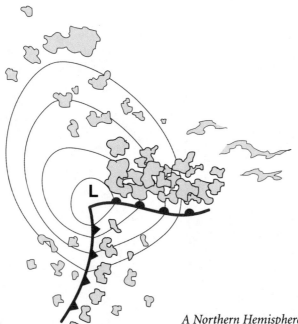

A Northern Hemisphere low pressure system can be roughly divided into quadrants, each with their own characteristic cloud types, wind directions and progressions as they move over a particular location.

As Quadrant 2 approaches us, the barometric pressure will begin to drop. The winds will be some form of easterly. They could be SE to NE. In the idealized version of our system, if the pressure continues to drop, and the wind doesn't shift either right or left, the center of the system is headed over our position. Initially the cloud cover may be high, wispy cirrus cloud. But as time passes and the system gets closer, the clouds will get thicker and lower in the sky. If, as the pressure continues to drop, the wind shifts to the left, becoming more northerly, the temperatures should drop, and the skies should gradually clear. Cold air can't hold as much moisture as warm air, so the skies may eventually take on a clear blue, with scattered clouds. We're getting closer to Quadrant 1. If, however, the skies are getting cloudier and the elevation of those clouds is getting lower and the wind is shifting to the right – becoming more southeasterly and southerly – then we are headed toward the warm front and Quadrant 4.

During the Winter of 2002-2003, Southern New England experienced a lot of Quadrant 2 weather. low pressure systems formed off Cape Hatteras and traveled toward the northeast, frequently passing just to the south of Cape Cod. Cirrus clouds with increasing low-level cloudiness typify the weather initially and extended drizzle (or snow during the winter) and winds can gradually increase. If someone asks me what the weather will be like tomorrow, and the only information that I have is that I see that we're going to be in Quadrant 2, I suggest they get ready for an entire day of rain or drizzle. That may not always be correct, but it's a good first assessment.

Once the warm front has passed with the center of the low to your north and you are in Quadrant 4, the skies become partially clear, leaving scattered cumulus clouds. Temperatures are generally warmer and humid with winds from the South to Southwest. Barometric pressure will fall if the center of the system is getting closer and as the cold front gets closer separating Quadrant 3 and Quadrant 4. As the low pressure system continues to move over your position, the cold front will be approaching, and winds will typically continue to shift to the right – going from southerly to southwesterly to west southwesterly. Often as the cold front approaches, squall lines will form along the leading edge of the front. If they're high enough, the jet stream may blow them out ahead of the front, and the squalls can be a hundred miles or more before the front. The towering cumulus (cumulonimbus) clouds in these squalls associated with the front can reach 40,000 feet or more if conditions are "right." Large, developing cumulonimbus clouds such as these can have extremely powerful downbursts preceding the cloud. Telltale signs of extreme winds under the clouds include ragged, "bubbling" structure to the clouds, flat cloud tops and wind-driven white caps on the approaching seas. They're not to be taken lightly, and quick wind shifts can accompany the downbursts.

Starting again in Quadrant 2, if the wind does shift left from easterly to northerly as the pressure drops, the air will become colder as you go into Quadrant 1. Once into Quadrant 1, the pressure will begin to

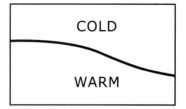

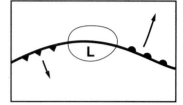

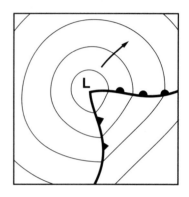

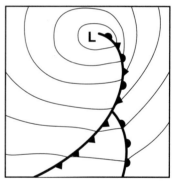

A surface low pressure system goes through an evolutionary process from birth, to maturation to eventual decay.

rise, skies will clear, perhaps leaving some relatively small puffy cumulus clouds with puffy wind gusts to accompany them. Winds will go from northeast to northwest.

As the low pressure system moves past your position, and you get into Quadrant 3, pressure will continue to rise, and winds will move into the west or northwest behind the cold front. The rising pressure and generally cooler air will not support moisture in the air, so skies will generally be clear or mostly clear.

Clouds are convective systems and a result of moisture and temperature differential as the air rises. Understanding which quadrants pick up warm, moist air with winds from the south and which Quadrants tend to cool that air, creating clouds and moisture will help you understand where you are relative to the larger weather system. Watching how the barometric pressure and wind direction changes will help you to understand the movement of that system and what to expect next.

Lifecycle of extra-tropical low showing fronts changing with time

low pressure systems can pop up, seemingly in the middle of "nowhere." Often they can start as secondary low pressure systems

Relatively young low pressure systems can form as secondary lows along a front. As they occlude, age and decay, the wind speed near the center will decrease.

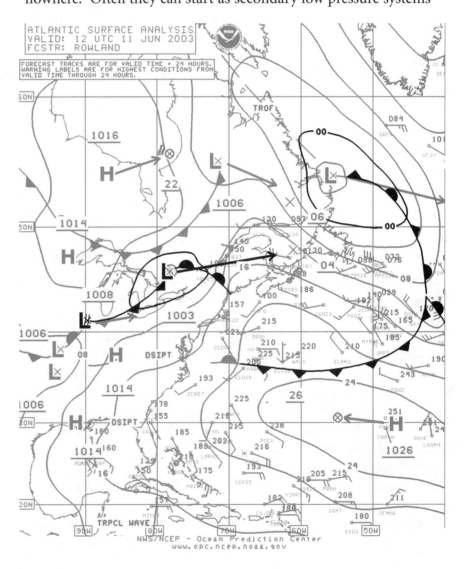

along a frontal boundary that comes off an existing low pressure system. Somewhere along the front, circulation begins to close a loop of pressure and the new secondary low starts its life cycle.

Some geographic locations such as off Cape Hatteras seem more prone than others to spawn low pressure systems. Other times, rising air forms a standing "heat low" with consistently warm air forming its own circulation system.

The newly developing low pressure system is generally characterized by a large temperature gradient. As the storm matures and occludes during the aging process, the temperature gradient diminishes. Remember that one of the ingredients in extra-tropical storm development is the mixing of warm and cold air. As a general concept, the greater the temperature differential is, the stronger the storm will become.

You may note that off Cape Hatteras, we have elements of the cold Labrador Current and the warm Gulf Stream. And we have land protruding into the ocean. The unsettled nature of the local environment and the natural temperature differences create a location ripe for low pressure development.

How to locate and track fronts

The easiest way to locate and track fronts is to look at a surface weather map that clearly indicates the fronts.

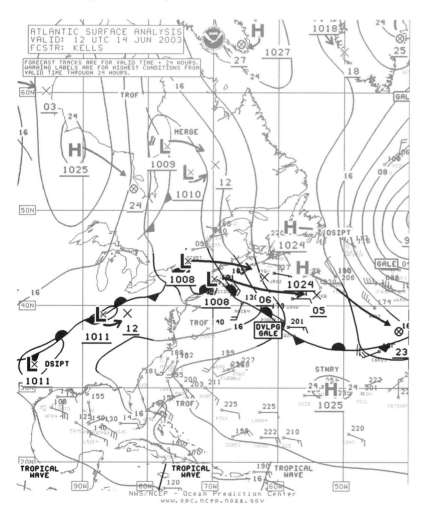

Often on surface pressure maps, fronts are relatively easy to identify. The centers of the associated lows on some maps are projected to relocate 24 hours after the Valid Time, and the new fronts will morph into new shapes.

Occasionally, surface pressure maps don't indicate the fronts, so you will have to find them yourself. If you think of the surface isobars as similar to contours on a topographical map (technically they are NOT contours because they represent pressure differences at a given height, NOT elevation differences), the front will generally be located along the distorted isobars representing a "depression" in the pressure. It would be like a "valley" on a contour map.

If you are looking at a satellite image, you can often find the front by locating the cloud line with the highest, coldest clouds. Following a cold front, as an example, there will often be a general clearing in the skies as the air turns cool and clear.

Remember that cold air doesn't hold as much moisture, so the cold air following a cold front will be clear or mostly clear. The air preceding a warm front will generally be cloudy and rainy, but the clouds may not be quite as high as the clouds preceding a cold front.

Generally, the higher the cloud, the colder they are, and by comparing infrared satellite imagery of cloud cover you should be able to find the tall, cold, tower cumulus clouds often associated with squall lines near cold fronts and somewhat lower, thick clouds associated with warm fronts.

Using weather maps to illustrate synoptic weather patterns

Western Atlantic Surface Pressure Analysis, Valid 12 UTC, 30 June 2003

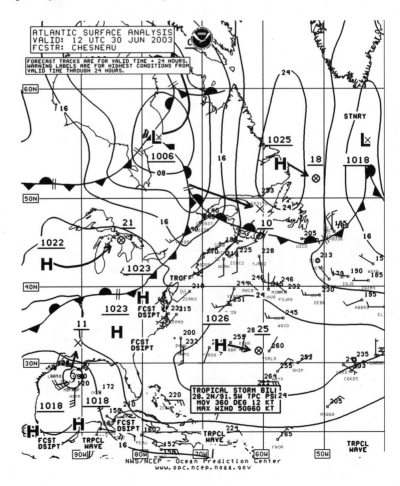

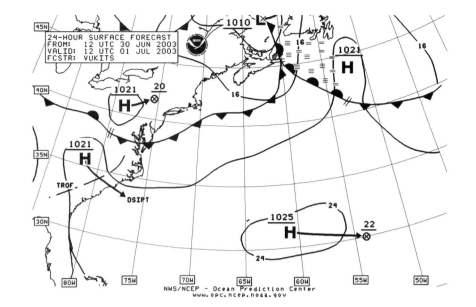

Far Western North Atlantic Surface Pressure, 24 Hour Forecast, Valid 12 UTC, 01 July 2003

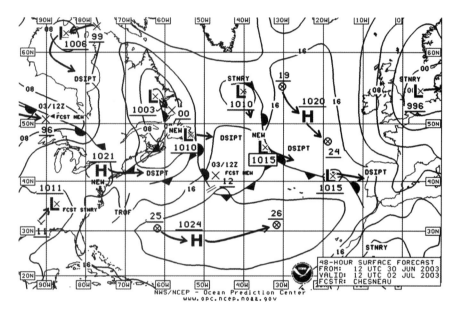

North Atlantic Surface Pressure, 48 Hour Forecast, Valid 12 UTC, 02 July 2003

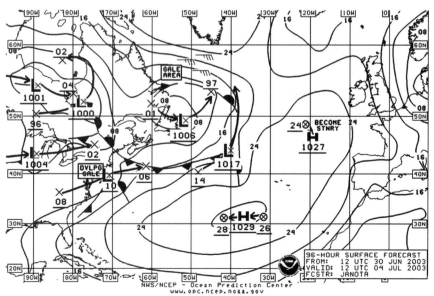

North Atlantic Surface Pressure, 96 Hour Forecast, Valid12 UTC, 04 July 2003

To illustrate the various synoptic weather characteristics we cover in this Chapter, we will use a specific type of weather map (or weather chart, we'll use these terms interchangeably) called a surface pressure chart. There are quite a few types of weather maps available. Some are tropical streamlines, showing the movement of clouds. Some are nephanalyses, indicating the types of clouds present in an analysis. Some provide wind, sea state, ice, or current information.

Surface pressure maps also come in a variety of "flavors." There is the Preliminary Surface Analysis, Surface Analysis, 24 hour Surface Forecast, 48 hour Surface Forecast, and 96 hour Surface Forecast. Generally, the Surface Analyses come out 4 times per day. The 24 and 48 hour Surface Forecasts come out twice per day, and the 96 hour Surface Forecast comes out once per day. These, of course, are subject to change and should be checked prior to departure on any long passages.

For purposes of our discussions we will primarily use U.S. charts, although there are very high quality charts available from other government weather services, as well.

High and low pressure systems

High and low pressure systems are expected to be in the locations indicated by their respective letters at the time that the weather map is (or "was" in the case of a Surface Analysis) valid. The arrows indicate the direction and forecast position for that system 24 hours after the Valid Time. On forecast maps, sometimes there will be arrows pointing toward the letter from the system's assumed position 24 hours prior to the Valid Time.

Although surface analysis maps indicate current conditions, they can also "forecast" the movement of H and L systems by indicating the direction in which a High or Low pressure system is expected to move and where it is expected to be located in 24 hours.

If you look on the Surface Analysis map, you'll see "H" (marked with an encircled X) representing the center of the high pressure systems and "L" (marked with an X without a circle around it) representing the centers of the lows. The presence of the letter implies some circulation. It can be reasonably assumed that some wind will be circulating around that center at varying distances from the center.

On most of the highs and lows there are bold arrows pointing toward the "H" or "L" and away from them. If the arrow is pointed toward the H or L, the arrows indicate where the high or low was located 24 hours PRIOR TO the valid time shown in the box.

If the arrow is pointing away from the "H" or the "L," it indicates where the system will be located 24 hours AFTER the valid time in the box.

In essence, the arrow away from the high or low on a surface analysis map is a 24-hour forecast position for where the forecaster thinks the system will move. In fact, some maps even include the following note: "Forecast tracks are valid time + 24 hours."

Next to the "H" or "L" you will see a number that corresponds to the center pressure of the system. It may contain 4 digits, such as 1024 mb (millibars), or there may only be two digits, such as 99, indicating 999 mb. The only time 3 digits will be used is when the meteorologist is describing the center pressure of a low pressure system of less than 1000 mb of pressure.

You may notice that the forecast location 24 hours hence also has a number associated with it. The high labeled as a 1024 mb high may have an arrow indicating its position 24 hours hence and have a 26 next to the expected position, indicating that the high will become a 1026 mb high, thus strengthening slightly. The higher the reading, the stronger the high pressure system. The lower the reading for a low pressure system, the stronger the low pressure system generally.

Keep in mind that there are several ways to measure pressure. Using millibars is the most common way on marine weather maps. However, some countries such as France use hPa (hectopascals) which are equivalent to millibars. And some inland areas use Hg (inches of Mercury).

Directional flow around high and low pressure systems in the Northern & Southern Hemisphere In the Northern Hemisphere because of the Coriolis Effect, the wind goes in a clockwise direction around the highs and in a counter-clockwise direction around the lows. Rather than flowing along a tangent to the isobars, due to surface friction the wind toes out away from a high by about 15 or 20 degrees and in toward the center of a low by about 15 or 20 degrees. If you follow the isobars around, making little arrows canted in toward the low and away from the high, you'll see that it all works together.

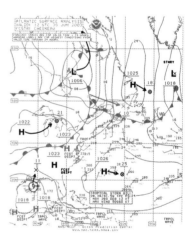

Center pressures for the respective systems are also indicated. The 3 or 4 digit underlined number is the assumed pressure at the valid time of the weather map. The 2 digit underlined numbers refer to the previous or projected pressure for the system. (Either a "9" or a "10" is assumed to precede the 2 digit number). By comparing the past pressures with the current and future pressures, one can determine if the system is getting stronger or weaker.

In the Southern Hemisphere, the wind circulates in a counter-clockwise direction around the highs and in a clockwise direction around the low pressure system.

Fronts

Earlier, we discussed the structure of fronts and how they differ. Looking at the accompanying map, you can see cold fronts, warm fronts, occluded fronts and stationary fronts. Regardless of whether this is a forecast map or an analysis, it is a graphical representation of how the weather is interpreted for the particular valid time indicated.

Weather is dynamic, however. It is constantly moving. Parts of the fronts may be moving at different rates than other parts of the front. The low may be getting deeper (lower pressure reading) or weakening (higher pressure reading). The high may be getting stronger (higher pressure readings) or dissipating. Weather is constantly evolving even as it moves over our position.

Areas of lots of wind

As H and L pressure systems move and the air masses collide into one another, sometimes the pressure gradient between two systems gets very steep. The pressure increases over a smaller distance. As the pressure gradient increases, the wind increases.

Some areas of wind build up include the regions between high and low pressure systems and in cold fronts.

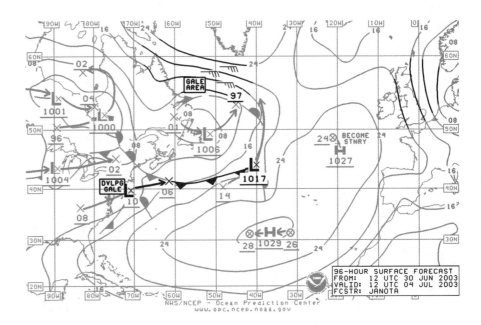

It's like there's a lot of air "packed" into the high pressure system, a bit like a balloon. When there is a big difference between the high and the low over a small distance, like between a balloon and the rest of the room, there is a great deal of wind taking place in order to attempt to equalize the pressure. The Coriolis Effect turns the wind to the right in the Northern Hemisphere (clockwise around the high) and toward the left (counter-clockwise) in the Southern Hemisphere.

If you were looking at a surface pressure map, finding areas where there is a great deal of wind, first you would look to see where the isobars are packed closely together. When judging which places have

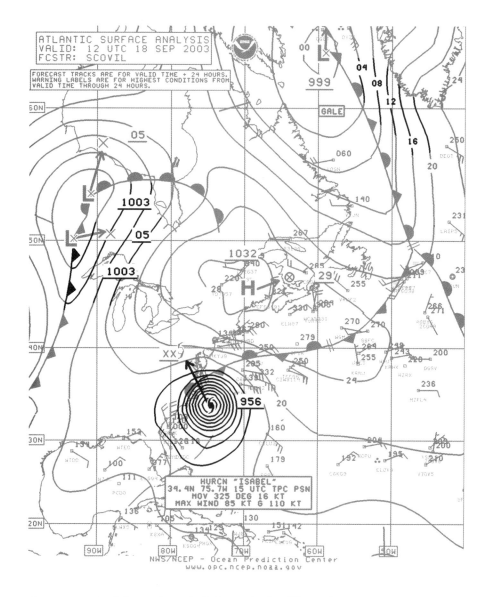

ATLANTIC SURFACE ANALYSIS
VALID: 12 UTC 18 SEP 2003
FCSTR: SCOVIL

FORECAST TRACKS ARE FOR VALID TIME + 24 HOURS.
WARNING LABELS ARE FOR HIGHEST CONDITIONS FROM
VALID TIME THROUGH 24 HOURS.

HURCN "ISABEL"
34.4N 75.7W 15 UTC TPC PSN
MOV 325 DEG 16 KT
MAX WIND 85 KT G 110 KT

NWS/NCEP - Ocean Prediction Center
www.opc.ncep.noaa.gov

Extra-topical lows may have high winds near their centers, but in aging, occluded lows, more wind will exist further away from the centers. Tropicals, on the other hand, have most of their winds near the eye wall and in the leading right hand quadrant.

the most wind, keep in mind that wind will accelerate as it goes around curves. So if isobars are equidistant in places where they are straight, as well as in places where they are curved, there will probably be more wind where the isobars are curved.

Often there are high winds around low pressure systems. In a tropical low, the areas of greatest wind are located near the center of the low. Hurricanes, as an example, have their highest winds near the eye of the storm. Extra-tropicals can also have their highest winds close to the center of the low, but it depends on the age of the low pressure system and how it is developing, as well as what is happening with high pressure systems in the low's proximity. The highest winds often occur in the region of the greatest temperature differential. As the temperature suddenly changes, so also does the pressure. And as the pressure changes suddenly, the wind speeds increase.

Because of this phenomenon, winds will often be gusty along a cold front. The temperature changes suddenly as the winds go from the southwest to the northwest (in a typical Northern Hemisphere cold

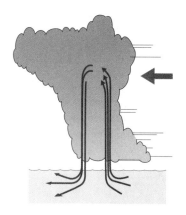

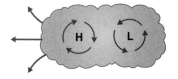

Even on a local level, winds can be excessive. Rapid cooling of air at the top of a towering cumulus cloud can lead to downbursts at the bottom of the cloud.

front), and the sudden change in temperature creates a sudden change in air pressure.

Areas of high wind aren't just associated with synoptic scale gradient wind patterns, however. They also exist on the local level. Often associated with tall, cold clouds, the warm, moist, rising air feeds the cloud's development. As the air rises, the upper atmosphere air can suddenly cool it. The cold, dense, dry air then begins to fall, rushing out at the bottom of the cloud, potentially as a downburst.

Squall lines and towering cumulus clouds can often precede cold fronts, but they also exist in tropical areas. Knowing the types of clouds, their structures and characteristics will help to differentiate between the ones that foretell of good weather and the ones that may be potentially destructive.

In summary, the following are often indicators of generally higher wind areas:

❶ Isobars closely spaced together
❷ Curves in isobars will often have somewhat higher wind speeds associated with those areas than straight, parallel isobars similarly spaced
❸ Near the centers of low pressure systems for young low pressure systems; Somewhat further away from the centers of older, occluding low pressure systems
❹ Cold fronts
❺ Local tall, cold clouds

Areas of relatively little wind

Areas that have relatively little wind include the centers of high pressure systems, ridgelines, the relatively small centers of low pressure systems – including the centers of both tropical and extra-tropical low pressure systems – and areas between low pressure systems called "cols." All of these areas have relatively little pressure change over a given distance. In the case of the centers of lows, the distance is pretty

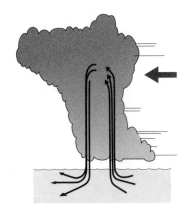

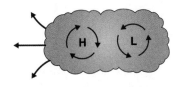

The centers of clouds can also have relatively little wind if one is caught in the updraft area. Wind speeds and directions directly under a cloud can be extremely light or confused.

The centers of high and low pressure systems as well as along ridgelines can be areas of little wind.

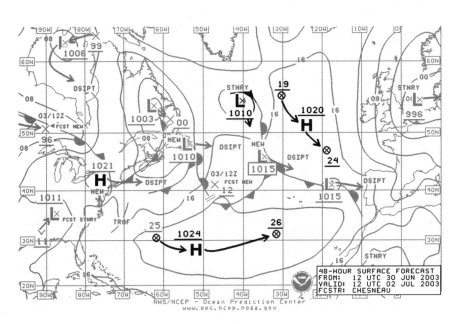

small. If you look at a low with wind swirling around in a circular direction, at some point it seems almost logical that there must be an area where little or no air is moving in the center. In fact, that is the case.

While crossing the North Atlantic, I've gone through the center of low pressure systems. On the eastern side of the center, wind was blowing out of the south. There was little or no wind for about 6 hours as I sailed through the center of the low. And on the western side of the low's center the wind was northerly and a similar wind speed.

Areas of little wind aren't just on the synoptic scale, however. They also exist on the local level, not unlike areas of high winds and gusts. Large clouds often set up their own wind circulation patterns. The warm, rising air can set up a kind of "mini-low pressure system" with counter-clockwise circulation around the edges and a center with little or no wind. Whether we're out day sailing on dinghies or in mid-ocean, the cloud can have wind from one direction on one side and from a completely different direction on the other side. In the middle, sails can be slapping back and forth as you wait to find out whether you will be forced to tack or gybe when the wind gusts back up.

In summary, the following are indicators of low wind areas:
❶ centers of high pressure systems
❷ ridgelines
❸ relatively small centers of low pressure systems – including the centers of both tropical and extra-tropical low pressure systems
❹ area between low pressure systems called a "col"
❺ under the center of some local clouds

OCEANOGRAPHY

Oceanographic features affect us as sailors on more than just the global climatological scale. We need to be aware of what's happening with the water below us just as we need to be aware of the wind around us. The two are inter-related and they affect each other and ultimately us and our vessels. Currents and tides play a significant role in how efficiently or competitively we sail. And they play a large role in modifying or even helping to create the weather around us.

Current

Current is the movement of water. There are large-scale currents such as the Gulf Stream (in the N. Atlantic), North Equatorial Current (in the N. Atlantic, N. Pacific and Indian Oceans), Kuroshio Current (Japan Stream in the N. Pacific), East Australian Current (EAC - offshore eastern Australia), and others created by global wind patterns.

There are also local wind drift currents produced by storms. There are currents created by tides – the gravitational pull of the moon and the sun. And there are currents produced by river run-off.

Both warm and cold currents affect local, mesoscale, and global weather patterns.

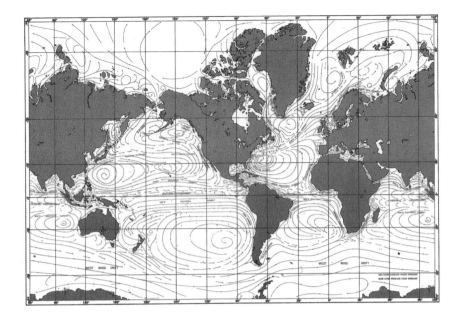

The flow rates of each of these currents can – to one degree or another – affect each other. As an example, a storm surge or excessive river run-off can alter a tidal flow in coastal regions. While tides don't seem to have much of an impact on large-scale currents, they can have some interaction in areas such as the north side of the Bahamas as tides flow on and off the Bahama Banks.

Warm and cold currents affect mesoscale meteorology

Both warm and cold currents affect the local, mesoscale, and global scale weather patterns. Winters are generally warmer in Scandinavia than they are at similar latitudes in Canada and Siberia largely because of the warm water the Gulf Stream transports across the North Atlantic.

On a smaller scale, the heat energy from the Gulf Stream can often add power to squall lines forming along the leading edge of cold fronts coming off the U.S. East Coast.

Gulf Stream in winter Since extra-tropical low pressure systems derive a great deal of their power from the mixing of cold and warm air, the greater the difference in the temperatures of the air mass, the more potent the low can become. Winter over the Gulf Stream provides numerous examples of how a little extra heat energy combined with cold air can create havoc at sea.

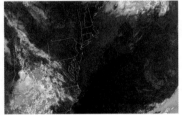

Infrared satellite image that distinctly shows the warm current of the Gulf Stream in the Western North Atlantic.

In New England during the late fall, frontal passages often take place about every 3 days more or less. As the lows, driven by the cold jet stream parade their way across North America, boats heading south to the Caribbean from New England are usually advised to time their departures so that they cross the Gulf Stream prior to a cold front going across the Stream.

If we look at a surface pressure map, we can get a feeling for how much wind speed we can expect in a particular place by looking at the spacing between the isobars. The closer they are together, the more wind we can expect to find in that location, generally. If the gradient weather pattern prior to the cold front arriving over the warm Gulf Stream implies that there would be 30 to 35 knot winds from the south with relatively warm air, following the frontal passage when the wind direction often shifts to the northwest, the cold northerlies could push the wind speeds up to 45 or 50 knots. Increased air volume and gusting can sink down from aloft. The cold, dense air at somewhat higher altitudes sinks along the north wall of the Gulf Stream's warm air. Getting caught on the Stream in a fall or winter northerly is definitely to be avoided because the gradient wind speeds are enhanced by the cold, sinking air.

Structure of the Gulf Stream Although I'm neither a professional meteorologist nor an oceanographer, I've spent more than the average amount of time experiencing the interaction between currents and weather first-hand. It has become obvious over the years that it would be in my best interests to understand something about both.

If you were to take a running water hose and put it in a swimming pool, you'd have a pretty good starting point for understanding what the Gulf Stream and other currents are up to. If you were to toss some grass into the pool in the area of the stream, you'd be well on your way to getting a simplistic and primitive idea of what goes on with drift buoys. While these are "experiments" I did at about 5 years of age, they may give you a point of reference as they have given me.

You would notice that the flow of the water doesn't stay in line for very long after coming out of the nozzle. After a short distance it starts to snake around, meandering from one direction to another. As it turns out, these varying directions are called just that, "meanders," in large currents as well. And as the water "squirts" between Florida and the Bahamas, it doesn't take very long before the stream starts to meander or form eddies.

For the most part, though, the stream remains distinct from the rest of the water in the pool (or ocean).

How cold and warm eddies are formed As the meanders go from side to side, they occasionally become exaggerated enough that they form first a "U," and as the open end of the "U" closes, it forms a complete loop – an eddy. In the small scale of the swimming pool, the eddies look like little whirlpools.

If the meander dips to the south and the water in the middle of the meander is from the cold, north side of the Gulf Stream, we call this a "cold eddy." When we say "cold" we are referring to the center – the core of the eddy. Since the water in the core is actually from the north side of the meander that forms the eddy, it is a "cold core eddy." Due to the original flow of the water in the meander, the current in a cold eddy flows in a counter-clockwise direction.

If the meander dips to the north and the water in the core is from the warm south side of the Gulf Stream, we call this type of eddy a "warm eddy." Similarly to the above, the warm eddy has the water in its core from the south side of the meander. The warmer water of the

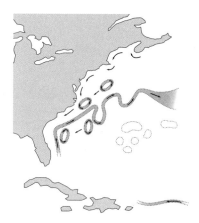

Here is an illustration showing the direction of the Gulf Stream as well as the warm eddies to the north of the Stream and the cold eddies to the south of the Stream.

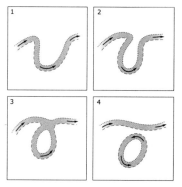

The eddies to the south of the Gulf Stream start as meanders, entrapping cold water in their centers, hence their name of "cold eddies" or, more specifically, cold core eddies.

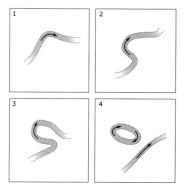

The eddies to the north of the Gulf Stream start as meanders, entrapping warm water in their centers, hence their name of "warm eddies."

core is what we're referring to when we call it a warm core eddy or just "warm eddy." The water flows in a clockwise direction.

Current profile If we were to measure the current going from south to north off the coast of Florida at West Palm Beach we would find that the flow is actually going in the opposite direction within the first mile of the shoreline. The counter-current along the Florida coastline varies in both distance offshore as well as speed, but it is often between .75 and 1 knot toward the south for the first mile off West Palm Beach.

If we were to take another reading a mile or mile and a half off-shore, the current would often be as high as 4 to 5 knots flowing to the north! Continuing toward the east, if we took another reading, the speed would be somewhat less. As we continue toward the Bahamas, the current flow eventually gets as low as 1 to 2 knots as we get to the Bahama Banks.

Surprisingly enough, current speeds can be almost as high even as we go further to the north in the Gulf Stream. I've sailed in parts of the Gulf Stream south of Rhode Island that had current speeds of between 3 knots to as high as 5 knots on several occasions.

How we track the currents There are a number of ways that oceanographers locate and track the Gulf Stream and other currents in the world. The principal way of locating the currents is using remote sensing – infrared satellite (IR) imagery.

❶ *Thermal imaging* Because the currents remain distinct from the water they flow through, IR imagery can show up the temperature differences. These can then be transferred to charts and people can use the charts to find favorable currents or avoid unfavorable currents. Sometimes the charts are presented as a series of lines (isotherms) indicating the same temperature. Sometimes they are presented as color-enhanced images that are colored to show the major temperature differences.

Often the greatest flow is along the sharpest temperature gradient. Also, as you might expect, flow tends to be somewhat faster around the outside radius of the curves. Generally, however, the fastest current speeds are along the north or west walls of the Gulf Stream (GS) where the temperature between the GS water and the cooler slope water is greatest.

Thermal imaging has a number of advantages. It is global. It can be disrupted by cloud cover but, by using composite pictures, taken over several days, the latest clear pixels showing the sea surface can help to eradicate most of that problem.

One difficulty worth noting, however, is that thermal imaging only takes note of the surface temperatures. In the case of a cold eddy, the colder, denser water in the center tends to sink. Warmer water then tends to fill in above the core water. As the warmer water fills in, the thermal imaging has a bit more difficulty showing up the temperature differences and location of the cold eddy.

❷ *Drift buoys* Another way currents are located and measured is by using drift buoys. Buoys are set adrift in various parts of the world's oceans and they transmit their positions, water temperature and other information. As their positions change, the location and speed of the current is noted.

❸ *Altimetry data* Additionally, altimetry data is measured remotely by satellite to help locate various currents and their features. Not unlike whirlpools forming in a swimming pool, eddies tend to be lower as they circulate. By comparing the height of the overall ocean surface with the height of a suspected eddy, its location can be confirmed. Using all of the tools available, skilled and trained oceanographers have considerable success at locating the various features of the world's currents.

El Niño, La Niña Ocean currents are not necessarily constant. The El Niño phenomenon may be one example of that. Although there is still a great deal to be learned about the causes and effects of El Niño and its opposite number, La Niña, there are some characteristics that are known.

It is a roughly cyclical weather pattern that occurs approximately every 3 to 5 years. The western Pacific trade winds fail to develop sufficiently, and the degree to which El Niño becomes severe or not depends on the degree of trade wind failure.

Warm water normally pools in the western Pacific, pushed there by the trade winds. When the trades fail, the temperature of the warm surface water is more uniform across the Pacific.

As a result, western Pacific waters are cooler than they otherwise would be and eastern Pacific waters are warmer than they normally are. From a climatology standpoint, that creates a situation in which there are higher pressures in the western Pacific and lower pressures in the eastern Pacific.

The results from the 1997-'98 El Niño give us a few examples of some of the side effects. That year, the eastern Pacific underwent the largest temperature departure from the norm ever measured. There was record rainfall in Peru (normally dry) and drought in Brazil (normally wet). There was record high pressure in Indonesia during the summer and very dry conditions. And there were above normal number and strength of hurricanes experienced in the eastern N. Pacific while there was virtually no hurricane activity in the N. Atlantic. There was record rainfall during the winter in California, and there were record high temperatures from N. Dakota to New England in the U.S. The following summer, in 1998, the temperatures were hot and dry in the northeastern U.S. and there were more hurricanes.

Why do I care? What does this mean to those of us who sail? For one thing, it means that both the sea surface temperatures and the climatological averages are skewed. If we know that the averages are out of alignment and we are planning for a passage, shouldn't we take the anomalous features into consideration? Whether we're on a

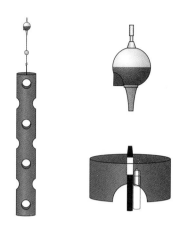

With a buoy that measures approximately 2 feet across and a drogue that can be 40 feet long, the instrumentation can follow the currents of the world, record various weather data, and transmit that information back to analysts ashore.

trans-oceanic passage or planning a weekend regatta, we're going to have to live with those anomalies.

Meteorologists from Commanders' Weather have worked up climatology studies for various sailing events up to 6 months prior to the actual event. Rather than use the average for all years, they selectively chose years that seemed to more closely emulate the anomalies of the year the event was going to take place. In other words, if a Transpac was going to take place in an El Niño year, the climatology study was based on averages taken only from El Niño years. Skewing the data by eliminating years that seemed less relevant appeared to provide results that were remarkably accurate.

Another aspect to knowing how the averages are skewed helps us to understand the greater or lesser probability of strong tropical storms for a given year in a given ocean. Understanding the oceanographic and climatological averages helps us understand the global weather patterns. Understanding how those averages vary from one year to another helps us to refine our knowledge for a given time frame.

Current can work for or against you by improving or hindering speed or heading Current, of course, can work for you as well as against you. It can add to your boat speed, helping to get you to a more favorable position for developing weather. It can also slow your advance. And, of course, it can widen or narrow your tacking angles and gibing angles as it adds to your speed and heading on one tack, or impairs your speed and heading on another.

Changing wave shapes and frequencies Another consideration on how current can help or hinder our sailing is how it changes wave shapes under certain circumstances.

Wave shapes and frequencies are the result of a number of factors. Wind speed, fetch, duration, water depth, current, reflected patterns induced by regular or irregular coastlines and other factors each play their role in creating wave patterns and shapes. The greater the wind

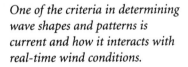

One of the criteria in determining wave shapes and patterns is current and how it interacts with real-time wind conditions.

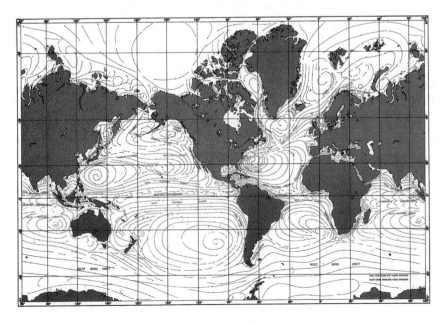

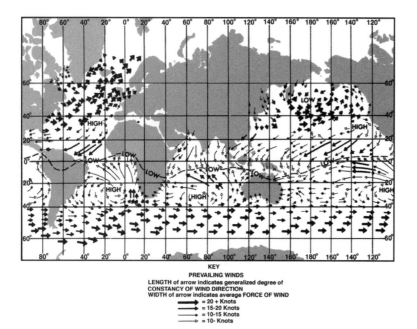

Global generalized wind patterns for the months of January and February

KEY
PREVAILING WINDS
LENGTH of arrow indicates generalized degree of
CONSTANCY OF WIND DIRECTION
WIDTH of arrow indicates average FORCE OF WIND

➤ = 20 + Knots
→ = 15-20 Knots
─ = 10-15 Knots
⟶ = 10- Knots

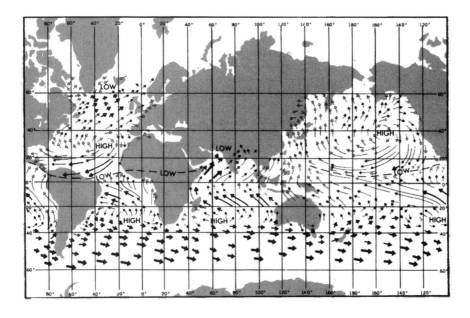

Global generalized wind patterns for the months of July and August

speed, the longer the fetch and duration, the larger the waves. The shallower the water and faster the current pitching against the wind, the steeper the waves. And the more irregular the nearby coastline that is reflecting the waves or the faster a low pressure system moves, the more confused the seas.

The shape of the waves generated by a 35-knot wind blowing from behind our boat with a 5-knot current also from behind our boat will be considerably different from the shape of the wave if the wind is pitching directly against the current. In that case, the 180-degree wind shift can make a nightmare out of a sea state. If that case is in the Gulf Stream, the ride can be gut wrenching. Wind blowing against the current can make waves both larger and steeper as the wave frequency is increased.

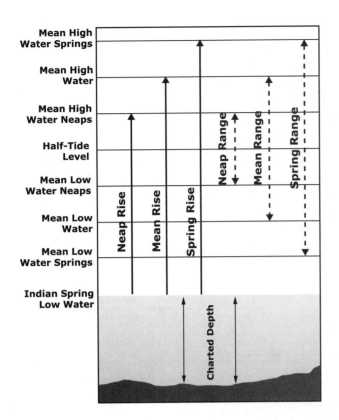

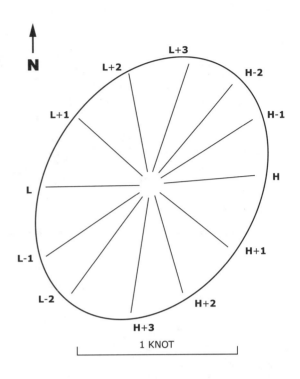

Above: Tidal Terms and What They Mean

Right: Rotary tides, direction and flow rates for Nantucket Shoals relative to high and low water

Tidal situations can be even worse than the Gulf Stream at times. The wind direction may not shift, but the direction of the tidal flow may change radically over a period of time. Additionally, the water in tidal areas is almost certainly going to be much shallower than in the Gulf Stream. A coastal tidal situation in which the wind continues from the same direction, but a 5-knot tide shifts and the water is relatively shallow can be disastrous. Even shorter frequency and steeper waves can be created. In the tidal situation you may loose steerage and end up on the rocks.

Currents can be wind driven in both the large and local scales

As we discussed, large-scale ocean currents are generally created by the prevailing winds. It should be mentioned that winds associated with storms also cause currents. Other currents, such as those that occur in the Straights of Bonafacio also can be largely wind driven currents. As the wind shifts – or surprisingly sometimes before the wind shifts locally – the current also changes direction.

Tides

While tides may affect the weather locally in subtle ways, the weather can also have a great effect on the tides. Furthermore, the tides can have a profound effect on how we can safely or efficiently move or route a boat.

One instance in which weather changes the tides includes inland rainfall. As an example, if there is heavy rainfall in parts of Georgia, upstream from Savannah, the actual tidal flow characteristics offshore from that city will be changed.

Storm surges are another example of how weather affects the tides. Severe storms often push a "mound" of water in front of them as they advance across the ocean. When the rise of water approaches coastal areas, the tides can reach substantially higher levels than normally predicted. As a result, hurricanes that make landfall during high tide are often more devastating than if they had hit during low tide. The resultant high tide, combined with the storm surge, can substantially exceed normal heights, causing moorings and anchor lines to be raised more vertically. High winds combined with increased water depth can cause anchors or moorings to drag. Floating docks can be raised above their pilings and drift free.

Tides can also radically affect the routing of a vessel in coastal areas. If the wind is pitching against the tide, the resulting waves will increase in steepness.

Sailing in fast moving tides or currents can often be tricky. Going against a strong tide, the boat may be making virtually little or no speed over the ground. When going with the strong tide or current, the boat may be moving quite quickly relative to the ground under the water, but the boat may only be going as fast as the current, leaving little water actually moving across its rudder. The result is that the boat has little or no steerage, and it can easily be swept onto rocks or into bridge abutments.

Here are a few quick things to keep in mind about tides and how they may or may not affect the routing of a vessel.

❶ Usually there is less current in shallow water and more current in the deeper water.

❷ In inland tidal situations, the speed of the tide will generally be greater in mid channel than along the shorelines.

❸ The time of the tide change will vary on average, as well. The tide will generally change along the shoreline earlier than in mid channel.

❹ The variation in the height of the tidal fall is not necessarily related to the speed of the current. You can have a fast current with little tidal range, or a relatively slow current with a high tidal height range.

❺ In open water, such as the Gulf of Maine, tides are rotary in nature, changing direction throughout the tide cycle. In confined areas, they tend to be more linear due to the confinements.

❻ Tidal characteristics are unique to a particular location and the prudent navigator makes himself aware of the tide's characteristics in his own area.

Upwellings

Upwellings are essentially currents in the ocean that flow in the vertical. Often caused by seamounts or other underwater features, they create a change in the water temperature at the surface as well as throughout the various depths of that area of ocean. The temperature change may affect the type of sea life in the area, perhaps attracting whales or other animals seeking various kinds of food.

Water, like air, moves in three dimensions. Water can sink or rise due to convection or upwellings caused when currents run up against seamounts. The result can be erratic wave patterns at the surface of the ocean.

Because upwellings flow upwards, eventually they have to flow in the horizontal plane as well. They can accelerate, slow or otherwise alter other currents from flowing in the horizontal plane. As they change the horizontal currents, the upwellings also tend to alter the degree to which wind and current interact. Wave patterns and temperatures can abruptly change in and around upwellings.

Wave patterns

Wave patterns and shapes are a complex mixture of a variety of factors. Each factor adds to or cancels out part of the other factors. And the various waves can be traveling in a variety of directions, further adding to the complexity of the pattern.

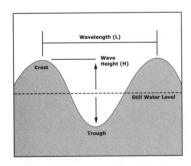

Waves are described by wave height, measured from trough to crest, and wave length, measured from wave top to wave top. Time between successive wave crests would be called the wave period.

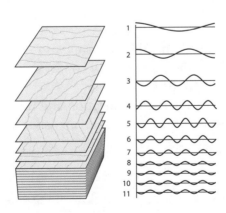

Wave patterns are a summation of a variety of waves of varying frequency, height and direction.

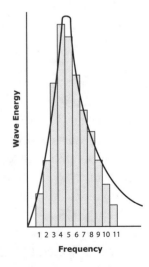

With a variety of simple waves combining to form a wave pattern, waves can assume complex and towering configurations.

Factors that create wave patterns

We can think of wave patterns as a series of sine waves, one superimposed on another. The result is the actual sea state in which we sail. Here are a few of the factors that have implications for wave height or shape:

❶ Wind speed. The more wind, the bigger the wave – to a point.

❷ Wind duration. The longer the wind blows, the more developed the wave becomes.

❸ Fetch. The further the wind blows across open water, the more developed the waves become. In the lee of an island, as an example, the fetch is short, so even if there is substantial breeze, the waves may be relatively small.

❹ Current. If a wind is blowing directly against a current, the wave will become steeper and the frequency will increase.

❺ Water depth. As a wave goes over shallower water, the wave will become steeper. An example of that would be waves breaking on reefs or shoals. But it is also true in other areas. The waves in the Irish Sea, the Tasman Sea or the Great Lakes are often generally steeper and closer together for a given wind strength and duration than open ocean waves.

❻ Reflected waves. Just like in a ripple tank, waves will reflect off a coastline, adding further complexity to the total wave pattern.

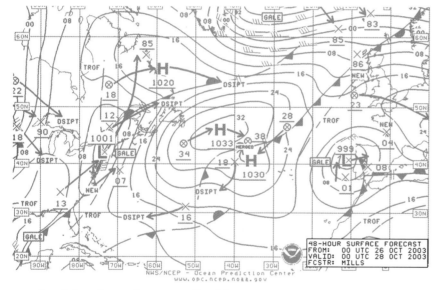

Surface pressure maps will give you ideas about wind speed and direction all over the map once you're adept at reading them. If you're in doubt about the actual wind speeds and directions, you can compare your interpretations with those listed on a wind/wave map for the same time frame listed below.

Each of the above factors will add to or modify the combined wave pattern. Since sea state, especially in severe conditions, will dictate much of what we can do on a small vessel, it becomes increasingly important to understand how each of these factors changes the waves. If we're coming onto soundings, making an approach to an island, what kind of waves will await us? How should we position the boat relative to the waves for the approach?

Sea state charts

Sea state charts show us the height of the waves we can expect to find in a particular part of the ocean. They will be affected by the various factors that create waves, but the sea state charts will do little to warn us about the actual shape and nature of the waves.

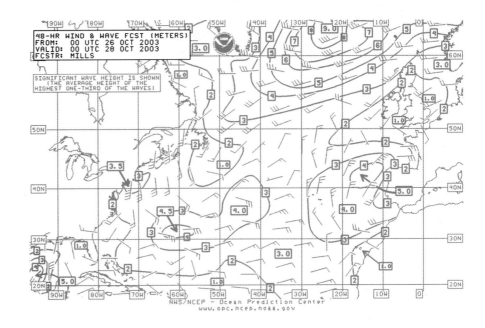

There can be large 20 to 25 foot swells that are relatively harmless to small boats. Storms or hurricanes hundreds or even a thousand miles away may create them. And those waves may do little to impede the progress of a boat. On the other hand, 10 or 15 foot waves that are in shallow areas can drive a boat up onto the rocks, and there may be little that can be done to keep the vessel off the rocks once she is controlled by the waves.

How various vessels relate to sea state

Since sea state is an important consideration in routing a vessel, it is necessary to understand how a vessel may relate to a particular type of seaway. A particular ship may find most conditions acceptable, even if not totally efficient. Often ships are routed based on the hydrodynamic characteristics of the vessel and the sea state that is to be encountered. If the wave pattern is too high and the frequency such that the vessel may span only two waves, it's not inconceivable that the vessel could snap in two. Ships off the eastern coast of southern Africa have encountered huge standing waves and plunged head-long down the waves, blowing out hull plates in the bow and creating holes 12 feet or more in diameter.

Some smaller, 150 foot steelhulled motor yachts may be able to sustain some waves, but similar sized aluminum-hulled motor yachts may not be able to avoid hull damage without taking evasive action.

Similarly, monohulls and multihulls have their own respective sailing characteristics. Multihulls perform more efficiently in relatively flat water. Given the fact that they don't have great masses of lead hanging down in the form of a keel, they can often achieve higher speeds in lower wind speeds. Multihulls derive their stability from their shape. Their form stability creates righting characteristics that are quite a bit different than monohulls. In steep waves and at high

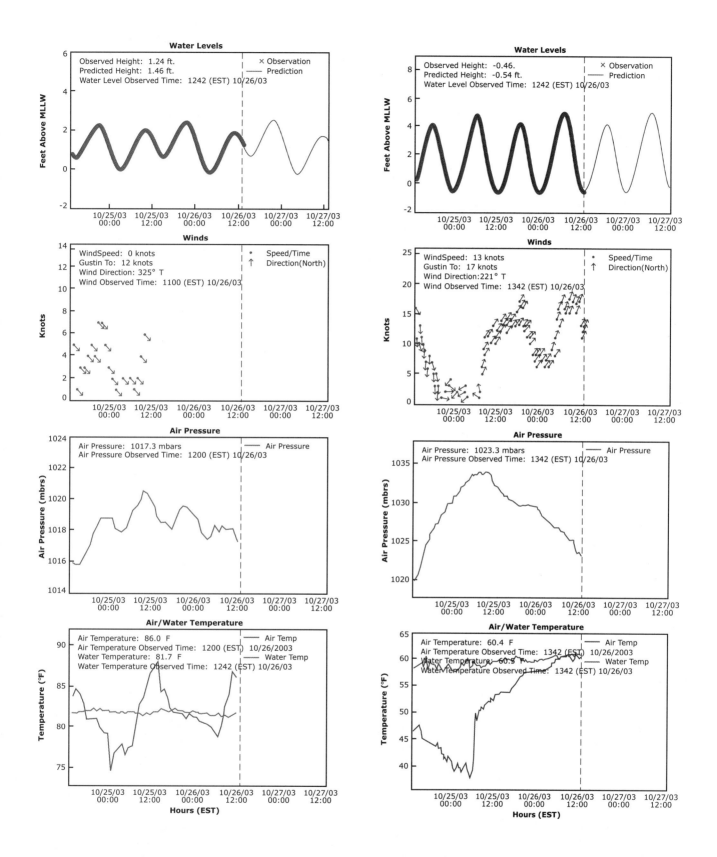

Observing several types of data simultaneously will sometimes give us clues that might not otherwise be obvious by looking at one type of information alone. As an example, as a storm approaches, it may or may not drive a storm surge ahead of it as it approaches a bay or sound. Much will depend on the wind direction and how that relates to the body of water. Another thing to look for is how temperature changes throughout the day affect the wind direction of a potential sea breeze.

speeds, multihulls run the risk of burying their leeward float in a wave, and perhaps pitchpoling. Once upside down, the multihull probably isn't coming back upright anytime soon.

Monohulls, on the other hand, may slam over some steep waves, but they are much less likely to pitchpole than a multihull. The ballast in their keel helps to keep them upright under all but the most severe conditions.

Because each kind of vessel has its own set of construction and stability characteristics, it is necessary to understand the strong points as well as the limitations of the vessel when looking for an optimal route.

Weather and oceanography affect the sea state, and they all affect the vessel. Each type of vessel is unique in the way it deals with its environment.

Water temperature versus air temperature

Air temperature and water temperature have a profound and multi-faceted effect on each other and the creation of weather. We know that warm air rises and cold air sinks. We also know that instability in a column of air creates low pressure (rising air) and high pressure (sinking air). And in the case of the Gulf Stream in the winter, the sinking cold air of a winter northerly breeze blowing across the Stream adds more wind to a gradient wind pattern.

There are other additional effects of warm currents. As a cold front approaches the warm current of the Gulf Stream, the added heat energy of the water can accelerate the formation of squall lines. On a larger scale, the heat energy can add to the strength of both tropical and/or extra-tropical low pressure systems and storms, or warm Northern European winters.

Cold currents can create a marine layer of still near-surface air. The differences in those temperatures can add to the smog and marine layer in Los Angeles or bring the fog into the San Francisco Bay area, keeping it cool even in the summer.

As seasons change, from summer to winter, the jet stream, extra-tropical storm track and sub-tropical high pressure regions migrate away from the pole and closer to the equator. In the Northern Hemisphere, the systems go south, and in the Southern Hemisphere the systems go north in the winter.

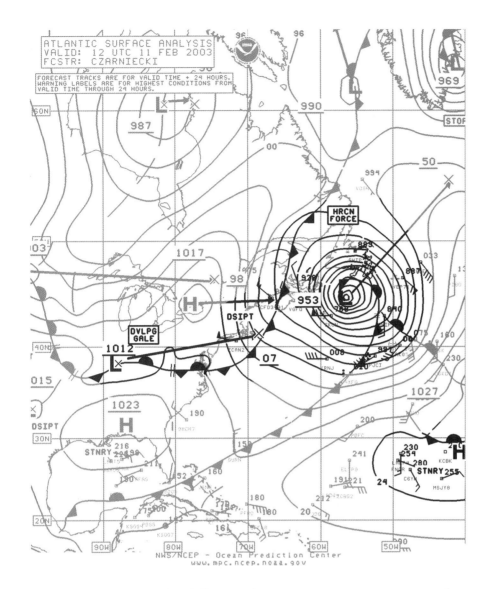

In extra-tropical low pressure systems, the greater the difference in temperature between the warm and cold air masses, the stronger the storm. In winter, the temperature gradient along the jet stream is more pronounced than during summer, leading to more fierce storms in the winter, late fall or early spring.

On a smaller scale, the difference between water temperature and air temperatures can also cause or inhibit the presence of a sea breeze or cause wind sheer over our sails and from the masthead to the surface of the water.

Wind shear is defined as a rate of change in wind speed or wind direction that takes place over a given surface or between separate layers of wind. In other words, the flow of air is not the same throughout a particular column of air. The wind at the top of the mast may not be at all the same as the wind speed or direction on the water. Higher up in the atmosphere, the wind speed and direction of the air in the jet stream may be completely different from the conditions only a few hundred feet or less out of the jet stream.

SEASONAL EFFECTS IN SYNOPTIC SCALE METEOROLOGY

Intuitively, we all know that there are differences in weather pattern between the seasons. Even if we live in the tropics, summers are different than winters. If we live outside of the tropics and further north in the Northern Hemisphere or further south in the Southern

Hemisphere, the weather changes that take place are radically different.

When you understand the mechanics of the various weather features, you can begin to have an understanding of how those differences occur. Understanding how they occur will help you understand how they can become more or less severe within a particular season. Here are a few of those differences.

Extra-tropicals are more severe in winter than in summer

Extra-tropical low pressure systems are generally more severe in the winter than they are during the summer. Lows occur more frequently in the winter. On average they are stronger and larger during the winter than they are during the summer. And they occur further to the south (in the Northern Hemisphere) during the winter. In the U.S., the lows pass more frequently and, rather than tracking across the northern U.S. and southern Canada as they do during the summer months, they more often travel across the middle of the country.

Understanding that extra-tropical low pressure systems are mixtures of cold and warm air masses, we can begin to understand why their characteristics change from winter to summer. Since they also occur along the boundary between the greatest temperature differential, we can also understand why they tend to track more south during the winter.

During the winter months the jet stream is located further to the south. That is the overall steering mechanism for the extra-tropical lows. As the jet stream brings down substantially colder air from the winter polar regions, that air mixes with the still relatively warm air located nearer to the sub-tropical high pressure systems. During the winter, the temperature differential between those two air masses is considerably greater than it is during the summer months. The greater the temperature differential, often the greater the severity of the low.

Furthermore, it is not an accident that some of the most severe storms occur during October or November, and also during March or April. These months, weather patterns are beginning to be in transition from summer to winter or vice versa. Air masses can have hugely different temperatures as the polar regions are very cold and the regions further to the south (in the Northern Hemisphere) can have very warm weather.

In winter, the jet stream tends to dip further to the south, bringing colder air to the south than during the summer months.

Both low and high pressure readings tend to be higher during the winter months

Pressure readings tend to be higher during the winter months. On average, the air is colder and denser during the winter. Regardless of whether that air is in a low or a high pressure system, the package of air is going to "weigh" more because it is denser. The molecules are more tightly packed together. With the cold air masses weighing more, the pressure readings will – on average – be higher during the winter.

Temperature gradient is more pronounced in winter

The temperature difference between higher and lower latitudes is more pronounced during the winter. As an example, in the summer it's not uncommon to have 95 degree F temperatures in Florida and Georgia. At the same time, there could be 70 degree temperatures in upstate Wisconsin or New York. During the winter, however, it wouldn't be an unlikely event if the temperatures in the southern U.S. were in the 70's or 80's while in the northern U.S. the temperatures were zero or even sub-zero. The temperature gradient across that distance is significantly greater during the winter than during the summer. And the temperature differential in air masses is ultimately one of the critical factors in determining the strength of an extra-tropical low pressure system.

Timing can be more critical in winter

From a routing, sailing or other marine application perspective, timing can be more critical during the winter months.

Low pressure systems are more frequent and more severe than during the summer months. Temperature gradients are more pronounced. Because the probability of severe storms is increased, timing offshore passages can become more critical during the winter months than during the summer months.

Along the U.S. east coast, there may only be 2 or 3 days on average between low pressure systems during the late fall or winter months. If one is trying to attempt coastal cruising even in mid-Atlantic or New England states, finding a suitable window of opportunity to get from one place to another may be a problem.

Timing can be even more critical if attempting offshore passage making. Boats leaving New England bound for the Caribbean will need to time their departure to allow enough time to get well south of the north wall of the Gulf Stream, prior to the arrival of the next cold front or low pressure system. Given the warm temperatures of the Gulf Stream and the potentially extreme cold air of a winter cold front, conditions in that region would be ripe for heavy weather compounded by steep seas caused by wind pitching against the current.

Springtime wind shear

During the spring and early summer months, with water temperatures still cold, the warm air is more likely to set up a marine layer. The cold, denser air, cooled by the water, forms a kind of boundary between the warmer air aloft and the surface of the water.

The flow characteristics of the cold, dense air are different from the warmer air aloft, and wind shear takes place. At the masthead of a 50-foot sailboat, wind speeds may indicate 12 or 14 knots of wind, while the water's surface is mirror flat, indicating no wind on the water. The wind direction may indicate an apparent wind angle of 50 degrees at the masthead but, if you were to attach telltales periodically along the cap shrouds, you would find that the wind angle and speed change over the height of the mast.

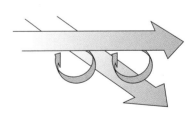

During the spring and early summer months, with cold water still present in many locations and warm air overhead, springtime wind shear and turbulence can be evident in how the wind affects our sails and instruments.

Wind shear, of course, can distort the actual wind that the sails are subjected to, leading to improper sail selection and trim. From the navigator's perspective, wind shear can also distort our expectation of what kind of performance we can expect from the boat.

Wind shear can take place any time of the year, but certain areas are more prone to it during particular times of the year. Since it is caused by warm air over cold water, it can occur quite frequently and may be more pronounced in places like California or Maine, where the water is frequently cold.

Wind shear can be broken down by sustained winds causing a mixing of the various layers of air. The sun warming the lower levels of cool air and creating a more even mixing of temperatures can also break it down. As a result, it is often best to calibrate instruments prior to the start of a race to make sure that wind shear isn't affecting tacking angles. The best time of the day for polar development and sail trials would be generally during the afternoon on days when the flow of air is uniform from masthead to the surface of the water.

Tropicals

Tropical storms can occur throughout the year. In the North Atlantic, the only month that has never had a recorded hurricane is April, but even in that month, in 2003, we had a tropical storm reported.

Tropicals, of course, don't rely on the mixing of cold air into a mass of warm air. Rather, they are solely fed by heat energy – warm, moist air. There are seasonal conditions that are more conducive to their creation. The warm months of the summer heat the water that feed the tropical low pressure systems. And, in order for them to fully develop, they require that there is no wind shear aloft. All of these conditions for their development point toward a season in the late summer. It's not a surprise, then, that the month of September is considered the height of the North Atlantic hurricane season. The water has had the entire summer to fully warm up to its potential, and there is relatively little upper atmosphere wind shear in the tropics.

The region of formation of tropical systems also tends to be somewhat seasonal, based on which regions achieve the suitable conditions at a particular time of year. There are, however, exceptions to these "rules," so it should be noted that tropicals can occur in somewhat "unusual" places and at somewhat "unusual" times.

Chapter 4
Local Conditions

How do local conditions affect overall weather patterns? In general, the following local conditions affect overall gradient, synoptic scale weather patterns:

❶ Unstable air masses
❷ Time of day
❸ Friction caused by air moving over the earth's surface
❹ Sea breezes
❺ Land breezes
❻ Clouds

Ultimately, the weather you experience will be largely determined by these conditions, working in conjunction with the synoptic scale weather. Some of these conditions will affect coastal sailing more than offshore sailing that takes place 20 miles or more out to sea.

NOTE ABOUT LOCAL CONDITIONS: Local conditions can be such that they grow into synoptic scale features, such as relatively small local features developing into a secondary low pressure system forming off Cape Hatteras and evolving into its own system. But more frequently, local conditions play a role in distorting or modifying a larger synoptic scale feature. Don't be misled by the physical size of local features. They can be significant players in how you experience the weather. A particular towering cumulus cloud can qualify as a localized condition but, if it is large enough, it can pack 45 or 50 knots of wind and change the wind direction by 90 degrees or more. That alone could be a significant factor in how you experience the weather on a particular day.

Stability

Vertical stability or instability has significant implications for the mariner. Stable air implies little or no wind. Unstable air implies breeze. Clouds, discussed separately, create their own form of instability. Sea breezes rely on instability in order to work.

Signs of stable air include light or no wind, little or no low-level cloud cover, hazy air at the surface level that may abruptly clear at higher altitudes, hot days and often the presence of cold water.

Signs of unstable air include low-level cloud cover, skies that are not hazy, but rather can range from clear to cloudy, and plenty of wind.

What causes unstable air masses at the local level?

When we talk about air stability, we are talking about how buoyant the air is – how likely it is to rise when heated or sink when it is cooled. Unstable air indicates air movement up and down, and it also

Relatively stable air can become unstable as the sun warms up the land and air begins to rise and condense, forming small cumulus clouds.

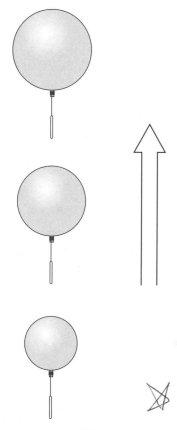

In a standard atmosphere, a balloon carrying a thermometer can expect to have the temperature drop about 3 degrees F. for every 1,000 feet it rises.

Inversion layers are characterized by light surface winds and low level hazy conditions.

implies an interaction between upper level air currents and lower level air currents. A stable air column indicates little or no air movement up and down, and implies little or no interaction between upper and lower level air currents.

Under normal circumstances you could expect that temperatures would drop as you go higher in altitude. If, for example, you tied a thermometer to a balloon, it would normally drop in temperature about 3.5 degrees for every 1,000 feet in altitude.

There are local factors that can inhibit the buoyancy of air, however, causing it to become relatively stagnant (stable). One such factor is an "inversion layer" which acts as a lid on rising air.

Here's an example of an inversion layer. In this example, the air temperature at 1,500 ft. is warmer than the surface air due to cold-water temperature keeping the lower altitude air "artificially" cooled. And up at 1,500 ft. the air temperature is actually 78 degrees.

When the air package at the surface begins to warm in the daylight and it starts to rise with a temperature of 76 degrees F, the temperature will drop as the air rises. As it goes up to 1,000 ft. the temperature of the air package will decline to about 72.5 degrees (76 − 3.5 = 72.5). As the air continues to rise to 1,500 ft. the temperature of the air package continues to drop another 1.75 degrees, cooling the air package to about 70.75 degrees. At that point, the air layer above 1,500 ft. has a temperature of 78 degrees, and the rising air package is actually cooler than the air above it. The inversion layer acts like a lid on the rising air. Air at 2,000 ft. may actually have a horizontal gradient wind speed of 15 or 20 knots but, because there is no interaction between the two layers, the air in the surface layer – under 1,500 feet – is not dragged along at 15 to 20 knots. Therefore, the forecasted, gradient wind may not be experienced locally at the surface.

Physical mixing of the air can break down the inversion layer. But the gradient breeze must be strong enough to force the warmer, higher altitude winds to mix down to the surface. Alternatively, if the sun can warm the lower levels of air sufficiently and eliminate the temperature differential with the inversion layer, mixing can also occur.

On those days when an inversion layer is present, you might do well to think that the wind shift is not necessarily located hundreds of miles away in the next state. It can be as close as 1,500 or 2,000 ft. away and located overhead. You would want to be prepared for the gradient wind shift as soon as the conditions causing the inversion disappear.

Where are inversion layers typically found?

In the U.S., inversion layers can be common in Southern California, Long Island Sound, and the Great Lakes, among other places. The reasons that inversion layers can be experienced in these regions include the potential presence of warm upper level air, hot days, and cold water.

Time of day

The time of the day has significant implications in how local conditions can affect the gradient wind pattern on the local and synoptic scale. The rising and setting of the sun adds to the warming and cooling of the land, water and air at differing rates. The increased rising and sinking of the warm or cool air modifies the surface barometric pressure.

Offshore, experience tells me that shortly after sunrise and sunset, there is an unsettled nature to the wind. It seems to be somewhat gustier. And at night the breeze frequently picks up between 2 and 5 knots. Clouds seem to develop late at night as the warm, moist air of the day cools down and condenses. The cloud formations often set up their own little circulation systems or there may be upper level lightning generated.

Dawn may cause these clouds to start to disappear in the warming air. The moisture can return to a gaseous state as the condensation from the night before is reversed. As the clouds disappear, in some places, such as the Pacific on the route to Hawaii, great lull spots can be left as the breeze seems to evaporate in conjunction with the clouds in the early morning.

Frictional forces of wind over land and water

Friction affects the direction and speed of the wind. Wind blowing over water, and even more so over land, will shift to the left in the Northern Hemisphere. So, a boat approaching from offshore beating toward the land can generally expect the wind to lift on port or head on starboard as it gets close to the shore. Local terrain may alter that generalization but, if all other considerations are nullified, friction will cause the wind to shift left.

How does friction change wind direction?

At the synoptic level, the Coriolis force, over great distances, bends the wind to the right in the Northern Hemisphere as air travels from high pressure to low. It bends it to the left in the Southern Hemisphere. Over shorter distances, friction bends wind in the opposite direction than the Coriolis force works. In the upper atmosphere, a relatively frictionless area, winds travel directly along the contours. Over water, the wind blowing across the surface of the water toes in from the isobars toward the center of a low pressure system by about 15 or 20 degrees. Friction bends the wind to the left (going from a high pressure to a lower pressure) in the Northern Hemisphere. It works in the opposite direction in the Southern Hemisphere.

Over land, increased friction slows the wind even more, causing it to bend even more to the left. Wind coming off the land will tend to turn to the right (viewing it from the land) and generally increase in speed due to the reduction in surface friction.

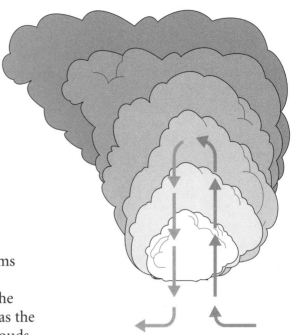

Throughout the day, the sun can create a convective action in air as it rises from the surface of the water. Clouds can then set up their own circulation patterns as areas of low pressure and high pressure are created with accompanying shifts under the cloud.

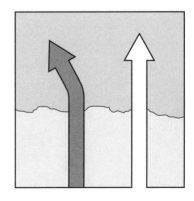

Although upper level gradient winds may continue straight, lower level surface winds are more affected by the increased surface friction as they approach and blow over land.

Winds that are funneling together are considered "convergent," and winds that are spreading out, are considered "divergent."

Convergent and divergent winds

Wind bends differently in different areas; for example, it can be funneled down valleys toward the shoreline or redirected around mountains or buildings. Local geography will cause wind streams to converge with each other, resulting in higher wind speeds, or they will tend to diverge from each other, resulting in lower wind speeds.

Think of convergence like you were on the expressway, and there was traffic trying to converge from a six lane highway to a two lane highway. If the expressway were going to actually be able to process as much traffic, the speed of the cars would actually have to increase. Similarly, if the expressway is going from a two lane highway to a six lane highway, in order to process as much traffic in a given amount of time, the cars can slow down, It can be said that the cars are diverging from each other – spreading out from each other – resulting in slower traffic.

Another way to think of convergence and divergence and how it affects speed would be to think of a water hose. In order to move a certain amount of water through a hose, if you narrow down the nozzle on the hose (forcing convergence of the water molecules) the water flows faster. If you open the nozzle or widen the end of the hose (allowing for divergence of the water molecules) the flow of the water slows.

Convergent (accelerating) and divergent (slowing) air flows take place in many places in the atmosphere. It happens in upper atmosphere as well as on the surface and in both the synoptic as well as the meso- and local scales.

As an example of local convergence, if the gradient wind is approaching the Connecticut shoreline from a southeasterly direction, as it gets to the shore along the coast the increased friction (link) of the land will cause the wind to slow and bend to the left (e.g., east southeast) along the beach. The southeasterly wind offshore will converge with the east-southeasterly wind along the shoreline, causing somewhat higher wind speeds along the beach in the zone of convergence.

Conversely, when the gradient wind over the land is west-north-westerly – say after a frontal passage – the land breeze will be west-northwesterly but the breeze over the water will be more northwesterly due to the effects of friction, leaving the two wind currents diverging from each other and causing a reduction in the breeze along the beach.

Another example of divergence might be a lack of wind in the middle of Lake Michigan caused by sea breezes on all shorelines with divergence in the middle of the Lake.

In general, convergent winds add to the overall wind speed, and divergent winds reduce the overall wind speed. To be exact, converging winds that are tangential to each other will lead to bands of stronger wind speeds. This will occur around islands, in river valleys, etc., and are generally not associated with cumulus clouds. Converging winds that are nose to nose to each other will build cumulus clouds and lighter winds underneath the clouds – you must be on one side or the other for breeze. Divergence of wind always leads to lighter wind speeds.

Sea breeze

A sea breeze is a local condition that results in an onshore breeze (wind traveling from the sea towards land). A pure sea breeze develops when the land heats faster than the ocean water and the air starts to rise over the land. The ability for the air to rise over the land, which is caused by the instability of the air over land, will determine whether a sea breeze circulation will develop, whether it will grow in vertical size, and also whether it will grow in area over the ocean.

An air mass that is unstable typically has outstanding visibility since it is well mixed. The air is not hazy. This well-mixed, unstable air mass frequently, but not always, forms cumulus clouds along the shore. This is a key indicator that a sea breeze condition exists. Conversely, a hazy sky, which implies air is not mixing (i.e., stable air), usually means that conditions are not right for the formation of a sea breeze.

The optimum temperature differential for the formation of a sea breeze is often around 8-12 degrees Fahrenheit. It is important to note, however, that temperature differential can help a sea breeze, but it is not the primary cause of a sea breeze. It is the instability and ability of the air to rise along the shoreline that allows a sea breeze to form. Although the difference in temperature between land and ocean can enhance a sea breeze, technically, you can get a sea breeze – albeit, a weak one – when the land temperature is cooler than the ocean.

When there is an extreme temperature difference between land and water, then a strong inversion layer will form over the ocean extending into the beach area, preventing the rise of heated air over the land. The hot land temperature creates a stable air mass, and shows up as haze. This condition can also cause a great deal of wind shear on the rig due to the temperature differential between the two adjacent – and unmixed – air masses. This condition often happens in the springtime in the early morning when cold water is present.

Basic mechanics of a sea breeze

If we remove gradient wind as a factor for a moment, the following sequence of events will help to gain a basic understanding of how a sea breeze works. Basically, the steps are:

❶ Air rises over the land – When it cools, the moisture that the air held while warm begins to condense, forming small fair weather cumulus clouds over the land along the shore and somewhat inland. This is one of the sure telltale signs of a sea breeze.

❷ The rising air comes to a state of equilibrium, then diverges seaward away from the rising (heated) land air at between 500 and 3,000 ft. Since sea breezes frequently form below 2,000 feet, they are considered low level/mesoscale weather systems.

A sea breeze is a local condition that is typified by clouds forming over the land due to air rising as the land heats up. Meanwhile, the skies over the water tend to remain largely clear at lower levels due to the air subsiding – dropping – over the water.

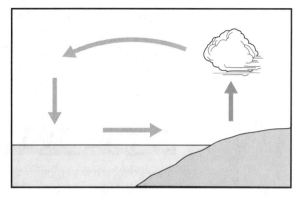

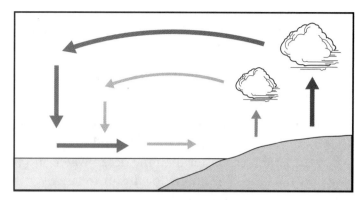

A sea breeze should be looked at as an entire system of actions. If successful, it can build and work its way progressively further offshore. But due to the fact that it is bringing cool air in towards the land that is heating up, it can tend to be self-defeating.

❸ The air then sinks over the ocean and diverges towards the land and also seaward.

a) This divergence (caused by the air hitting the water and scattering in different directions) is seen as a large wind hole on the water.

b) As that upper level wind sinks, the skies are clear of any cumulus clouds or lower clouds. This is the other sure telltale sign of a true sea breeze.

❹ The downward moving air begins to take the place of the air that is now moving across the surface of the water in toward the beach, which will in turn feed and replace the warming air on the land that continues to rise.

❺ As the basic sea breeze develops, it typically spreads out from the beach progressing further offshore throughout the day.

❻ The end of the sea breeze will be noticeable when the small fair weather cumulus clouds over land begin to dissipate or start to move offshore – caused by an increase in the gradient wind.

Quadrant theory and the relationship between coastline and gradient wind

Sea breezes are seldom simple affairs of heat rising, going out to sea, falling and returning to the shore. There are usually complicating circumstances. Often the complications take the form of gradient wind coming from one direction or another and irregular coastlines. The result is that each location will have its own peculiarities for a particular wind direction.

That doesn't mean, however, that we can't come up with some generalizations that will apply in most situations. In order to do that, we will create a series of four possible scenarios.

Imagine a coastline running east and west with the land to the north and the sea or water to the south. We will look at wind coming from each of four quadrants across that coastline. As we look at the four scenarios, realize that this orientation can be rotated 360 degrees to fit any coastline. The important factors are how the gradient wind relates to the coast, and the actual compass directions become secondary and in these cases are merely used to illustrate the situation.

Quadrant Effects on Gradient Wind In general, sea breezes will affect gradient wind from each quadrant in the following ways:

Quadrant 1 Sea Breeze:

A quadrant 1 sea breeze tends to be the strongest and most stable sea breeze. The strongest breeze during the afternoon will be the sea breeze within 10 miles of shore. There will be a calm zone where the sea breeze ends and inshore of the northwesterly gradient.

Quadrant 2 Sea Breeze:

A quadrant 2 sea breeze can develop into a reasonably good sea breeze, but it will tend to be puffy and shifty.

Quadrant 3 Sea Breeze:

The speed of the gradient wind will determine which one wins out: the gradient wind or the sea breeze. A faster gradient wind will choke off the sea breeze circulation pattern aloft.

Quadrant 4 Sea Breeze:

A quadrant 4 sea breeze will rarely develop as a true sea breeze.

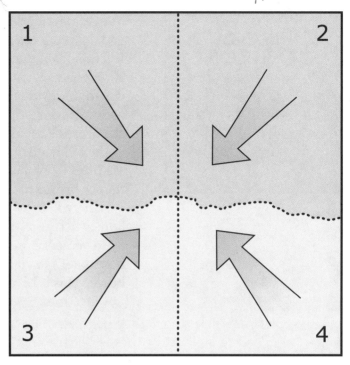

Quadrant 1 Sea Breeze Description The gradient wind is NW. Friction from the land slows the wind and shifts it to the left, resulting in a WNW wind. When the WNW approaches the water, it turns right due to the lower significance of friction over the water; i.e., unaffected by the forces of friction over land, it becomes the NW gradient wind. When the WNW meets the NW wind, it causes a natural divergence within 1-2 miles of the shoreline.

As the sun heats the land, air rises over the land and sinks in this area of divergence (low pressure) near the shoreline. Even if the NW gradient wind is blowing offshore at 10-12 kts, a huge wind hole develops along the shoreline.

The NW gradient wind enhances the offshore flow of the sea breeze circulation aloft. The first puffs of the sea breeze are generally perpendicular to the coast and in this case a southerly wind will develop.

If the air continues to be unstable, the sea breeze circulation will grow larger and the sea breeze will become stronger, expanding further offshore. There will always be an area of wind holes between the inshore sea breeze and offshore gradient wind during a Quadrant 1 sea breeze. Do not get stuck in-between and in the wind holes.

As the speed of the sea breeze increases and thus the forces of friction over both land and sea become more significant, the sea breeze over the water will rotate right, becoming a SW wind.

Quadrant 1 sea breeze circulation can go through a cycle of strengthening and weakening as it builds. If the ocean is cool, then a surge of sea breeze will cool and stabilize the land, choking off the circulation. The sea breeze weakens, then waits for another surge of rising air, which will be accompanied by a significant left oscillation, then builds again, etc. This is the self-defeating nature of sea breezes: the cooling air from the water slows the sun's warming process of the air over land.

When considering a sea breeze and its ultimate probability of success, think of a typical coastline arranged as above with Quadrant 1 in the upper left hand corner and the gradient wind from the northwest. The example can be rotated in any direction to adapt to your own situation. As an example: in Chicago, where the coastline runs north and south, rotating the quadrants 90 degrees counterclockwise would mean the Quadrant 1 example would rotate and the wind would be from the southwest.

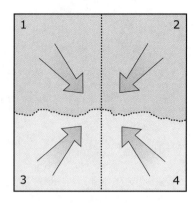

Sea breeze – quadrants

A Quadrant 1 sea breeze is generally the strongest of the sea breezes.

Quadrant 2 Sea Breeze Description The gradient wind is NE. Friction from the land slows the wind and shifts it left, resulting in a NNE wind. When the NNE wind approaches the water, it turns right due to the lower significance of friction over the water, causing a natural convergence within 1-2 miles of the shoreline. This causes a band of stronger winds just away from the shoreline.

The NE wind does enhance the upper altitude offshore flow of the sea breeze circulation, but there is no natural area of divergence for the sea breeze circulation to sink into.

There will be two areas of wind holes with quadrant 2 sea breezes. Somewhere 2-5 miles offshore, wind holes will develop, slowly, from the divergence. Inshore, there will also be wind holes since the inshore portion of the circulation will actually be slightly seaward of the beach. This is because of the band of NE wind along the beach.

A Quadrant 2 sea breeze develops slowly and is weak and generally full of wind holes. This is a much trickier wind to make good tactical decisions.

If there are increasing clouds, the sea breeze remains light, and the sea breeze does NOT rotate right as the effects of friction over both land and water become less significant. Frequently, the wind moves left late in the day as it continues to die.

A Quadrant 2 sea breeze is generally the second strongest sea breeze, although puffy and shifty.

Quadrant 3 Sea Breeze Description The gradient wind is SW. By true definition, a sea breeze occurs when rising air over the land causes a sea breeze circulation. However, Quadrant 3 wind is characterized by competition between the offshore flow of warm land air aloft and the onshore flow of the gradient wind, also aloft. This results in the circulation being choked off aloft and a weak or non-existent sea breeze.

Typically, the gradient wind builds throughout the day, eliminating the chance for sea breeze circulation to begin.

❶ SW wind with a west to east shoreline is an onshore wind. It is caused by low pressure to the NW or over land.

❷ There is a diurnal rise in pressure from daybreak to mid-morning, so you would expect the SW wind to weaken if there are no other influences.

❸ There is a sharp diurnal fall during the afternoon, so you would expect the SW wind to freshen during the afternoon and freshen a bit right of the previous SW wind direction. This is because the diurnal pressure fall is faster/larger over land than over water.

However, if the gradient wind is sufficiently light enough, generally under 10 kts, then the circulation will begin; rising air over land will lead to sinking air over the ocean. The sinking air will cause an ever-increasing area of wind holes due to divergence. The offshore component of the sea breeze circulation is fighting the onshore, gradient SW wind, so the wind holes will become larger and lighter.

The light sea breeze will allow further heating of the land, more rising air, and a larger pressure fall. Over time, the offshore flow of the sea breeze circulation will become strong enough for a significant onshore flow at low levels or a developing S-SW wind. This wind begins left of gradient (S), but readily and actively clocks to the SW and even W-SW with the increasing speed of the sea breeze.

There may be large oscillations, from S-SW to SW, as the sea breeze circulation tries to become established, but once this breeze starts to build quickly, the breeze will move right and the wind speeds will increase quickly.

How can you tell if the SW wind is a sea breeze or gradient wind?

❶ If the SW wind diminishes to under 4 or 5 kts and redevelops from the S, then it is a sea breeze.

❷ If the SW wind increases without a significant left turn and only a minor drop in wind speed, then it is a gradient wind.

Finally, the strategy is key. If it's a sea breeze, you want to stay offshore and play the old, diminishing SW wind and avoid the wind holes. If it's the SW gradient wind, you don't need to worry about wind holes and can stay inshore.

A Quadrant 3 sea breeze is one of the weaker forms of a sea breeze.

Quadrant 4 Sea Breeze Description SE gradient is another onshore gradient wind that will "fight" the offshore component of the sea breeze circulation. A SE wind on a west to east coastline is caused by high pressure to the NE or low pressure to the SE. Diurnal pressure increase during the morning will lead to a strengthening high pressure area, so the SE wind frequently increases a bit after sunrise. Diurnal pressure fall will lead to a weakening high during the afternoon with the SE wind frequently dying off, if the high pressure is driving the wind pattern. Sea breezes rarely develop in quadrant 4.

If the SE gradient wind diminishes to nil during the afternoon, then that will allow the S sea breeze to develop. This is typically a late developing and weak sea breeze. Once again, there will be a transition to wind holes before the sea breeze develops.

If low pressure is causing the SE gradient wind and the low moves closer to the race course, you will see increasing clouds which will limit the heating over the land, the rising air, and the sea breeze circulation. The SE gradient rarely becomes a S sea breeze with increasing clouds.

Let's say the low is approaching, but at a lower speed, which will allow the sea breeze to develop. The sea breeze will be reluctant to move right and frequently moves left, with increasing wind speed as the clouds increase.

Sea breezes and enclosed bodies of water

Sea breezes in enclosed bodies of water get progressively more and more specialized. However, broken down into their components, they can begin to make sense. We could be talking about Lake Michigan, the Chesapeake Bay, Long Island Sound or The Solent. They will each have their own unique qualities, but they will also have some similarities.

Physics will ultimately tell the tale. Each coastline can set up its own sea breeze, drawing wind in toward the beach and creating a pattern of calm zones in the middle of the body of water.

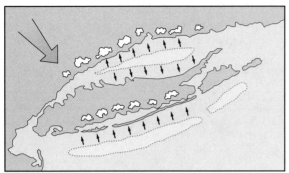

Sea breezes can be complex affairs with wind being drawn in several directions. The clouds will ultimately tell the story about where air is going up, and calm patches may help to understand where it is coming down.

Not unlike Long Island Sound, here's another example of that happening. Lake Michigan runs north and south. Over Chicago, the prevailing wind is generally southwesterly, a quadrant I wind if we rotate the above example around. Over on the Michigan side of Lake Michigan (the eastern side of the lake), the same gradient wind out of the southwest would provide a quadrant IV wind, the weakest wind. The middle of the lake would likely see relatively calm conditions as the sea breezes tried to pull wind toward both the eastern and western shores. Typically, quadrant I sea breezes are the most reliable and quadrant IV are the weakest. Keep in mind, however, that there may be local effects from the concrete and structures of Chicago. That material can absorb quite a bit of heat, distorting the airflow over the city and into the near shore of the Lake.

Sea breezes and islands

Low-level cumulus clouds will again tell the story about what is happening with a sea breeze and islands.

Long Island Sound adds a further complication: one of the shores is actually an island. Sea breezes can break down over Long Island as the gradient south-westerly builds and the CT mainland sea breeze develops all of the way across the Sound and over to the Atlantic Ocean. Prior to that happening, however, the Sound can be extremely light with a series of light spots, dictated by the general rules of sea breeze quadrant theory.

The sign to watch for to see if the sea breeze is breaking down over Long Island is the cloud cover over Long Island. If the clouds begin to streak toward the Sound and eventually break down, the gradient southwesterly, combined with the CT sea breeze, is beginning to dominate.

Stand-alone islands or island groups such as Madeira or Bermuda also have their own set of peculiarities. During the day in Bermuda, if conditions are right, the air over the land will begin to heat up and rise, condensing as it cools at the higher altitudes. The upper level air radiates out from the islands. It gets about 5 to 8 miles offshore, and the air begins to sink, returning to the shore at the surface. The rising air causes a kind of "mini-low pressure system" with a counter-clock-wise flow to it. I've seen satellite imagery over Madeira with clouds indicating the same kind of flow. The rotation of the wind at the surface can cause an easterly component in the winds along the northern side of Bermuda. When the offshore gradient wind is generally expected to be southwesterly, in the presence of a sea breeze the winds can actually be southeasterly on the final approach to the north side of Bermuda.

Land breezes

Land breezes are not like sea breezes in reverse. They do, however, result from the changing temperatures over land. In the case of a night land breeze, the air – especially at higher altitudes – tends to cool and spill down the side of the hills or mountains. The cool, dense air drains or flushes down the side of the mountain, down the valleys and out to sea, tending to follow the contours of the land. The greater the temperature differential between the warm air at the bottom of the mountain and the cool air coming down from the upper parts of the mountains – as well as the shape of the mountain itself and its proximity to the coast – the stronger the land breeze. Land breezes therefore tend to be relatively strong in places like Sicily, some of the Caribbean islands and along parts of the western Mexican coastline.

Clouds

As we go through our daily lives, often tucked away in an office cubicle, it's easy to lose touch with what's happening with nature. Clouds seem to drift by, almost capriciously and with little or no cause. The winds blow. It's sunny or it's raining. There often seems little cause and effect to most of us, but the reality is that there is, in fact, a pattern. Understanding weather patterns and their elements will help us to understand what's in store for us.

How can I tell where I am located in a system by the clouds?

Even though there are countless variations, we can break down a "typical" low pressure system into four rough quadrants. Numbering them from left to right and from top to bottom, Quadrant 1 of a low would be northwest of the center of the system. A warm front lies along the line dividing Quadrant 2 and 4 and a cold front lies roughly along the line dividing Quadrant 3 and 4 in our "idealized" low pressure system. We can look at each of the quadrants and deduce what kinds of typical sky, clouds and other characteristics they would each have. If we are in a boat in the upper right of the chart and this idealized Low Pressure system is headed towards, over, and past us, here is what we can expect to find and the types of clouds that will give us the warning of what is in store.

As Quadrant 2 approaches us, the barometric pressure will begin to drop. The winds will be some form of easterly. They could be SE to NE. In the idealized version of our system, if the pressure

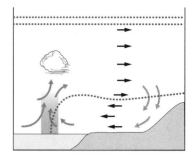

Land breezes are not sea breezes in reverse. They are generally weaker than sea breezes, and often rely on the topography of the land to make them work. If cooling is taking place in adjacent mountaintops, the cooler air at night-time can roll down the hillside and accelerate the land breeze.

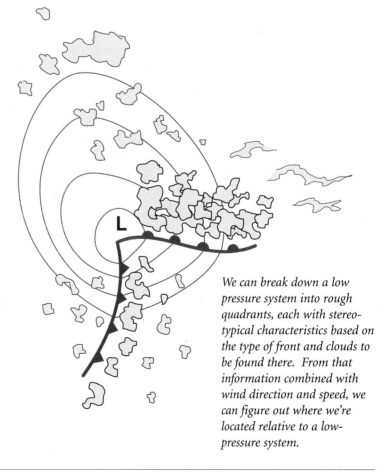

We can break down a low pressure system into rough quadrants, each with stereo-typical characteristics based on the type of front and clouds to be found there. From that information combined with wind direction and speed, we can figure out where we're located relative to a low-pressure system.

Knowing the wind direction and type of clouds, it becomes relatively easy to figure out where the weather systems are located. Knowing where we are relative to the weather helps us to better understand what to expect.

continues to drop, and the wind doesn't shift either right or left, the center of the system is headed over our position. Initially the cloud cover may be high, wispy cirrus clouds. But as time passes and the system gets closer, the clouds will get thicker and lower in the sky. If, as the pressure continues to drop, the wind shifts to the left, becoming more northerly, the temperatures should drop, and the skies should gradually clear. Since cold air can't hold as much moisture as warm air, the skies may eventually take on a clear blue, with scattered clouds. That means we're getting closer to Quadrant 1. The skies will be getting cloudier and the elevation of the cirrostratus, altostratus, and nimbostratus clouds will be getting progressively lower. And, if the wind is shifting to the right – becoming more southeasterly and southerly – then we are headed toward the warm front and Quadrant 4.

During the winter of 2003 Southern New England experienced a lot of Quadrant 2 weather. Low pressure systems formed off Cape Hatteras and traveled toward the northeast, frequently passing just to the south of Cape Cod. Cirrus clouds typify the weather initially, with increasing low-level cloudiness and extended drizzle (or snow during the winter), and winds can gradually increase. If someone asks me what the weather will be like tomorrow, and the only information that I have is that I see that we're going to be in Quadrant 2, I suggest they get ready for an entire day of rain or drizzle. That may not always be correct, but it's a good first assessment, especially if we are located close to the approaching warm front.

Once the warm front has passed with the center of the low to your north and you are in Quadrant 4, the skies become partially clear, leaving scattered cumulus clouds. Temperatures are generally warmer and humid with winds from the South to Southwest. Barometric pressure will fall if the center of the system is getting closer, and as the cold front gets closer separating Quadrant 3 and Quadrant 4. As the low pressure system continues to move over your position, the cold front will be approaching, and winds will typically continue to shift to the right – going from southerly to southwesterly to west southwesterly. Often as the cold front approaches, squall lines will form along the leading edge of the front. If a squall develops high enough into the atmosphere, the jet stream may blow it out ahead of the front, and the squall can be a hundred miles or more before the front. The towering cumulus (cumulonimbus) clouds in these squalls associated with the front can reach 40,000 feet or more if conditions are "right." Large, developing cumulonimbus clouds such as these can have extremely powerful downbursts preceding the cloud. Telltale signs of extreme winds under the clouds include ragged, "bubbling" structure to the clouds, flat cloud tops and wind driven white caps on the approaching seas. They're not to be taken lightly, and quick wind shifts can accompany the downbursts.

Starting again in Quadrant 2, if the wind does shift left from easterly to northerly as the pressure drops, the air will become colder as you go into Quadrant 1. Once into Quadrant 1, the pressure will begin to rise, skies will clear, perhaps leaving some relatively small puffy cumulus clouds with puffy wind gusts to accompany them. Winds will go from northeast to northwest.

As the low pressure system moves past your position, and you get into Quadrant 3, pressure will continue to rise, and winds will move into the west or northwest behind the cold front. The rising pressure and generally cooler air will not support moisture in the air, so skies will generally be clear or mostly clear.

Clouds are convective systems and a result of moisture and temperature differential as the air rises. Understanding which quadrants pick up warm, moist air with winds from the south and which Quadrants tend to cool that air, creating clouds and moisture, will help you understand where you are relative to the larger weather system. Watching how the barometric pressure and wind direction changes will help you to understand the movement of that system and what to expect next.

Thunderstorms and their development

Clouds often indicate an unstable air column. They are often convective systems. Cumulonimbus or "towering cumulus" clouds are the types of clouds that we often associate with thunderstorms, the high winds of downbursts and a great deal of turbulence if we're riding in aircraft. Here is a quick list of requirements for their development:

❶ Warm, moist air must be present along the ground or surface of the water.

❷ Instability in the air column must be present as the warm air rises and cools. That action creates an updraft, and either water droplets or ice crystals form.

❸ When the water drops or ice crystals cool, they release latent heat energy, which in turn slows the cooling of the rising air and increases the likelihood that it will continue to rise.

❹ The water droplets or ice crystals get so large that they begin to fall, dragging the cooled, more dense air down and starting a downdraft, a kind of avalanche of air.

❺ Rain and downdrafts fan out at the bottom of the cloud in a variety of directions with strong winds.

❻ Eventually, the downdrafts grow and choke off the updrafts, cutting off the supply of warm, moist air and beginning the degradation of the cloud system.

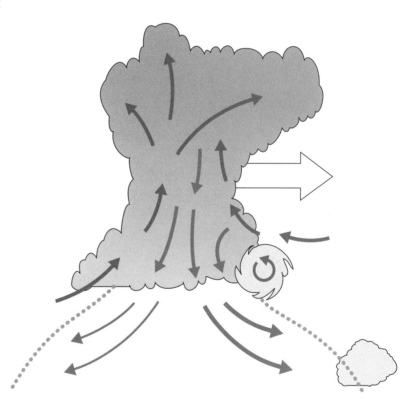

Thunderstorms can take on a variety of characteristics, but there are some generalizations that apply and means by which we can determine their strength by looking at them.

Here are a few things that increase the strength of a towering cumulus cloud:

❶ A steady supply of warm humid air from down below keeps the whole system fed. A typical severe weather outbreak will see warm, moist southerly winds coming out of the Gulf of Mexico with a cool dry, westerly coming off the Rocky Mountains. In New England, a warm, humid southerly ahead of a cold front with a strong, cool NW jet stream will produce the greatest severe weather.

❷ Shear contributes to instability and thus increases the threat of severe weather. The best example of this is the effects of high winds and shear that cause a cloud to "spin" and help form a tornado. Shear is important for severe weather.

❸ High altitude cold air, blowing across the cloud top, ventilates the system and allows it to grow higher into the atmosphere. The rising air is quickly cooled, and creates a more rapidly moving downdraft. You can often see this condition by identifying the flat top of the cumulonimbus cloud that may be streaking from high winds aloft. Very cold air will produce a strong downdraft and large hail, but frequently the cloud tops are very high into the atmosphere.

❹ Warm ground wind can be forcefully "shoved" aloft by an approaching cold front with cold, dense air forming a kind of wedge under the warmer air. Another way that warm air can be "shoved" aloft is by having the warm air mass run up against hills or mountains as the air mass moves across the ground.

❺ Thunderstorm severity is related to updraft strength. Whatever is going to strengthen or increase the updraft flow and height of the cumulonimbus will eventually increase the severity of the thunderstorm.

Wind circulation around thunderstorms

As thunderstorms develop, the warm moist air begins to create an updraft. The rising air results in a decrease in air pressure, setting up a kind of "mini-low pressure system" under the cloud. Often the surface winds around the base of the cloud start to shift in a counter-clockwise direction (in the Northern Hemisphere) at the base of the cloud, if you were looking down from the perspective of being above the cloud. In the middle of the cloud, there is little or no wind, just like in the middle of a full-sized, low pressure system.

As the cloud develops, the downdraft creates an area of high pressure. From above, those surface winds would generally be circulating in a clockwise direction.

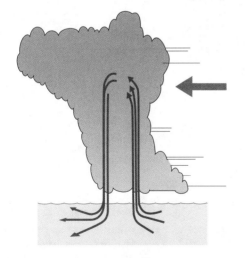

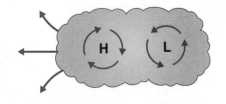

Although winds can appear confused under and around large towering cumulus, there is a rough pattern that can help to better understand them and how to use or avoid them.

Location of the best winds and visual clues for approaching clouds

Frequently the most brisk winds are in front of the cloud. Lighter winds are often in the track, behind the cloud. The absolutely worst winds for a sailboat to get caught up in are directly under the cloud. With both high and low pressure centers under the cloud, that area becomes a quagmire of wind shifts, gusts and calm patches. The winds can go full circle, shifting 90 or 180 degrees at a time.

Cloud characteristics can tell us a lot about the wind underneath them.

In races such as the Transpac, frequently crews will attempt to ride in front of the cloud, gybing back and forth in order to remain in the strong breezes and "catch a ride" with the cloud. One caution is that since clouds often form at night and the best rides may be in the very early hours of the morning after midnight, the same cloud may evaporate at daybreak. As the cloud breaks down and evaporates, often the only thing remaining when the cloud is gone is a very calm patch with no wind. If that's the game you're playing, make sure you get away from the cloud at daybreak.

For those on deliveries or cruising, if it is impossible to avoid going directly under the cloud, you might consider running the engine as you go under the cloud. It may be a good time to charge batteries but, more importantly, if the wind shifts suddenly, you will immediately have the option of motoring back to course or taking the wind shift down and heading off to avoid an accidental tack or gybe. The main consideration is to avoid being caught unaware and have to make an unplanned maneuver that results in damage or injury. Wind shifts under clouds can be sudden and violent.

Here is a brief list of some visual clues that will help you understand the nature of the cloud and how windy it may be near the cloud.

❶ Look at how tall the cloud is. That is not always an indicator of how much wind there is underneath it, but it may give you a clue.

❷ If the cloud is very tall and the top is flat, you will probably have a very brisk downdraft caused by the cooling at the top of the cloud. The wind speeds and shifts will be quite brisk.

❸ If the cloud is billowing and actively growing or looks like it is "boiling," there is a great deal of convection, indicating wind underneath.

❹ If the line of clouds is uneven and tilted, there is also probably good convection inside the cloud indicating wind.

❺ Look to see if there are streaks under the cloud. They may indicate rain. In order to confirm that it is rain and not just shade, figure out where the sun is located and make sure that the streaks aren't merely streaks of light coming through the cloud.

❻ If there is rain coming from the cloud, there is a good chance that there is also wind, but that is not always necessarily the case. Notice if the rain streaks are slanted or falling straight down. If they're straight down, there's probably not much wind under the cloud. If the streaks are slanted, it could be caused by one of several things.

❼ If the rain is slanted, check to see if the cloud is moving. Sometimes there is relatively little wind under the cloud, but upper air currents are pushing it along. The rain droplets may be getting dropped progressively as the cloud moves over calm areas. More than likely, the cloud may be moving, but the streaks don't necessarily indicate cloud movement. Check to see which way it's moving.

❽ As the cloud gets closer, notice the color of the water. The water may be darker merely because the cloud is shading it. Alternatively, the water may be darker appearing because the wind over the water is stirring up the surface.

❾ Check for wind driven waves and whitecaps as the cloud gets closer. If those are present, there will be gusting associated with the approaching clouds.

The next step, of course, would be to make sure that you have prepared to reduce sail area. Preparation to reduce sail area, of course should be started as soon as you begin to think that there may be breeze under the cloud. Depending on your type of boat, readiness and skill level of your crew, and how easy or difficult it is to reduce sail, you can allow more or less time. The point is, however, to make sure that you're prepared and capable of maintaining control of your boat regardless of how much wind is present with the cloud. There can be as much as 45 or 50 knots of wind in some storm cells, and being prepared will go a long way in keeping things under control.

Areas of increasing cloudiness

Because of the structure of clouds, we can conclude that there are probably areas where there may be an increase in cloudiness. One such area is near or over the Gulf Stream. Any substantial warm current will accomplish the same thing. The warm water provides an energy source for the formation of the clouds, whether they are fair weather cumulus clouds – those little "cotton ball" type of clouds we associate with trade winds – or whether they are tall, cumulonimbus clouds we associate with thunderstorms.

Clouds will also be arranged around low pressure systems. For typical cloud structures associated with particular areas of a low, refer to the above information and illustrations. Towering cumulus clouds often are associated with cold fronts, and they can precede a cold front by as much as 100 miles.

Clouds will form when there is a reason to do so. Warmer water provides one of those "reasons" or a source of additional energy to do so. As a result, the location of the Gulf Stream can often be seen 10 or 15 miles away by looking for the band of low-lying cumulus clouds.

Headlands

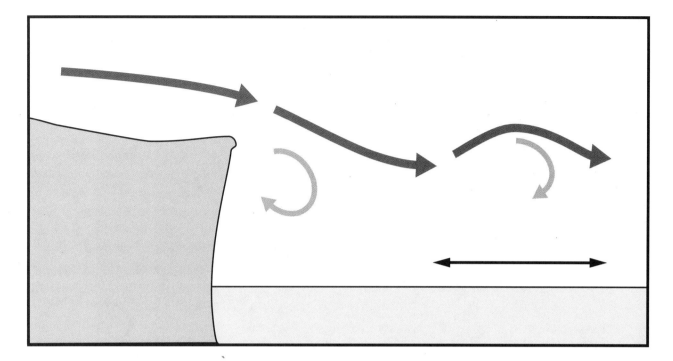

When wind is blowing along a shoreline that has cliffs and head-lands, there is relatively little change in the characteristics of the wind. If the wind is blowing toward the cliff or headland or from the cliff out to sea, there are changes to the wind on the water adjacent to the shore.

The effect on the wind will depend greatly on the height of the headland, the speed of the gradient wind and the temperature. Similar situations can take place in lakes or ponds when dealing with large buildings near the shoreline.

If the wind is blowing onto the shore, there can be a calm area close to the shoreline. The greatest air current goes up and over the obstruction, leaving a narrow area of calm.

Winds blowing offshore over headlands can create lees immediately below the cliff, and there can occasionally be eddies down on the water at the base of the cliff that are in opposition to the normal wind flow.

Lees can extend out a great distance. If the wind is light and moun-tains are high, such as on some of the Canary Islands, the lee may extend out 20 or 30 miles or more.

Heat can also extend a lee. Heat build-up in Chicago, Tokyo or on mountainous islands can increase the distance that the lee extends. The heat rising over the buildings, concrete or rocky mountains can distort the flow of the light gradient breeze and deflect it upwards. If the gradient is light and the surrounding temperatures warm, the gradient breeze may not come back down to the surface for an extended distance.

Gradient wind pouring off a land mass can sometimes form a back eddy. The resulting wind shift could unexpectedly create a lee shore.

The above satellite photo shows the Canary Islands with disturbed cloud formations pouring to the south-southeast for a hundred miles or more. Wind eddies can extend for considerable distances.

Oceanographic features and how they affect local conditions

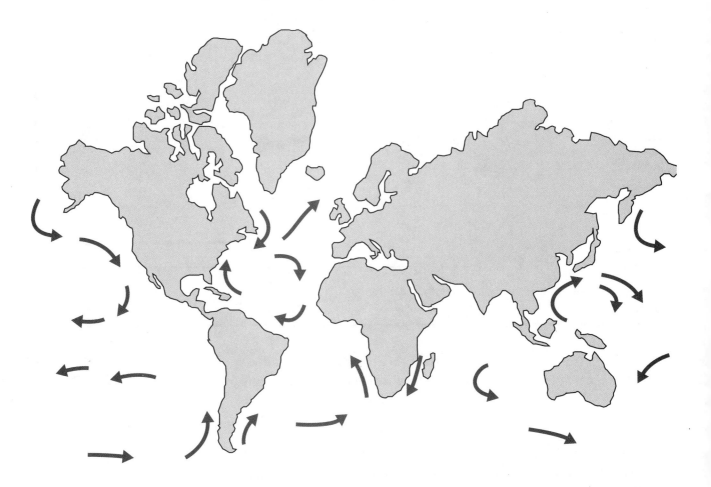

Warm and cold currents do more to affect local conditions than we sometimes think. They can alter the amount of energy available to create clouds, make gradient weather patterns more extreme and change wave patterns.

Tides and currents affect us on a local level. As the tide turns and increases in flow, wave patterns change for a given wind speed and direction unless the wind is perpendicular to the flow of the tide. Wind and current of any kind interact with each other to help determine wave shape and frequency.

Warm currents also play a role in adding to the creation of an unstable air column. The Gulf Stream is a prime example of how warm water can add to the formation of clouds. Frequently, the Gulf Stream can be located by identifying fair weather cumulus clouds on the horizon. If you look closely, often you can even follow where the meanders are located by the clouds overhead. You can do this from the deck of a sailboat, 5 miles or more before you get to the Stream.

In the winter, cold northerlies blowing across the north wall of the Gulf Stream will add ferocity to the surface weather as cold air from aloft sinks to the surface over the warm water. The warm current is adding a local effect to the gradient wind pattern.

When the current modifies the weather, much of that local effect is ultimately due to the temperature differential between the air and the water, and how the temperature changes either over time and distance.

Chapter 5
How Global Climatology, Synoptic Meteorology and Local Conditions Relate to Each Other

There is inter-relatedness to global climatology, synoptic scale meteorology and local conditions. Each one affects all the others to varying degrees.

As an example, in the winter the jet stream moves to the south. The low-pressure systems more frequently track across the middle of the U.S. As fronts move over the mid-Atlantic states, local conditions near Cape Hatteras, combining warm water temperatures from the Gulf Stream plus cold arctic air from the north, can be conducive to the formation of secondary low-pressure systems. To fully understand local conditions, it is necessary – or at least very helpful – to understand weather in its other scales of time and geography.

Norm to actual continuum

As sailors, we need to understand what constitutes "normal" weather, how the norm may deviate within expected parameters, and how local conditions can distort even those parameters over time or given certain circumstances.

The continuum from "norm" to "actual" starts with global averages, then considers synoptic variations, and finally local anomalies.

As an extreme example, hurricanes in the North Atlantic in December are not the norm (global average), but they do occur from time to time (synoptic variation). Conventional "wisdom" is that hurricane season is finished after November 1st. On those occasions when hurricanes do occur late in the season, they frequently behave in erratic ways (local anomaly). One such hurricane moved from its formation over Jamaica east toward the British Virgin Islands and on to St. Maarten and Antigua. It went into the trade winds! Because it was an unusual weather feature, computer-based forecast models, based on very limited historic data, had relatively low reliability.

Sailors had to make decisions. Based on the fact that the hurricane was an odd occurrence behaving in an unusual way, the best course of action was to try to stay as far as possible away from it. Few would have expected it to stay over St. Maarten for the best part of 4 days!

Global averages

Climatology is the study of global weather patterns and averages. It is the study of large-scale trends and anomalies. Sometimes the trends relate to each other. Sometimes they may not.

As an example, all El Niño years are similar in the sense that the eastern South Pacific Ocean is warmer than normal. The years may differ in the degree to which the water is warmer. There may be other associated variations or similarities from one year to another, such as

CHAPTER HIGHLIGHTS

• Norm to actual continuum

   • Global averages

   • Synoptic variations

   • Local anomalies

• Future to now continuum:
  The planning stages

   • Stage 1:
     Global averages

   • Stage 2:
     Synoptic variations

   • Stage 3:
     Local effects

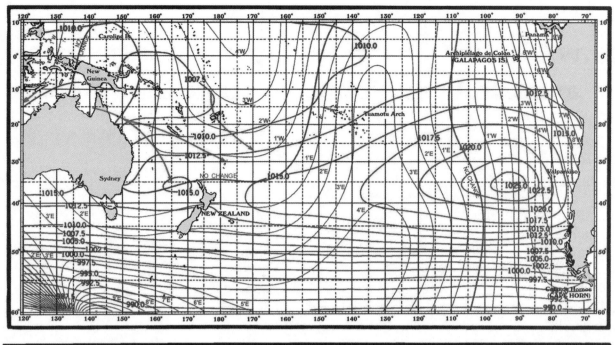

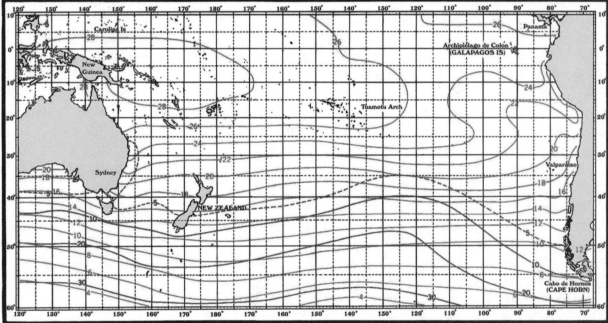

Pilot charts can help us to understand some broad averages and concepts about the weather or sea state of a region for a certain time of year, but there are more refined ways to get more specific sets of data.

the location and strength of the eastern North Pacific high or the amount of rainfall in Brazil. And those may have some correlation to the water temperature in the eastern South Pacific – or they may not.

Averages can be deceptive, like most information we can collect, so the conclusions should be arrived at cautiously.

Once, not too many years ago, a boat designer had been commissioned to design a boat for the Whitbread Round the World Race. Because of my experience in several previous round the world races, he met with me as well as with a meteorologist known for his marine forecasting abilities. The sailor who had commissioned the study had researched the pilot charts of the world and had deduced that winds would never be less than 6 knots and never above 45 knots, so he proposed the boat be designed within those parameters. Both the meteorologist and I begged to differ with the conclusion.

Pilot charts can be fair weather biased. Since ships, given the option of avoiding storms or drifting conditions (for sailing ships a hundred years ago), will opt to go where weather suits their purposes, the data collected over time tends to avoid the worst weather. The averages can be somewhat tilted. From my own personal experience, I've seen wind speeds hover between 0 and 2 or 3 knots for the best part of a week in the doldrums (Inter-Tropical Convergence Zone – ITCZ). Conversely, I've seen winds in the Southern Ocean regularly exceed 55 or 60 knots. Those spikes may not necessarily show up in the climatological averages, but those are things we have to live with when we untie the dock lines. For that reason we need to understand the synoptic variations and how they affect the averages.

How does global climatology help the coastal cruiser? Global climatology helps the coastal cruiser by informing him about what kind of conditions can be expected under normal circumstances. He understands what kind of weather frequently exists in an area. It is the norm, but it is not always the situation he will confront due to synoptic variations or local anomalies.

As an example, if a coastal cruiser is going to go to Maine in May or June, he can have a pretty good expectation that the water will be cold and there may very well be fog along much of the coast. An understanding of climatology will tell that coastal cruiser that, later in the summer, the jet stream is typically in a summer pattern located further to the north. The storm track may have low pressure systems moving further to the north, as well. The water is probably warmer, and in September there is a lower probability of fog.

That is not to say, however, that if you go up to Maine on a particular weekend in the middle of September that it won't be raining. Often there can be low-pressure systems approaching from Cape Cod and the coastal cruiser can still have a cold, wet weekend. Those conditions may be less likely in September than in May, but they are not off the list of possibilities.

How does global climatology help the dinghy sailor? The dinghy or day sailor may understand from global climatology that conditions in the Chesapeake Bay may be relatively light in July with a prevailing wind direction out of the southwest. Statistically, the sub-tropical high is probably located to the east southeast, and the weather is quite warm. That will often be the case.

Actual conditions may be temporarily altered, however, from the "norm" as low-pressure systems come up from the Gulf of Mexico or fronts reach down from lows tracking further to the north. The changes can be dramatic and even severe, but the norm will generally prevail much of the time.

Understanding climatology helps all of us better understand what the "normal" weather is expected to be so that we better understand the implications of changing weather.

Climatology provides all of us with a baseline of information. That baseline can have variations from one year to another, however. Have you ever noticed that some summers seem to have consistent wet weather in some locations and consistent warm weather in others? Trends can persist throughout a season but, in order to understand the trend and how that is going to affect us, we should first understand the norm.

Synoptic variations

We can have all the averages we want but, when it comes down to it, the particular weather we're going to be faced with can throw out all the averages. I've heard it said that, "There are lies, damned lies, and statistics." In that particular continuum, I guess the most reprehensible category is "statistics."

The fact is that global averages (climatology) give us a basis for our understanding. Synoptic scale meteorology helps us to refine that understanding and apply it to a particular near-term time frame.

From a practical stand-point it's nice for me to know that in New England the prevailing wind direction may be southwesterly in June, but it may be more important for me to know that on Saturday there will be a cold front that goes through in the afternoon and the wind will go from 15 knots out of the southwest to 30 knots out of the northwest. Climatology will tell me the first piece of information, and synoptic scale meteorology will help me with the second piece of information.

How I apply that information can take many forms. I may be trying to figure out how I'm going to get my boat down to Newport, RI from Maine – a heading that will take me on a heading to the southwest. I may not really like 15 knots of southwesterly, so my planning could perhaps allow for some flexibility in my scheduling. Perhaps I can leave after the front and, if weather forecasts suggest the wind direction holds constant while the wind speed drops, I might have the best of all possible situations.

If I was in a hurry, and with a well found boat I'd prefer to reach in 30 knots of wind rather than beat in 15. I may still elect to depart Maine, knowing that most of the time the wind direction favors southwesterly.

If I was interested in cruising in one location with my family, my decision process is completely different for the same set of criteria. If I know that winds are usually moderate out of the southwest, I may decide that I needn't subject them to 30-knot northwesterlies on Saturday. We can go sailing another time. Both an understanding of climatology and synoptic scale meteorology help with that decision making process.

Local anomalies

Understanding the local conditions further refines the decision making process. As the actual weather pattern we are facing gets closer in both time and distance, our understanding of the local conditions sheds further light on the topic.

Local anomalies can be created by:

❶ Heating of local land masses
❷ Local storm cells
❸ Local topography
❹ Stable or unstable air columns
❺ Tidal or current conditions

Local conditions may include heating in the land that will create a sea breeze, shifting the wind in a more favorable or unfavorable direction. The presence or absence of storm cells may make the approaching front in the above example worse. The local conditions may include tidal considerations. As an example, if we were expecting to leave in the southwesterly and beat to Newport, and the tide was very fast but pitching against the wind, would we still make the same decision? Would we leave in the 30-knot wind speed? Under some tidal conditions, standing waves can be created and make some channels impassable or in those conditions a loss of steerage can put a boat on the rocks.

Local conditions can include storm cells approaching our boat.

How are local anomalies relevant to offshore sailing? Local anomalies occur offshore as well as inshore. The immediate causes for the local conditions are, of course often different, but we need to understand that the offshore gradient weather pattern can be greatly altered by local conditions at sea.

Storm cells offshore can change wind speeds and directions for a large area around us. Currents such as the Gulf Stream, Brazil Current and others provide not only different wave patterns but also different energy sources for weather systems in their vicinity.

You may be led to expect certain wind conditions for a particular gradient weather pattern but, if you are under a huge cumulonimbus cloud or entering a warm eddy north of the Gulf Stream, you will understand that local anomalous conditions can very definitely alter the gradient pattern. In order to fully grasp what you are dealing with, you will need to understand both the gradient pattern and the local condition and how they affect each other.

When do we start to plan for local anomalies? We should always be aware that the larger scale gradient pattern could be affected by local conditions. In some areas such as at the base of mountains or buildings, near warm currents, or as cold fronts approach, we may experience an increase in local anomalies. Nightfall may bring an increase in the number, size and convection associated with some cloud formations. Daybreak may bring an increase in calm patches as those clouds evaporate. But we should always be alert to possible changes, realizing that the changes may only be taking place on a local level rather than on a synoptic scale.

Future to now continuum: The planning stages

At different stages of planning and execution we can use different types of weather information to our favor. We can break down the time continuum into several rough time categories:

Ocean Temperatures (°C)

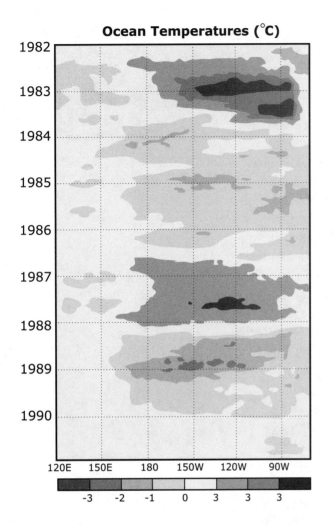

850-mb Zonal Winds (m/s)

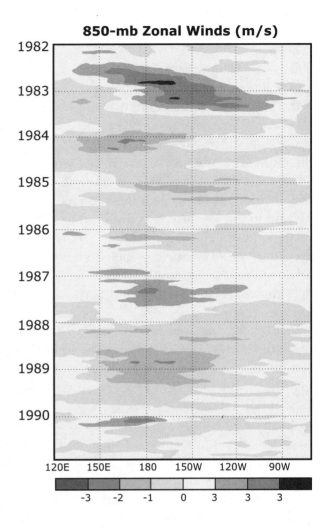

Different years have their own set of anomalies. Here a comparison is made between winds aloft at 850 mb, and the ocean temperatures. Warmer years may imply more tropical storms, stronger surface winds in some locations, displaced high pressure systems or other things that will certainly affect the conditions in which we sail.

Stage 1: studying global averages months or years prior to departure,

Stage 2: analyzing synoptic conditions 10 days to immediately prior to departure, and

Stage 3: factoring local conditions based on real-time or near real-time data.

Stage 1: Global averages

We can start to get a sense of the weather conditions months or even years prior to departure. Using global climatology and an understanding of general conditions we might expect to encounter, we can plan an entire route around the world. Naturally, as the time draws near, we will probably want to modify some of the original assumptions.

Months before a competition or passage is to be undertaken, meteorologists have successfully looked at trends particular to a certain year or how one year related to another. By skewing the averages to reflect an assumed trend, the resulting deductions seemed to be more accurate. For example, on several occasions, 4 to 6 months prior to Transpacs or Bermuda Races, meteorologists studied climatological data to compare similar El Niño or La Niña years to help predetermine what kind of conditions would be prevalent during those competitions. Rather than solely relying on an average of all years, the meteorologists were recognizing a trend and looking at averages from other years that complied with the pre-existing trend. Tilting the data that way seemed to provide long-range forecasts that were considerably more similar to the conditions that eventually took place during those races. Meteorologists can be a great help in Category 1 analysis.

Stage 2: Synoptic variations

Climatological averages are all well and good, but all it takes is one strong frontal passage or low pressure system pressing against a strong high and averages don't mean much to the person on the water in 45 knots of wind. They may primarily be interested in how long it takes before things return to "normal."

Synoptic scale meteorology tells us what is expected to happen in near real time. Forecasts can be created that go out 9 or 10 days that provide us with some notion of what may happen. As we get closer to the valid time for the forecast – say 5 or 6 days – the forecasts are beginning to have some real relevance. There will still be errors, however, and those should – to a certain degree - be expected. Weather forecasting is not, as it turns out, a perfect science at this point.

As we continue to get closer to real-time, the 96 hour and 48 hour forecasts continue to improve. And with the 24 hour forecast we should have a reasonably good expectation that the weather tomorrow will be as expected. It isn't always, but odds are good that the forecast will generally be close if not perfect.

All of that may seem pretty sketchy and hardly of value in planning strategy and certainly of minimal value in thinking about tactics. The fact is that it does have some value for both.

If we're on a long offshore passage, my general strategy is to be within some cone of positioning along a general course toward a mark. The further out from my position, the wider the cone. My information input – the weather forecasts – can help to widen or narrow that cone. If I have a great deal of faith in the forecast, the cone is narrower, telling me where I should go. If the forecast is in doubt, the cone is wider.

Within the 96 hour (4-day) window prior to departure, it's good practice to determine the reliability and accuracy of the forecasts (and forecasters) that you will be relying on for your planning and voyage. We can use the forecasts themselves to indicate to us how much faith they deserve. If we collect the 96 hour forecast, along with the 48 hour and 24 hour forecasts and later compare them to the surface analysis, we can begin to get an understanding of how reliable they may be. Does the 96 hour forecast map that I collected 2 days earlier look the same as the 48 hour forecast map I collected today? If it does, then I have an idea that perhaps the reliability of both are relatively high. My range of choices narrows as I develop a better defined set of conditions over time.

Occasionally, someone will ask me a few days before a regatta or start of a long distance race, "Where will we want to head after the start?" Usually my internal response is that I have no idea – other than what climatology would imply. I'll give some kind of answer that is rather general and based more on averages than on the reality we'll have to face a few days hence. It often strikes me that it's as if someone asked a skeet shooter where he's going to aim when the clay pigeon is launched next Tuesday. It kind of depends on the conditions at the time.

Studying the synoptic scale forecasts will help you get a more refined understanding of what has been happening and what is most likely to happen in real time. The closer the valid time of the forecast, the more likely it will be accurate for that scale of understanding. But to get a highly refined understanding of what is going to happen to you aboard your boat, you will want to have a thorough understanding of local effects.

Stage 3: Local effects

Local effects are best studied in near real time or real time. You can't tell what the puffs will be like under a cloud two days before the squall line approaches. Even with something as predictable as tides, you either don't know your exact time in the tide cycle if you are two days away from landfall or you can't be certain of the wind conditions and how they will affect the wave patterns.

Local effects can radically alter the gradient, large-scale wind pattern.

You can and should study and anticipate such things and the range of possible choices, but local conditions and anomalies will become more clearly manifest as time and distance decrease.

How radically will local effects alter the gradient weather pattern? Local effects can either present minor modifications or completely rearrange the gradient weather pattern on a local level. As an example, a sea breeze may accelerate by a knot or two and shift the wind approaching a coast by 10 or 20 degrees. In some sea breeze situations, you can be in one area, completely becalmed, and meanwhile in another nearby area have 5 knots of wind or more. In shore, the wind may be going directly toward the beach, and meanwhile well offshore the wind may be blowing away from the beach.

Even in mid-ocean, local anomalies can completely rearrange the weather you are experiencing. If you are directly under a towering cumulus cloud, you can have wind from almost any direction and speeds that vary between 45 knots and 0! When the cloud passes, you may be back in a relatively steady gradient pattern in which the wind may be a relatively steady 15 to 20 knots from the east-northeast. Keep in mind that local effects are often temporary. If you understand both the gradient pattern as well as the mechanics behind the local conditions, you will be better prepared to cope with the conditions that you actually do experience. You will then be empowered to make good, well-informed decisions accordingly.

Chapter 6
Gathering Data

In order for the decision makers onboard to come to informed decisions, they will need the relevant information to support their sailing objective.

What types of data we will deal with

Some of the weather data the decision makers will need to collect will be:

❶ Weather maps
❷ Satellite images
❸ Text forecasts
❹ Onboard personal observations, and instruments

And they will need to have an understanding of the validity and probability of its accuracy in order to base a decision.

How to read a weather map

The decision makers will need to have a basic understanding of how to read weather maps as discussed above. They will want to know how to plot the boat's expected position on the weather map. The forecast maps are for times in the future, so navigators and skippers will have to project out their assumed positions or at least a range of choices of where they may be located for the relevant time period and plot those locations on the weather map.

Useful weather maps for sailors

The following maps will be particularly useful in helping to understand the weather features and what can be expected along a route:

Surface analysis
24 hour surface forecasts
48 hour surface forecasts
48 hour wind/wave forecast maps
96 hour surface forecasts
96 hour wind/wave forecast maps
500 mb charts

Please turn to the next page for samples of these maps and for a listing of common weather map symbols.

CHAPTER HIGHLIGHTS

- **What types of data we will deal with**

- **How to read a weather map**

- **How to read a satellite image**

- **Text forecasts**

- **Read the weather while onboard using your senses and vessel's instrumentation**

- **Verify your data**

- **Barometers and using them**

- **Radar**

- **Predict future weather by plotting isochrones on weather forecast maps**

- **Obtaining the data**

- **Evaluating the data**

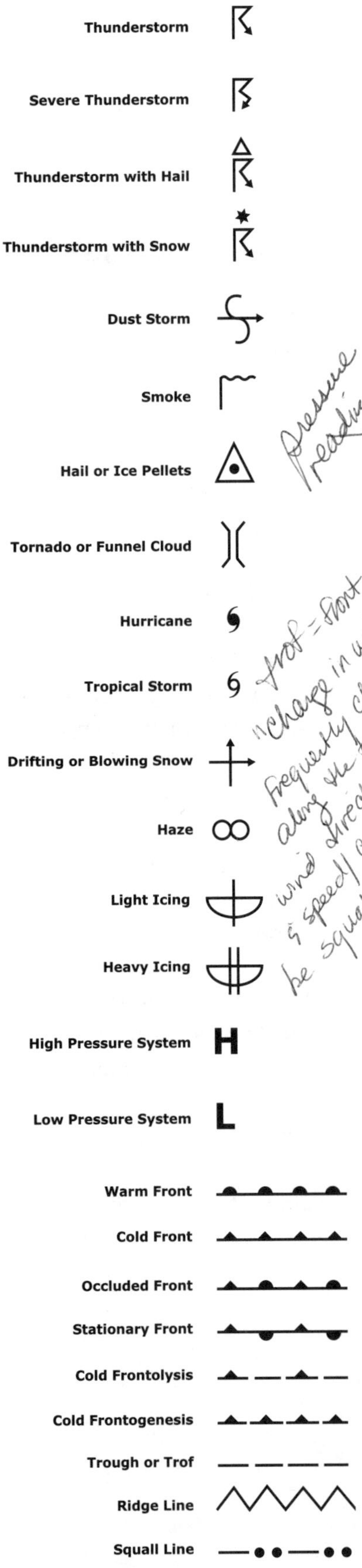

2 = Greenwich meantime (handwritten)

Look here first (handwritten, near top)

Thunderstorm	R
Severe Thunderstorm	R
Thunderstorm with Hail	R
Thunderstorm with Snow	R
Dust Storm	S→
Smoke	
Hail or Ice Pellets	▲ with dot
Tornado or Funnel Cloud	)(
Hurricane	6
Tropical Storm	6
Drifting or Blowing Snow	+
Haze	∞
Light Icing	
Heavy Icing	
High Pressure System	**H**
Low Pressure System	**L**
Warm Front	●●●
Cold Front	▲▲▲
Occluded Front	▲●▲●
Stationary Front	▲●▲●
Cold Frontolysis	▲ ▲ ▲
Cold Frontogenesis	▲▲▲
Trough or Trof	— — —
Ridge Line	∧∧∧∧
Squall Line	—●●—●●

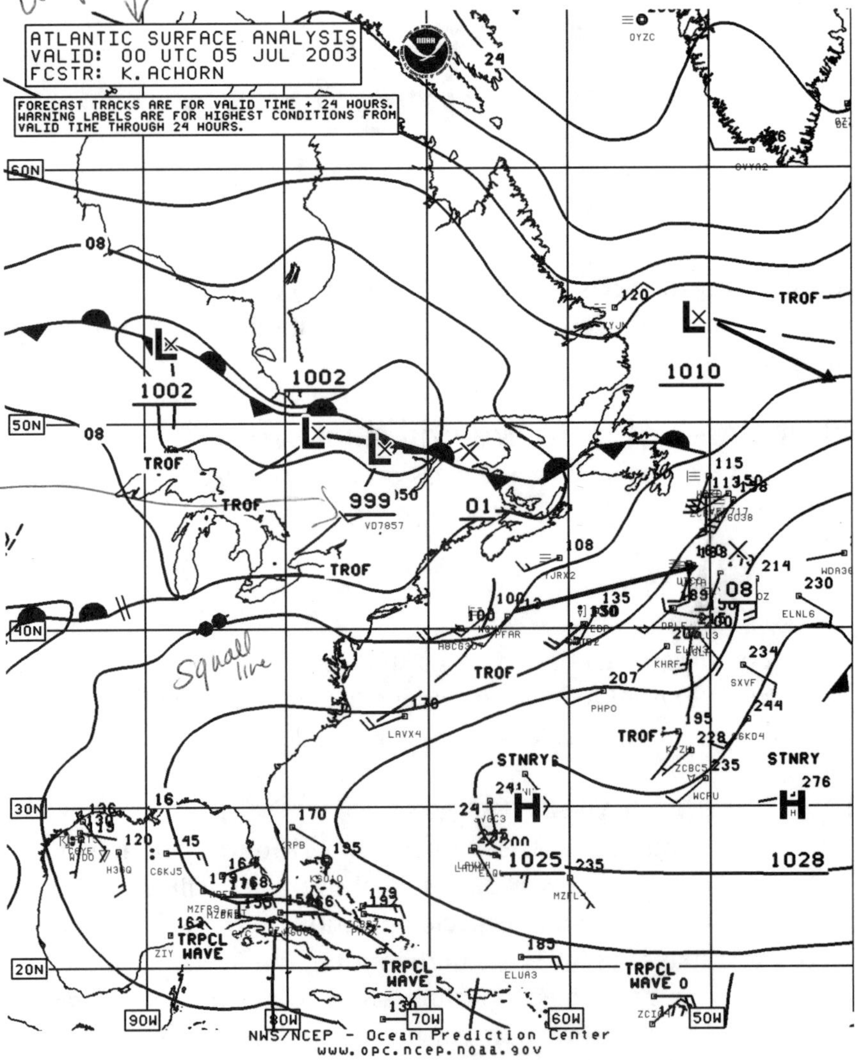

Pressure reading (handwritten)

Trof = front "change in wind" frequently cloudy along the trof - wind direction & speed can be squalls (handwritten)

ATLANTIC SURFACE ANALYSIS
VALID: 00 UTC 05 JUL 2003
FCSTR: K. ACHORN

FORECAST TRACKS ARE FOR VALID TIME + 24 HOURS.
WARNING LABELS ARE FOR HIGHEST CONDITIONS FROM
VALID TIME THROUGH 24 HOURS.

Squall line (handwritten)

NWS/NCEP - Ocean Prediction Center
www.opc.ncep.noaa.gov

Surface analysis:

Western North Atlantic Surface Analysis, Valid 00 UTC, 05 July 2003

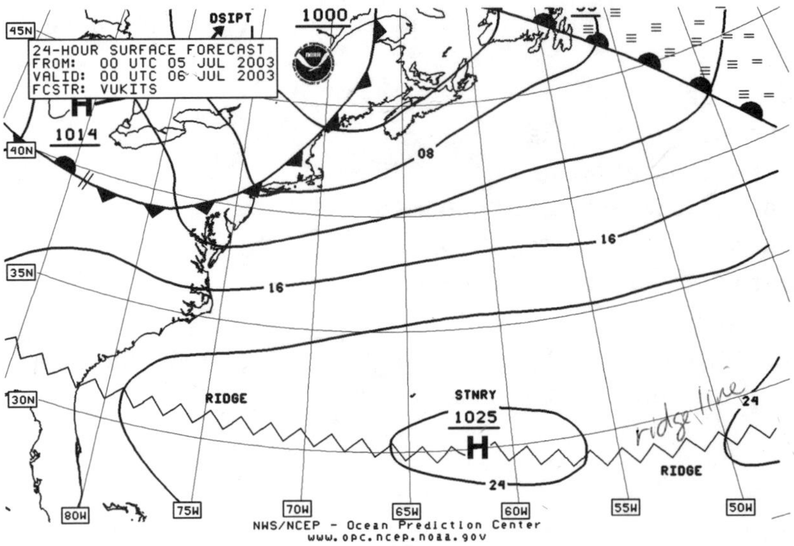

24-HOUR SURFACE FORECAST
FROM: 00 UTC 05 JUL 2003
VALID: 00 UTC 06 JUL 2003
FCSTR: VUKITS

ridge line (handwritten)

NWS/NCEP - Ocean Prediction Center
www.opc.ncep.noaa.gov

24 hour surface forecasts:

Far Western North Atlantic 24 Hour Surface Forecast, Valid 00 UTC, 06 July 2003

24 hrs. after they collected data - will be valid (handwritten)

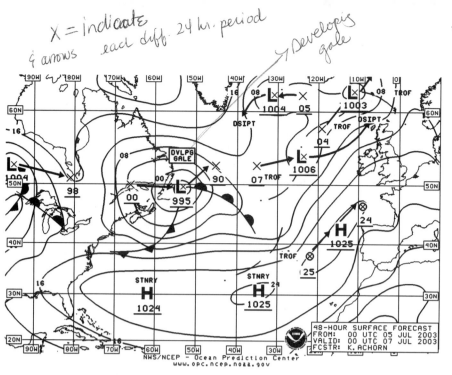

Handwritten notes:

X = indicate 4 arrows each diff. 24 hr. period

→ Developing gale

☆ Filing weather reports? by valid time

Isobars -lines of equal pressure - closer together = more wind

Ridge line? -middle of ridge line = no wind subtle wind changes top of H pressure?

48 hour surface forecasts:
North Atlantic 48 Hour Surface Forecast, Valid 00 UTC 07 July 2003

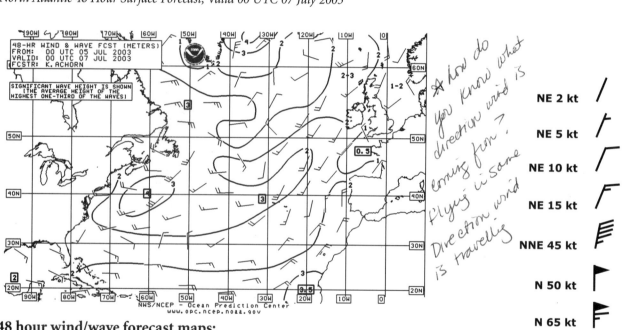

Handwritten notes:

★ how do you know what direction wind is coming from? Flying in some Direction wind is travelling

NE 2 kt		/
NE 5 kt		⊢
NE 10 kt		⌐
NE 15 kt		F
NNE 45 kt		⫤
N 50 kt		▶
N 65 kt		⊯

48 hour wind/wave forecast maps:
North Atlantic 48 Hour Wind/Wave Forecast, Valid 00 UTC 07 July 2003

	Symbol	Light	Moderate	Heavy
Rain	• •	• •	∴•	•ᛁ••
Snow	★ ★	★ ★	★★★	★★★★
Drizzle	❜ ❜	❜ ❜	❜❜❜	❜❜❜•

	Symbol	Light	Moderate	Heavy
Snow Shower	★▽	★▽	★▽	
Freezing Rain	∿	∿	∿	
Freezing Drizzle	∿	∿	∿	
Fog	≡	≡		≡

Various abbreviations:

- **SCT:** Scattered
- **ISOLD:** Isolated
- **NUMRS:** Numerous
- **HVY:** Heavy
- **STNRY:** Stationary
- **RPDLY:** Rapidly
- **FRMG:** Forming
- **MOVG:** Moving
- **DCRS:** Decreasing
- **INCRS:** Increasing
- **INTSFY:** Intensifying
- **Z. UTC, GMT:** Time in Zulu, Universal Coordinated Time, Greenwich Mean Time (all equivalent)
- **Mb, in Hg, hPa:** Millibars, inches of Mercury, hectopascals (formerly millibars)
- **DSIPT:** Dissipating
- **TROF:** Trough
- **TRPCL WAVE:** Tropical wave
- **GALE:** Gale (winds of 35 knots or more)
- **STORM:** Storm (winds of 50 knots or more)

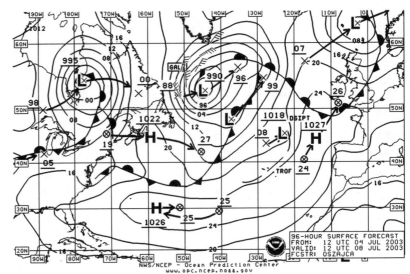

96 hour surface forecasts:

North Atlantic 96-Hour Surface Forecast, Valid 12 UTC 08 July 2003

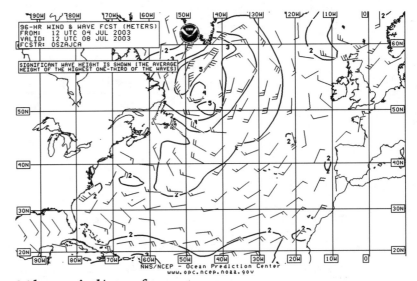

96 hour wind/wave forecast map:

North Atlantic 96-Hour Wind/Wave Forecast, Valid 12 UTC 08 July 2003

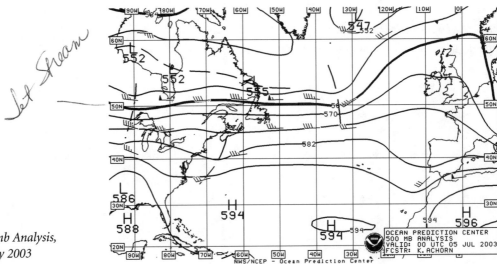

500 mb chart:

North Atlantic 500 mb Analysis, Valid 00 UTC 05 July 2003

Weather map symbols

Here are a few weather map features that you should know and be able to identify.

Cold fronts usually windier than warm fronts

one kind of front into another one

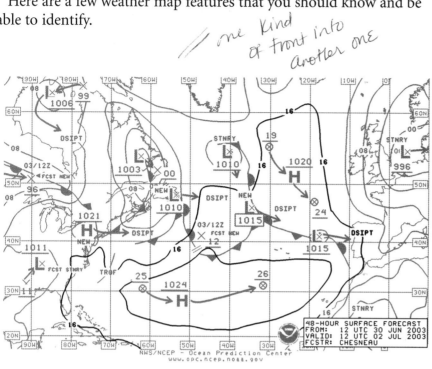

Isobar

An isobar is a line of equal barometric pressure, usually drawn on surface maps. In many cases, isobars differ by 4 mb of pressure.

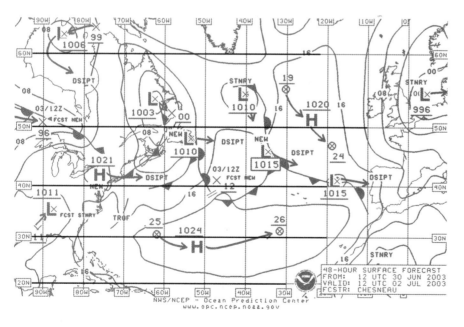

Latitude

Latitude is the angular distance from the equator, measured northward or southward along a meridian from 0 degrees at the equator to 90 degrees at the poles. It is designated (N) or (S) to indicate the direction of measurement.

U.S. vs. non-U.S. weather maps

Most of the symbols and conventions used in creating marine weather fax maps are internationally recognized. There are some differences, but generally, if you can read a British or Australian map, you can read an American or Chilean map. There may be a few things – such as the letters that represent highs and lows – that change in different languages or while using different conventions, but for the most part, learning to read the U.S. charts will help you in understanding weather maps around the world. For standardization and ease of access, we'll use U.S. charts for our initial discussions.

Top: Surface pressure map showing isobars. On most U.S. charts the isobars are separated by 4 mb of pressure.

Bottom: Although some U.S. weather charts are different projections, they all have lines showing latitude so you can estimate distances and locations. Note that there is some distortion in the distances as you move further north in this projection.

Lines of longitude are also shown on the U.S. marine weather maps.

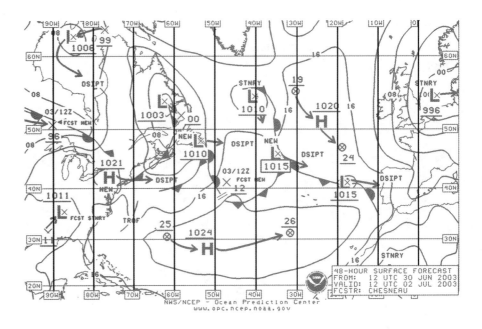

Longitude

Longitude is the angular distance between the prime meridian and the meridian of a point on the Earth, measured eastward or westward from the prime meridian through 180 degrees. It is designated east (E) or west (W) to indicate the direction of measurement.

The double hash marks between the two fronts indicates that the type of front changes at that point.

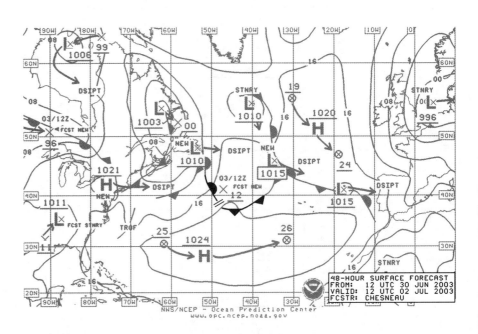

"Double hash mark on front"

Double hash marks indicate that the type of front is changing. In other words, a cold front is changing to a stationary front at a particular point where the double hash marks are located.

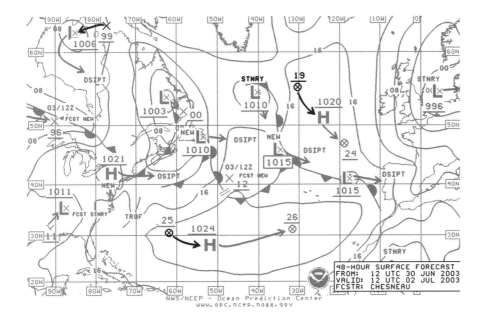

Arrow pointing toward the expected center for the pressure system indicates where that pressure system was expected to be 24 hours prior to the Valid Time indicated on the weather map, and the 2 digit underlined number indicates its expected previous center pressure. Either a "9" or a "10" is to be assumed in front of the 2 digits.

Arrow indicating where low came from 24 hours prior to valid time

On some surface maps, an arrow will indicate the location a low (or high) pressure system was located 24 hours prior to the valid time indicated on the chart.

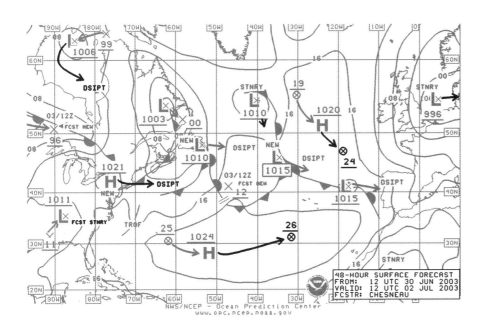

Arrow pointing away from the expected center for the pressure system indicates where that pressure system will be expected to be 24 hours after the Valid Time indicated on the weather map, and the 2 digit underlined number indicates its expected subsequent center pressure. Either a "9" or a "10" is to be assumed in front of the 2 digits. Noting how the center pressure is changing over time helps us understand whether the system is getting weaker or stronger.

Arrow indicating direction low is expected to move 24 hours after valid time

On some surface maps, an arrow will indicate where the a low (or high) pressure system will be located 24 hours after the valid time indicated on the chart.

Direction of general wind flow

Wind will flow in a clockwise direction around a Northern Hemisphere High Pressure system, toeing out about 15 degrees from the high. Wind will flow in a counter-clockwise direction around a Northern Hemisphere Low Pressure system, toeing in about 15 degrees toward the low. Wind will flow in a counter-clockwise direction around a Southern Hemisphere High Pressure system, toeing out about 15 degrees from the high. Wind will flow in a clockwise direction around a Southern Hemisphere Low Pressure system, toeing in about 15 degrees toward the low.

Top: Wind barbs indicate both wind speed and direction at the surface.

Bottom: Horizontal parallel lines indicate fog or heavy fog.

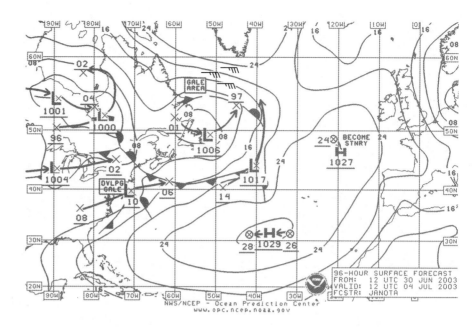

Wind barb and how to tell both wind speed and direction

Wind barbs can be likened to arrows flying through the air. The wind is flowing in the direction that the "arrow" appears to be flying, and the number of "feathers" indicates the wind speed. One "feather" is approximately 10 knots. Two feathers represents approximately 20 knots. A "half feather" is approximately 5 knots. A "black flag" is approximately 50 knots, and so forth.

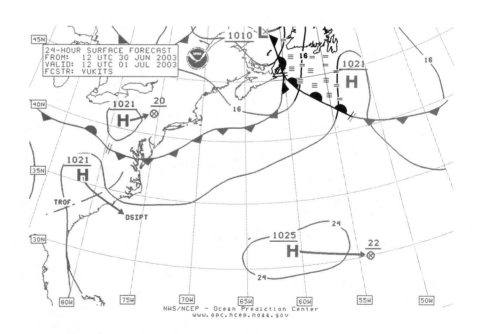

Icon indicating fog/heavy fog

Two or three horizontal parallel lines will indicate fog or heavy fog.

Icon indicating freezing rain/heavy freezing rain

Two or three vertical parallel lines will indicate freezing rain or heavy freezing rain.

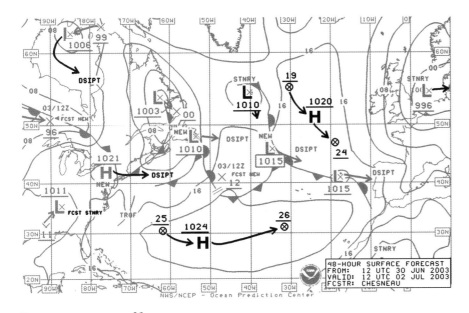

Center pressure of low

The center pressure of a low will be indicated by the 3 or 4 digit underlined number located beside the letter indicting the low's location (L on U.S. maps).

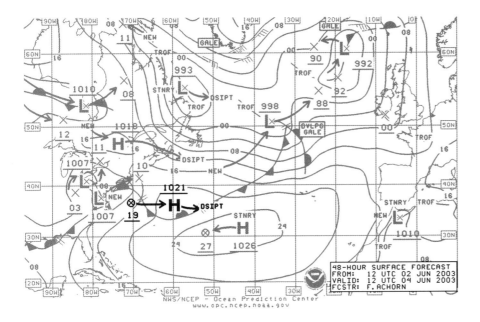

Center pressures of high

The center pressure of a high will be indicated by the underlined 4 digit number located near the letter indicating its position (H on U.S. maps).

Center pressure of "future" high and whether it is building or weakening

If there is an arrow indicting the future position of the high – 24 hours after the valid time indicated on the chart – there should also be a 2 digit number indicating the expected center pressure of the high. ("10" is assumed to be the first digits in the complete number

Center pressure of "future" low and whether it is building or weakening

If there is an arrow indicating the future position of the low – 24 hours after the valid time indicated on the chart – there should also be a 2 digit number indicating the expected center pressure of the low. (Either "10" or "9" is assumed to be the first digit(s) in the complete number for the future center pressure). By comparing the current center pressure with the expected center pressure, you can determine if the low is strengthening (numbers going lower) or weakening (numbers going higher).

Top: Arrows indicate where a system is expected to go 24 hours after the Valid Time.

Bottom: Systems will sometimes fade away or dissipate. Alternatively, new ones may spring up.

Center pressure of "previous" low and whether it is weakening or strengthening

If there is an arrow indicating the previous position of the low – 24 hours prior to the valid time indicated on the chart – there should also be a 2 digit number indicating the previous center pressure of the low. (Either "10" or "9" is assumed to be the first digit(s) in the complete number for the previous center pressure). By comparing the current center pressure with the previous center pressure, you can deter-mine if the low is strengthening (numbers going lower) or weak-ening (numbers going higher) as the time continues forward.

for the future center pressure). By comparing the current center pressure with the expected center pressure, you can determine if the high is strengthening (numbers going higher) or weakening (numbers going lower).

Center pressure of "previous" high and whether it is weakening or strengthening

If there is an arrow indicting the previous position of the high – 24 hours prior to the valid time indicated on the chart – there should also be a 2 digit number indicating the previous center pressure of the high. ("10" is assumed to be the first digits in the complete number for the future center pressure). By comparing the current center pressure with the previous center pressure, you can determine if the high is strengthening (numbers going higher) or weakening (numbers going lower) as the time continues forward.

Valid Time of the weather chart

Virtually, all of the weather fax maps will have a little box in one of the corners telling you what the maps represent. One critical piece of information is the "valid time." The box will give the following information:

❶ It'll say it's a particular kind of analysis – meaning it represents something that is happening (current analysis) – or it will tell you that it's a particular kind of forecast – something that will happen in the future (forecast).

❷ Depending on whether the map is a current analysis or a forecast, the box will also have one or two times.

An analysis map will indicate one time – the "VALID" time, indicating when the picture is a valid representation of the collected data. A forecast map will indicate two times – a "FROM" time and a "VALID" time. "From" will tell you the time that the weather data was collected that formed the basis for the forecast (i.e., when weather balloons were sent aloft, buoy data was recorded, ships' observations were taken and so forth). Meteorologists around the world then analyzed the data and created forecasts the would be "Valid" 24 hour or 48 hours hence from the time of the actual data collection.

As an example, a Surface Analysis with a valid time of 12 UTC, 03 June 2003, had the data collected at that time. UTC means the same as GMT (Greenwich Mean Time) and can commonly be written as 12Z or 12 UTC. At that time, around the world, the World Meteorological Organization (WMO) collected data from buoys, ships, airports, satellites and other sources and fed it into computers to crank out computer generated forecasts. The information was provided to meteorologists, and in some cases they created their own forecasts using the various tools of their trade. Naturally, it takes awhile to create all of these forecasts based on the data, so it may be a few hours before the actual weather map is created. But it is still based on the time indicated as the "valid time." By the time you receive the Surface Analysis from your onboard weather fax machine, the data and the representation on the map is probably about 4 or 5 hours old, so things may have advanced a bit in the interim.

```
48-HOUR SURFACE FORECAST
FROM:   12 UTC 30 JUN 2003
VALID:  12 UTC 02 JUL 2003
FCSTR:  CHESNEAU
```

The type of weather chart, its Valid Time, and the name of the forecaster are often on each chart. The Valid Time is the time at which the map is expected to represent reality.

Surface Analyses When looking at the Surface Analysis, the first thing that I determine is the location covered and the valid time – the time for which this "snapshot" of the weather actually was supposed to take place. If it is the current analysis, the time was actually probably several hours prior to when it was issued and came out of an onboard fax machine. Since it's based on data that is already several hours old, the actual conditions that are being experienced are probably somewhat changed.

After I've determined when and where the analysis is valid, I begin to look at the conditions around my own location. Are they reasonably accurate? Remember that we're only miniscule dots on the chart, and local conditions such as clouds, currents, inversion layers or other things may alter our conditions locally.

How do the weather patterns and conditions that are recorded as observations on the analysis compare to the expected conditions proposed by earlier forecasts?

24/48/96 Hour forecasts In a "perfect world," forecasts that are collected at different times but share the same valid time and region should look exactly alike. If the 96 hour forecast is exactly the same as the 48 hour forecast I collect two days later, I begin to develop a feeling that the

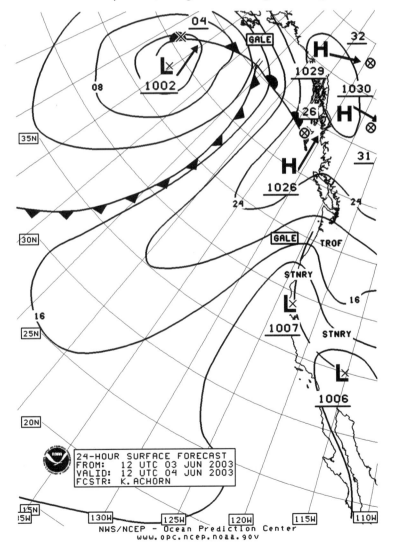

Eastern North Pacific 24-Hour Surface Forecast, Valid 12 UTC 04 June 2003. Note the location of the ridgeline, the cold front, and the low pressure system in the Gulf of Alaska. Look for other more subtle features.

occluded front

North Pacific 48-Hour Surface Forecast, Valid 12 UTC 04 June 2003. Even though the projections are different, in a "perfect world" the 24 Hour forecast above should provide the same information as this 48 Hour forecast, collected the day before the above 24 hour forecast.

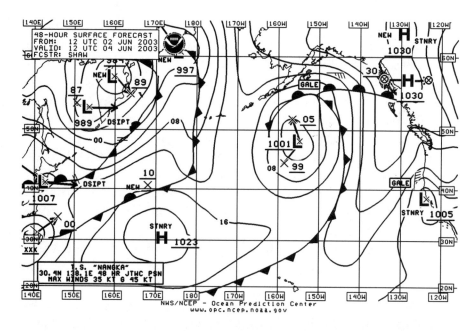

meteorologists and computer generated models have a relatively high confidence level in their forecasts. There is a heightened belief that two days after that 48 hour forecast, the Surface Analysis and conditions that I will experience will actually be quite accurate. If the 96 hour forecast and the 48 hour forecast valid for the same time period are wildly different, I begin to regard the forecasts with increased caution.

Check out the accompanying forecasts for similarities as well as dissimilarities. Remember that forecasting is still an art/science, and these things will probably not be perfectly the same. Note your own location or expected location on each of the charts. If one places a low to your east and the other places a low to your west, the wind directions could be 180 degrees different and wind speeds could be similarly different. One may show a front a bit closer to you or a high getting stronger rather than weaker and moving off. Each of these things will imply

North Pacific 96-Hour Surface Forecast, Valid 12 UTC 04 June 2003. Compare this forecast to the previous two forecasts, the 24- and 48-Hour Surface Forecasts valid at the same time. Are the maps getting more similar as time gets closer? If so, it would seem that the confidence level in the forecast is going up.

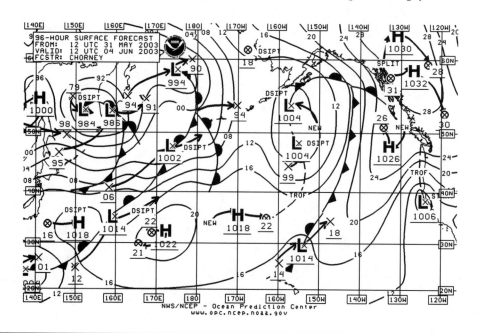

different things for the weather you can expect to experience at the time that the forecast becomes valid. Perhaps the wind shift associated with the front will get to you sooner, or perhaps with the high gaining strength and remaining stationary while the low approaches, you will experience more wind than previously anticipated.

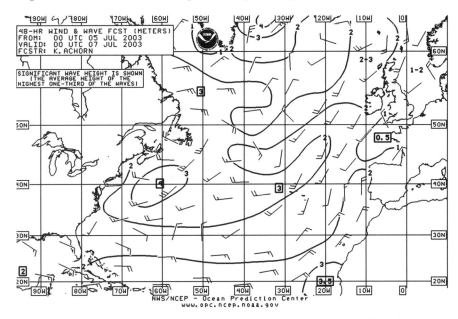

North Atlantic 48-Hour Wind/Wave Forecast, Valid 00 UTC 07 July 2003

Wind/wave map Wind/Wave forecasts will help me to understand exactly what kind of wind conditions the meteorologists expect me to have and approximately how high the seas will become. I sometimes use these Wind/Wave forecasts to fill in the blanks about wind conditions, but I generally find more information on the Surface Pressure forecasts. By reading the pressure maps, I can see what kind of wind conditions I'll get and why it is developing in a particular way. Wind/Wave forecasts show me the effects of a weather pattern. Surface Pressure forecasts show me the cause as well as the effect of the weather systems' movements.

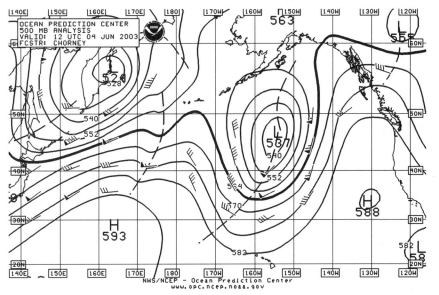

500 mb charts can be used to help verify surface weather movements and development.

upper atmosphere ridge

500 mb Chart I use 500 mb charts to verify surface forecasts, check-

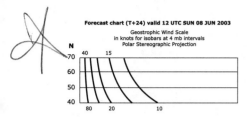

Forecast chart (T+24) valid 12 UTC SUN 08 JUN 2003
Geostrophic Wind Scale
in knots for isobars at 4 mb intervals
Polar Stereographic Projection

Geostrophic Wind Scale used on some British and other weather charts. By determining the distance between isobars at a given latitude (left scale), you can deduce the approximate wind speed.

ing for cut-off lows and jet stream tracks. These help me to understand why a system may tend to linger in one location, gain strength or move in a given direction or a given speed. The upper level charts help me to better understand why things are happening and how they are likely to continue to evolve.

Isobar distortion on weather maps

Charts can be somewhat deceiving. The projection of the map does not mean that all distances are equal in all parts of the chart. Take a look at how far apart the 10 degrees of latitude are between 20 N and 30 N and compare that to how far apart the distances are between 50 N and 60 N.

As navigators we know that 1 degree of latitude equals approximately 60 nm, 10 degrees equals 600 nm. And yet on a marine weather map the projection distorts the distances! The distances between isobars at 60 degrees N may appear the same as the distances between isobars at 30 degrees N, but in reality those distances are significantly different. In order to make sense of all of this and provide you with a reasonable idea of how much wind is in a particular place, some countries provide "geostrophic" wind scales on their charts. Along the vertical axis we have the latitude in degrees N, and on the horizontal axis we have wind speed in knots. The distance between the isobars is taken with dividers directly off a particular weather map and compared to the distance represented on the wind scale for the given latitude on the actual weather map. The result is read on the wind speed axis in knots.

Since geostrophic wind scales aren't generally available on U.S. weather maps; we either compare similar isobar spacing with known observations on the chart or sometimes refer to alternate charts such as the wind/wave analysis for further clarification.

How to read a satellite image

Interpreting satellite imagery is an art/science unto itself. We won't attempt to expound on everything known about it here. We will, however, offer the serious mariner a few insights into some of the things that will be most important to him and how this information can be used in conjunction with other information, such as a surface analysis, to gain even more insight into a situation than either one standing alone would provide.

IR

Infrared (IR) satellite imagery measures heat. Both high altitude geostationary (GOES) satellite images, as well as low earth orbiting satellites, can take IR images.

The images present a representation of how hot clouds, sea surface or land are at the time that the picture is taken. The images can be color coded for various temperature bands so that certain temperatures that might show up typically in cloud formations, as an example, are enhanced and more easily viewed and analyzed.

Generally speaking, clouds are colder as we get higher in the atmosphere. Also, as a broad generality, taller cumulus or cumulonimbus clouds often have gusty winds under them. Although high altitude cirrus clouds may not pack much wind under them at the surface, taller, colder clouds often have windier conditions at the surface. The surface gradient wind can be augmented or shifted by locally occurring storm cells.

We know that towering cumulus clouds can be associated with an approaching cold front. By identifying the cold front either on the IR satellite picture or on a surface analysis weather map, we can look at the IR picture and locate how high (cold) the associated storm cells may be hundreds of miles before they get to us. If there are relatively few extremely high storm cells, there may be a decreased probability of downburst and extreme high winds in squall lines approaching us. On the other hand, if there are huge, tall, cold clouds approaching us, we would want to be cautious about how violent those storm cells may be as they approach.

We can tell quite a bit about the approaching front by comparing the front on a surface analysis map to the clouds and front on the satellite imagery. If we can locate the front on the satellite picture, we can compare the respective locations and how they have changed from the valid time of the surface analysis to the valid time for the satellite image. From the advance of the front over the time difference, we can calculate the rate of advance for the various parts of the front. If we then see how that front will continue to move toward our own position, we can get a pretty good idea of how long it will take to get to us. And by noting how tall the clouds are relative to those that we are currently experiencing, we can get a good idea of how the weather will change in the very near term.

Another use of satellite imagery is to locate the shoreline and note if there are small, relatively low-lying fair weather cumulus clouds lined up along the coast. If the clouds line up along the coast, and the inland temperatures are significantly warmer than the sea temperatures offshore, we probably have the presence of a sea breeze. By studying the implications involved in sea breezes, we can get a good idea of how those local conditions are affecting the gradient wind along that coastline, perhaps hundreds or more miles away.

Satellite images can also be looped, allowing us to quickly see how a system is moving. We can deduce some of this information from surface analysis maps that indicate the direction a system is moving, but it sometimes seems clearer when we loop a satellite image, watching the actual movement of the system.

Low earth orbiting satellites can be very effective for picking out particular sea surface features in warm or cold currents. For help in understanding how to interpret this information, refer to the section on oceanography.

Visible light images

Visible light satellite images tell us a different story. As their name implies, they rely on the sun's light to show us the weather conditions

Low earth orbiting APT infrared satellite image. These satellite images can help to show cloud temperatures / heights, ocean currents such as the pictured Gulf Stream, and even help us deduce the presence of a sea breeze in some conditions.

Infrared GOES images can be looped for animation purposes, showing the progression of weather systems, and help us understand where the tall, cold storm cells are located which may have local gusting conditions under them.

below. Toggling between the IR picture and a visible light image can help us to understand some things that one alone doesn't clearly explain.

One such example is the identification of fog. The temperature of fog can be quite close to the sea temperature. The IR picture has some difficulty in differentiating between the actual sea and a fog bank. The visible light picture will show the fog bank as a white mass, not unlike higher altitude clouds. When you toggle between the two images, it becomes obvious which parts of the image represent high altitude cloud, lower level cloud, fog, sea surface and even warm ocean currents.

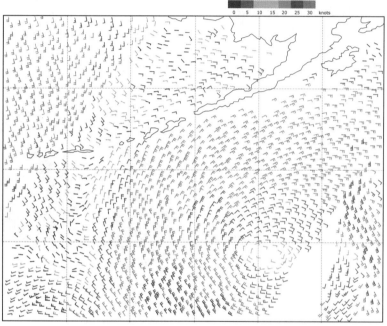

Scatterometer data, sometimes referred to as "QuikSCAT" can provide near real-time analysis of wind speed and wind direction virtually anywhere on the world's oceans or other large bodies of water.

Scatterometer

Scatterometer data is a relatively new form of satellite information available to the public for the last few years. The "quick explanation" of how it works is that reflected microwaves initiated from satellites measure the aeration in the water's surface. From that measurement, the wind speed can be deduced and, by doing a series of calculations over progressive images, wind direction can also be deduced.

Generally, the information is amazingly accurate. However, it's been my experience when talking with navigators on the water, that sometimes the wind directions can be off by as much as 30 degrees. Keep in mind that their observations may be subject to local condition, such as a cloud formation. The satellite image may pick up an average of the conditions that had been taking place earlier. However, when compared to actual buoy data, the Scatterometer data is very close.

Since it is available in near real time on the web, it can be useful in looking at wind conditions in remote locations offshore or other places that may not have buoys close at hand. It can also be used to determine how much wind is associated with various weather features defined in a surface analysis.

Text forecasts

Text weather forecasts are common around the world. They may be in the form of Navtex broadcasts, ECG messages over Standard C INMARSAT broadcasts or other means. They may also come to you by voice over VHF or HF radio.

Text broadcasts can be used to verify or update graphically displayed weather maps. While much of the information may be similar, telling you the same thing, occasionally you will find that the recent text broadcasts modify earlier maps. They can be very worthwhile to receive and use to confirm other types of weather information.

As words, it's sometimes difficult to get a sense of what's happening unless you plot the information out. In order to make it easy to keep track of what's been said during a voice weather broadcast, you might consider getting a small tape recorder to record the forecast. Then, when you're ready to analyze their comments, you can play the recording back if you have any questions about what was said.

Transferring the text information onto a chart

Here are a few helpful hints about how to transfer text weather broadcast information onto a chart. Seeing the information displayed on a chart will help you get a feel for where you are located relative to a weather system and how your respective tracks will affect your weather over time.

Get two pieces of clear acetate plastic approximately the size of your plotting chart. Tape the top of each piece of acetate to the top of the chart (north up). You will be able to flip the plastic up and plot your position on the actual chart. Flip the first (lower) piece of acetate down and, using grease pencils, draw in the various weather features mentioned in the weather broadcast. (Grease pencils tend to work better and be less susceptible to smearing than marking pens.) Use different colors for each day's forecast so that perhaps red is today's weather pattern, green tomorrow's and black the following day's and so on. The top acetate covers and protects the drawings that are written on the bottom acetate.

The weather features can be changed daily or whenever you are updated on the evolving weather situation. As you plot your vessel's position, you'll extrapolate out your expected position for the various days covered by the forecasts.

Many parts of the world don't have weather fax broadcasts easily available. Being prepared to thoroughly understand the text weather broadcasts may be your best or only source of outside information.

Read the weather while onboard using your senses and vessel's instrumentation

Ultimately, the weather we see is the weather we have. Your senses will tell you exactly what's happening, although from the perspective of a sailboat's deck, it can be somewhat confusing. It does, however, fit into a pattern. Our job, as sailors and decision makers, is to understand it and know how to act on that understanding.

Forecasts are not always right. Our perceptions are probably correct, because it's what we're actually experiencing. But our conclusions about our perceptions may not necessarily be right.

Understanding the surface analysis, upper level analysis and surface forecasts and putting our own current weather into a context that we understand will help us to decide how best to proceed.

Understanding our current weather situation using our own senses and onboard instrumentation is the first step in verifying our weather data.

Verify your data

As you collect your weather data, you will want to verify its accuracy by collecting supporting data. By collecting several forms of weather information, we achieve a number of things as we prepare for the decision/action stages of the routing process.

❶ We get our heads in the game. We need to shift our focus to achieving a set of desired results and, by looking at several sets of data, we begin to look at the forecasts with an eye toward determining what type of weather will suit our sailing objective most effectively.

❷ We begin to trust the data. By have several sets of supporting information, we begin to understand the degree to which it is reliable. As an example, if we collect Scatterometer images and also look at several buoys in the area and determine that the remotely sensed Scatterometer data is correct, we begin to have faith in its accuracy.

❸ By gaining a better insight into the weather data, we are more thoroughly preparing for action.

How to verify weather data, example 1

The following methodology is how I verify my weather data and prepare for a passage or race. Several weeks before the event, I begin

Eastern North Pacific Surface Analysis, Valid 12 UTC 04 June 2003

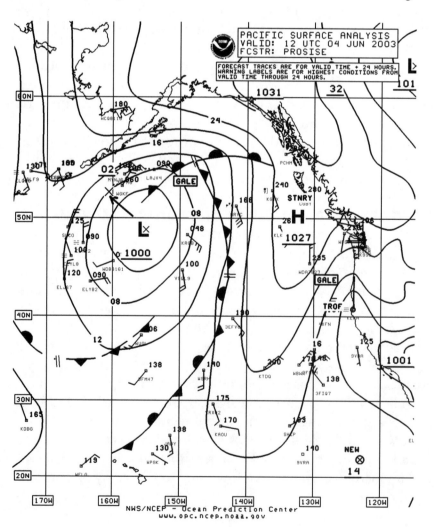

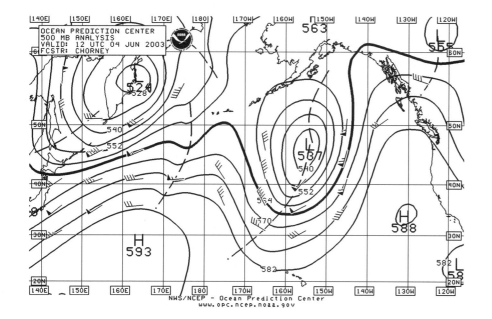

North Pacific 500 mb Analysis,
Valid 12 UTC 04 June 2003

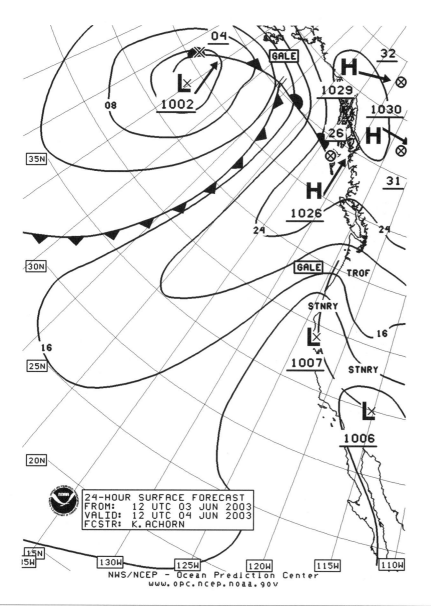

Eastern North Pacific 24-Hour
Surface Forecast, Valid 12 UTC
04 June 2003

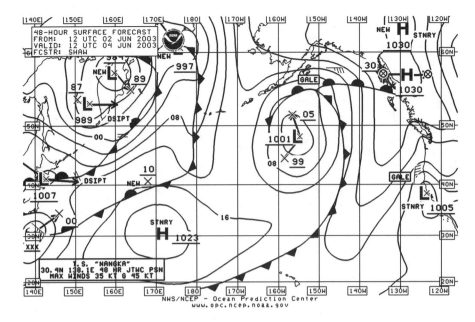

North Pacific 48-Hour Surface Forecast, Valid 12 UTC 04 June 2003

to collect weather information. If I am planning to cruise with my family over the weekend, I may collect information from Wednesday through the weekend.

Generally, the information consists of the 96 hour surface forecast, the 48 hour surface forecast, the 24 hour surface forecast, the surface analysis, the 500 mb analysis, relevant buoy data and Scatterometer images. The collection phase doesn't take too long on a daily basis, and I actually may not spend too much time analyzing the information until the final week before the event.

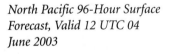

North Pacific 96-Hour Surface Forecast, Valid 12 UTC 04 June 2003

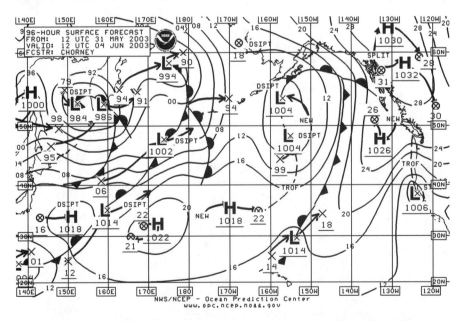

During the final week before the event, I start to collate the information and analyze it. Often I'll compare the 96 hour forecast with the 48 hour forecast I collected two days after the 96 hour forecast. They will have the same valid time. In a perfect world, both forecasts issued at different times but valid for the same time would look exactly the same.

If there are differences, it would imply that there may be some vagueness about what is about to occur in 2 days time. I will then compare those two earlier forecasts with the 24 hour forecast valid at the same time as the other two. How do they all compare? Is the 48 hour forecast very similar to the 24 hour forecast valid at the same time, implying that there is now increased clarity about the forecast? Have the computer models and meteorologists settled on what they think will occur? Then, I will compare all three of those forecasts with the surface analysis valid at that same time. The surface analysis is supposed to be based on actual observations. How close do the various forecasts come to the surface analysis? I may even check forecasts from different sources – perhaps British met if I'm going across the Atlantic or perhaps U.S. Navy models to see how the computer models had handled the situation. I'll compare the Scatterometer data with the buoy data and the surface analysis, all of which are valid at the same time. The process helps me to not only gain an understanding of the weather patterns, but it also helps me gain a faith in the forecasts and better understand both their strengths and weaknesses.

In the late 80's, prior to doing a leg of a Whitbread Round the World Race, I would collect surface analysis maps daily while we were still in port. I would highlight the lows in green or blue, and the highs in red or orange. Several days prior to departure, I would stack them on top of each other and flick through the pile, doing a crude kind of animation to see how the lows tracked across the Southern Ocean or how the high pressure system oscillated back and forth in the region of the subtropical high.

Now we have .gif image animation software that will do the same thing using maps we can collect off the internet. While the animations are rough, it gives us an idea of trends and tracks that the systems had been using for the weeks preceding the event.

When I have begun to understand the weather patterns and gotten a sense of what publicly available government sources are predicting, I will usually secure the services of a weather routing company such as Commanders' Weather to shed additional light on the particular weather I will face.

Private forecasting services are tasked with a different responsibility than government weather services. While the government weather services are given the duty to provide good general weather information for a region or general population, private weather forecasting services can zero in on my exact location, my proposed route, my vessel, and the type of task I am attempting to achieve.

Armed with my research and having a thorough knowledge of what I am trying to achieve, I can now enter into a productive dialogue with the meteorologists at Commanders' Weather, all of us seeking an optimal solution to the task.

The above process allows me to collect, analyze, verify and refine my understanding of the weather I will encounter.

Understanding the gradient pattern will help us to understand if a wind shift is permanent or, if it is caused by local conditions such as a cloud, how long that shift may be expected to last.

Comparing the forecasts to what we are actually experiencing, example 2

The process of analysis doesn't end with understanding the weather forecasts. In many ways, that's only the first stage. As mentioned earlier, the weather we see is the weather we have. That is telling us the real story, so we need to be able to put it into a context so that we can act appropriately. If the wind shifts 90 degrees and that hadn't been in the forecast, is it because the low-pressure system is going north of us rather than south as expected? Or is it because we're under a huge cloud, and the convection within the cloud system is causing a temporary shift? In these two cases, the actions we'll take could be very different and have significantly different implications.

One of our most important sources of on-board weather information is our own senses. Hints are also provided on what we're likely to get. Our immediate understanding of the weather situation through observation is further augmented and expanded through the use of a variety of tools to help us better understand what to expect in the near future.

By studying the clouds and how they are evolving around us, we can learn about the approaching weather.

Cirrus cloud is of particular interest in forecasting the weather from on-board. Storm centers, thunderstorm cells, and high pressure centers all tend to follow these high-level streamlines. Be sure you're looking at the cloud movements, however, and not the cloud orientation. Cirrus may band or streak perpendicular to the wind flow. Cirrus generally is a long-range signal of impending weather, but when it is the only cloud involved there will usually be a period of fair weather of 12 to 24 hours, since it will take that long for the rest of the lower-level weather to catch up. While cirrus clouds may have little immediate effect on wind direction and speed, others, such as cumulonimbus clouds, may have their own circulation and radically increased wind speed.

Cumulonimbus or thunderstorm clouds may be the most important cloud type to recognize because the winds can be rapidly shifting, and the sudden squalls can be a disaster to an over-canvassed boat. Winds can reach 60 to 80 knots, and the track of the approaching cloud can be difficult to predict. The prudent sailor prepares for the worst in order to remain in control of the situation, whatever it becomes, as he observes what is happening.

What is the approaching sea state? Are there multitudes of white caps and short, wind driven waves? When observing the sea state, be sure to take into account the depth of the water, the current or tide and the duration, fetch, and speed of the wind; all of these considerations will affect the resultant wave shapes. Is there rain falling from the clouds and what is the direction of the fall? Is that direction the result of the cloud movement or wind circulation? Is rain falling from other nearby clouds, and is the direction the same or is it different? Are there any flags or smokestacks on shore that can give an indication of what lies ahead? By seeing and understanding the various cloud types and observing what is happening, the sailor can anticipate the approaching weather and avoid problems before they occur. To confirm the visual observations, use a barometer or barograph (recording barometer). If you think thunderstorms are threatening, don't rely on sight alone; refer often to your barograph. Thunderstorms are almost always preceded by sharply falling pressures, perhaps 1.5 millibars or so per hour for 1 to 4 hours.

In addition to barometers or barographs, many sailboats are equipped with wind speed and direction instruments, and they can provide either digital or analog displays. When the wind instruments are interfaced with an on-board notebook computer most types of instruments such as Ockam, B&G, or Raytech allow the values to be recorded in logging software. The wind speed and direction, recorded over time, can perhaps be displayed in a strip chart that clearly indicates the changing wind patterns and trends. With the wind speed recorded at a 5 second interval and displayed over the past 2 hours, as an example, an increasing trend in the wind speed can be easily interpreted and a sail change can be anticipated. Regardless of whether or not the information is recorded by computer, you can sense the changes by feel. If the puffs are getting stronger, and they are coming more frequently, you may be in for a permanent wind change.

Regular recording of on-board weather information such as the barometric pressure, wind speed and wind direction help us to track the weather conditions and the rate of change as they are affecting our vessel.

Watching a barometer is a bit like taking a snapshot of the stock market. The most important information may be whether or not the pressure is rising or falling. A barograph will record the pressure over time and keep a record of how fast the barometric pressure is rising or falling.

Barometers and using them

Here is one example of how we have used on board tools to validate weather data we receive from other sources. Barometers provide an important tool to verify and understand what is happening locally.

Winter was fast approaching New England. It was time to move the 68' foot sloop south to the Caribbean for the winter. Normally we would want to be well to the east of Bermuda as we dove south of 32 degrees North in order to get east before we were too far to the south and into the Northeast Trades. But this year it looked like a low pressure system might be moving north out of the Gulf. How we negotiated that low pressure system could not only save days on the delivery, it could be the difference between a fast, comfortable downwind ride, or slamming to weather in a gale. The story would unfold across the paper of our barograph as the atmospheric pressure plunged 12 millibars over a few days.

Types of barometers

Barometers fall into two general categories: mercurial barometers and aneroid barometers. Mercurial barometers, invented in 1643, essentially consist of a column of mercury, the upper end of which is closed, and the other end, which is open to the atmosphere. A suitable scale indicating the atmospheric pressure in inches of mercury reads the height of the column of mercury supported by the atmosphere. The pitch and roll of a vessel, however, induces rapid shifting and rising of the mercury at sea. Because of this pumping, mercurial barometers have been largely replaced at sea with aneroid instruments.

Aneroid barometers measure atmospheric pressure by means of the force exerted by the pressure on a partly evacuated, thin metal element called a sylphon cell. A small spring is used to partly counteract the tendency of the atmospheric pressure to crush the cell. Atmospheric pressure is indicated directly by a scale and a pointer connected to the cell by a combination of levers. Measurements are in inches of mercury (in.), millibars (mb) or hectopascals (hPa), which are equivalent to millibars.

Reading the barometer

Watching a barometer is a bit like taking a snapshot of the stock market. The most valuable information is whether it's rising or falling and how fast. When it comes to wind speed, it doesn't matter very much whether the pressure is high or low. What does make a difference is how fast the pressure is changing, regardless of whether it's going up or down. Barographs record the atmospheric pressure over time and provide the trends that provide an observant navigator with important dynamic information.

Wind is caused by pressure gradients or differences in atmospheric pressure. When you blow up a balloon, you create a greater pressure between the air in the balloon and the air outside of it. When the balloon is released, the air rushes from the higher pressure to the lower pressure of the room. The pressure gradient causes air to flow from an area of high pressure to one of relatively lower pressure.

Since a barometer measures the amount of pressure, we can track the comings and goings of the various weather patterns by watching the rise and fall of the pressure readings. Like a depth sounder for the atmosphere, if we know that we're along the 1020 mb isobar because the barometer reads "1020," we can see how the weather system is progressing over our position by watching the change of both the barometer and the wind direction as the barometer goes to either 1021 or 1019 and the wind shifts to the right or left. A barograph provides a running graph of that rise and fall in pressure, while a barometer simply measures the current reading.

Gradient wind speed – the wind that is unaffected by local conditions – is generally a function of how great the pressure differential is, or, stated another way, how fast the barometric pressure rises or falls over a given distance. In order to visualize and better understand the use of the barometer, it's helpful to study and understand weather maps. Later, it's easier to form a mental picture of what's happening as the barometer rises or falls over time. Looking on a weather fax map, the rate of change will be indicated by the relative proximity of the isobars on the map. The closer together the isobars, the greater the pressure differential and the greater the expected wind speed. If the isobars around a low pressure system on a weather map are so close that it looks like someone left a thumbprint on the paper, you know that there is a very steep pressure gradient and there is plenty of breeze to spare.

Using isobars to determine gradient wind speed

To determine the gradient wind speed for a particular location, some weather fax maps include a "geostrophic graph" in the lower corner of the weather fax. For a given latitude and a given distance between isobars, a corresponding wind speed can be determined. If the distance between the isobars is halved, the wind speed is doubled at the same latitude on the weather map. Or, stated another way, if the rate of change in barometric pressure is doubled over a given distance, so is the wind speed. A faster rising or falling barometer means more breeze. Often, weather fax maps include barbed wind arrows with the number of "feathers" indicating the wind strength. If a wind arrow has one feather, a wind speed of 10 kts is implied. If there are two feathers, 20 kts. For a rough estimate of wind strength elsewhere on the map, compare the relative distances between the isobars along the same latitude and the wind strength will be approximately in the same ratio as the distances between the isobars. If you find a wind arrow with 2 feathers at a given latitude and in the area between two isobars, elsewhere on the map at the same latitude, a narrower space between the isobars will generally indicate more wind.

Law of Storms

The "Law of Storms" states that if you put your back to the wind, the low pressure (storms) will be on your left-hand side in the Northern Hemisphere. Flow would be the opposite in the Southern Hemisphere. As the wind swirls around the gradient weather patterns, the direction of the gradient wind (that wind produced by the pressure differential) will indicate the shape and/or location of the weather pattern. Simply stated, as the pressure rises or falls, we will be given good clues if a system is approaching or leaving and, the wind direction will provide hints about its shape and where we're located within the system.

Law of Storms

Barometric pressure and local conditions

Local conditions, however, can influence the gradient weather patterns. And these influences can tend to cloud the issues. To understand whether the gradient forecast is holding, you need to understand the effect of local conditions. Local conditions may include funneling wind down river valleys, local clouds or storm cells that may alter the pressure or wind direction by setting up their own circulation, the presence of a sea or land breeze, the proximity of warm currents, or diurnal effects on wind or pressure. When local effects are constant or well understood, atmospheric pressure and wind direction changes will clearly indicate trends in things to come. To confirm your visual observations use the barometer or barograph often. If you think fronts are approaching or thunderstorms are threatening, don't rely on sight alone; refer often to your barograph. Sharply falling pressures – perhaps 1.5 millibars per hour or so – almost always precede thunderstorms for 1 to 4 hours.

Northern hemisphere

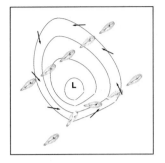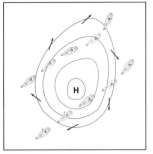

Southern hemisphere

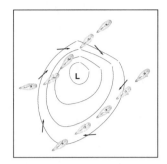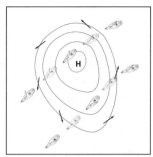

Using the barometer to determine where you're located in a weather pattern.

As the barometric pressure decreased aboard our yacht, we knew that we were getting closer to the low or front – it was approaching us. The wind direction was backing around – facing the wind, it was shifting to the left – as it should have been in a Northern Hemisphere Low passing to the southeast of our position. The wind direction was changing from Easterly to Northeasterly to Northerly. As the wind direction went to Northerly and began to go west of north, the barometer hit bottom and began to rise. We knew that the low's center had passed to our south and east, rather than to our north as forecast. We expected that the wind would then continue to shift to the left and become westerly as the system continued on its northeasterly track.

If the system passing to our south had been a Southern Hemisphere low pressure system, wind sequencing would have been reversed while the barometric pressure dropped. In the Northern Hemisphere, as a High passes to the south of your position moving from west to east, the wind will back from northerly to northwesterly to westerly to southwesterly.

In both cases the low and high pressure systems produced backing winds as it tracked south of our position. However, the low caused the pressure to drop as it approached us while the high caused the pressure to rise while it approached us.

Using barometric pressure to identify fronts

Once the large scale weather systems are understood, frontal passages can also be better understood and you can create your own forecasts or verify the forecasts coming to you by radio. Warm fronts, sweeping down from the low pressure system, contain warmer air that pushes across the earth's surface and displaces the colder, denser air as the barometer drops in the frontal passage. Often the wind shift in the warm frontal passage is less pronounced than in the following cold front. The cold front can be more violent in nature as squalls and towering cumulus clouds can precede the front. A falling barometer will precede both fronts, and winds in the Northern Hemisphere will often shift to the right. Local storms' cells, however, can exaggerate or delay the permanent wind shift.

Often the winds preceding the fronts are southwesterly in waters around the U.S. as the troughs emanate from the Lows and stretch from NE to SW. The wind in the front or following the warm front may be westerly and the post-frontal winds following the cold fronts can often be expected to go to the northwest. The gradient wind field will be the result of the pressure differential. As the pressure falls and rises, the wind field can be expected to shift unless the center of the high or low pressure system is headed straight towards your position. The weather fax maps will give you an idea about the shape of the weather systems and forecast to expect, and your observations should be able to confirm or refute those forecasts. But with or without maps, you should be able to visualize where you are within a weather system by tracking the barometer and wind direction.

Radar

There are numerous reasons to have radar on your vessel. Navigating through fog, avoiding collisions while at sea, and picking up unlit buoys while sailing at night are only a few of the reasons. I've made landfalls using radar, and used radar to verify my GPS position while sailing between two small islands at night. Much of the time, the radar display remains mounted in the nav station, unused. But when it's needed, there are few suitable substitutes.

Squalls may be widely scattered as an example, but they will provide a set of tactics all their own. In some cases, the extra breeze on the leading edge may induce the tacticians to try to stay with the cloud. In other cases, they may really want to stay out of the dead air zone in the middle of the cloud. The larger storm cells can set up their own circulation with updrafts, downdrafts and even downbursts. Rain gives a clue about the nature of the beast, and there are a few technological marvels that help the navigator keep track of what's coming as well as keeping an eye on the competition.

As the clouds approach, radar can be used to track the rain clouds. Although radar doesn't provide any information about rainless clouds, it can provide a great deal of information on clouds that are producing rain. The rain can be tracked and, even when the helmsman can't see his way to the other side of the squall, radar can let the crew know how far the squall extends. Whether it's for the recreational sailor or professional racer, radar provides very useful insights.

Getting the most out of the radar

Here are a few items that I look for in my "ideal" radar unit. They include screens that are both clearly visible in daylight and can be dimmed down low enough to allow me to retain some degree of night vision while using a radar unit in a cockpit at night. I want to be able to control the radar's features whether the unit is in the nav station or if it is a secondary unit in the cockpit. If I need to zoom into another level to find a landmark or buoy, I don't want to have to jump down to the nav station and then run back up on deck to see if I can pick up a buoy or squall line visually. There are times when I have better things to do than run back and forth to get the complete information. I would also like to have enough clarity from the unit to be able to discern the difference between rain and a land mass and

Radar can be used in a variety of ways for sailing. Whether you're at home, preparing to go sailing and accessing the information from the internet or using a radar unit aboard your boat, radar can be extremely helpful.

have the tuning controls easy and intuitive to use. And, I would like to have the unit mounted properly so that I can get maximum useable range from the radar.

Proper Mounting of Radar Correct mounting is the first step to insure proper functioning of your radar. The antenna should be as high as practical in order to increase the range to its maximum. The antenna mount should also be capable of being tilted so that, regardless of your angle of heel, the antenna remains level. Otherwise, it will alternately scan the sky or the surface of the water. Your goal is to scan a level plane, parallel with the surface of the water. And ideally, the bow of your boat should be in alignment with the top up display so that bearings correspond to a correct angle off the bow.

Furuno's Operator's Manual explains that "the maximum detecting range of the radar varies considerably depending on several factors, such as height of the antenna above the waterline, the height of the target above the sea, the size, shape and material of the target and atmospheric conditions."

They continue, "under normal atmospheric conditions, the maximum range is equal to the radar horizon or a little shorter. The radar horizon is longer than the optical one by about 6% because of the diffraction property of the radar signal. Rmax is given in the following equation: Rmax = 2.2 x (square root of h1 + square root of h2) where Rmax is the radar horizon in nautical miles, h1 is the antenna height (in meters) and h2 is the target height (in meters). For example, if the height of the antenna above the waterline is 9 meters and the height of the target is 16 meters, the maximum radar range is Rmax = 2.2 x (3 + 4) = 15.4 nm."

On the face of it, that appears rather straightforward. Mounting of the unit, however, can mean the difference between seeing 15.4 nm and considerably less. The radar antenna needs to be reasonably level in order to achieve those kinds of ranges. If the antenna is fixed to the mast there may be sufficient height, but the range can be substantially reduced when the boat heels over 25 degrees. If the antenna has a convenient means by which it is leveled, the range of the unit will be considerably enhanced.

Proper Tuning of Radar Properly tuning the radar is also of significant importance. Tuning the radar is an art form. It needs to be re-tuned for each range selected. When tuning the unit, be aware of what it is that you are trying to view. Are you trying to locate the rain in a squall or an approaching ship? Fine-tuning will help to pick out the ship from the rain.

While some radar units overlay the radar image directly on a digitized chart, some Raytheon units have a chart plotter side by side with the radar screen. Either arrangement will help you to understand what it is that you are looking at. Is that little "blip" an unlit buoy or a small fishing boat? A quick check of the chart on the plotter will help you to understand the possibilities.

When I know that the radar is properly aligned with the bow of the boat, the antenna is straight, and the unit is properly tuned, I can begin to have some faith in what I'm seeing on the radar screen.

Radar features I find useful

The features I most commonly use are the EBL (Electronic Bearing Line), Rings, and VRM (Variable Range Marker). The EBL gives me a bearing to a target at a particular point in time. The rings provide a fast reference point to a target. And the VRM marks the range to a target at a particular point in time. As time elapses, I can easily see if we are gaining or losing range and bearing to a target. Are we on a collision course with another vessel as we maintain the same bearing but continue to close range? Are we being swept to the wrong side of a buoy by a current or tide even as our compass heading implies that we are aiming toward the correct side of the buoy? The EBL and VRM will give you the answers. Units that acquire targets will continue to give you that information. Has the opposition just tacked? The new radar units will quickly give you the answer. In some cases, such as with a homespun software program used aboard Assa Abloy, it will even let you know if they're making a better VMG on the other tack – perhaps because of sea state or current.

Radar can provide invaluable information, but ultimately the quality of the information will be dependent on the operator. Mount it properly and spend some time to know how to use the radar to its fullest advantage. On that rare occasion when a tug pushing a barge is bearing down on you in a fog, you will certainly appreciate the time and effort you spent – and so will the captain of the tug.

Predict future weather by plotting isochrones on weather forecast maps

Here's the disclaimer: I'm not a meteorologist. I don't forecast weather. Rather, I've learned how to critically read weather maps, and figure out where I'm going to be located on that map. And from that information I can interpret what kind of weather I should expect.

As a sailor, I know what kind of weather my vessel will perform best in, and I try to position her in the most suitable weather, taking into consideration what my sailing objective is. As sailors, you can do the same thing.

Since I've been working with a variety of meteorologists and helping to route various boats for about 18 years, I've managed to become reasonably good at interpreting weather maps. But when I want to be better than "reasonably good," I prefer to work with a very good marine forecaster. Together we can both help each other achieve more than either of us would alone. It's my feeling that generally one should try to be their best, surround one's self with the best people, and that collaborative projects with those types of people tend to produce superior results.

Having said that, how do we as sailors still "predict" the future weather? My usual response is "to start out with the best forecast you can get, and don't trust it." What I mean is to look for additional ways to verify it, as discussed above.

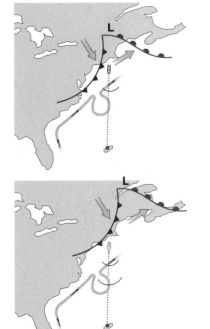

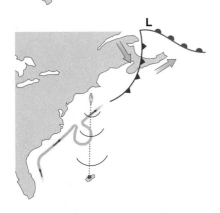

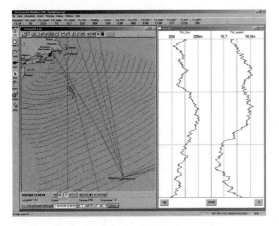

In order to figure out where you're going to be located when the forecast map becomes valid, you can plot your position by sketching isochrones to mark your assumed future position on the forecast map.

When I have obtained "the best forecasts," I then need to locate my position on that weather map. If I am in Newport, RI, and I am going to Bermuda and would like to know what the weather will likely be in two days, I'll look at a 24 hour forecast, 48 hour forecast and a 96 hour forecast. I'd also toss in a 500 mb chart to see if I really agree with the other surface charts. I might even check out some satellite images for the sake of curiosity.

As a hypothetical situation, if I was leaving Newport and it was dead calm, there was no current to consider and I was in a power boat doing 180 miles per day, I could scribe an arc 180 nm from Newport and 24 hours later, I'd be located somewhere along that line. Since that is a line depicting a distance traveled for a given amount of time, it's called an isochrone.

Sailboats, of course, don't work quite that neatly. In most cases we're going to try to sail to our destination, so if the wind is out of the southwest, say 225 degrees True, we can't sail toward the southwest. We might be able to sail straight south or to the SSE. If our boat was capable of sailing 180 nm while close hauled and hard on the wind, presumably we'd be a bit faster if we were cracked off a bit. If we were sailing to the SE, as an example, we might be able to cover 190 or 200 miles in a day. Our isochrone would be distorted a bit, elongating out toward the southeast going out maybe 200 miles toward the southeast, but still measuring about 180 miles straight south.

If I was doing a rough calculation to see where I might want to be after 48 hours, I'd probably pick some point on that isochrone, maybe SSE of Newport and about 190 nm from my starting point, and I'd draw another isochrone of similar shape and distance from the first isochrone. Assuming that the wind on the 24 hour forecast was also out of the southwest and of similar strength, I could assume that I might cover roughly the same distance.

Since I'm trying to figure out what the weather will be like in 48 hours, however, I've got to transcribe that second isochrone to a 48 hour forecast map. Looking at the 2nd line on the 24 hour forecast doesn't make much sense, since that would be the weather in that location the day before I arrived there! I've got to put my assumed position on the chart that has the same valid time that I will be at my expected position.

I can theoretically be anywhere along that isochrone on the 48 hour surface forecast map. I still realize, however, that I'm trying to get to Bermuda. So (assuming there is no current involved in this exercise), I would like to be as close as possible to Bermuda, but still putting myself in a good position for the expected weather for the rest of the trip. "Being as close as possible to Bermuda" is about the same as saying that I would like to be able to maximize my rate of closure

Computer programs such as this Deckman for Windows software can now quickly plot isochrones based on a computer generated forecast model, and the sailing potential of a boat if the computer has a known starting and finishing point.

with Bermuda. Or another way of saying it would be that I would like to maximize my Velocity Made good on a Course to Bermuda (VMC to Bermuda).

So, if I'm just trying to see what the weather will be along my route to Bermuda in 2 days, I should be able to look at the 2nd isochrone and pick out a point in the arc that is relatively close to my destination. At that point I can see from the shape and proximity of the isobars and/or from the wind/wave analysis what kind of wind conditions I'll have.

From other information we've studied so far I can tell that, if a cold front is approaching, there may be squall lines associated with the front. Or if I'm in the northeast quadrant of the low and a warm front is approaching, it may be steadily raining. And, I can confirm that on the next day's 24 hour forecast and I can verify the findings as the barograph reflects the approaching weather and the particular clouds begin to show up just prior to the valid time of the 48 hour forecast.

Obtaining the data

The well-informed sailor makes a point of knowing the forecast conditions well in advance in order to spend more time enjoying the sport and less time trying to solve problems.

Fortunately, there are a myriad of sources of weather information from which to choose, and they are presented in a variety of formats. While some of these sources seem to be fading from the scene, others are coming on line and gaining in popularity and reliability.

In many of the coastal areas of the U.S., taped voice weather broadcasts are continuously available from NOAA over VHF.
- WX1 (162.55 MHz)
- WX2 (162.4 MHz)
- WX3 (162.475 MHz).

Broadcasts are repeated every 4 to 6 minutes and updated every 2 to 3 hours.
- Coast Guard weather broadcasts on VHF channel 22 in many areas
- Private coastal radio stations such as Mobile, Alabama's WLO Radio provide VHF weather broadcasts over additional frequencies

Listings of schedules and frequencies for coastal as well as offshore weather broadcasts are available in a number of publications:
- "The Admiralty List of Radio Signals, Vol. III, Radio Weather Services and Navigational Warnings"
- "DMA Publication 117," Radio Navigation Signals,
- "Selected World Wide Marine Weather Broadcasts"
- "Reed's Nautical Almanac."

These and other publications are available through chart houses and marine bookstores and also online through www.WxAdvantage.com.

For vessels venturing further offshore, out of VHF range, voice broadcasts are also available over single side band HF radio in the marine band from 2 to 28 MHz. When receiving voice weather broadcasts, it's often helpful to record the broadcast using a small tape recorder. The tape can be played back for reference, and the location of the various weather systems can be more easily plotted from the recorded data.

In addition to voice-only weather broadcasts, there are a number of sources for text-based weather information.

NAVTEX

Broadcast on a single frequency, 518 kHz, the global NAVTEX system provides a variety of information services: weather, navigational warnings, ice reports, and search and rescue information are a few. The dedicated NAVTEX receiver accepts designated types of messages within a given NAVAREA, and some communications devices such as weather fax and satellite communications systems may already be equipped with the necessary capabilities to receive these broadcasts. Certain classifications of messages may be selected at the user's option, such as LORAN messages, while other types of messages, such as meteorological warnings, can be automatically received and printed out.

High seas telex

High seas telex provides another form of text-only weather information. When the vessel is equipped with the appropriate computer software that is interfaced with the SSB radio, weather forecasts can be received and stored in memory or printed out. One of the primary advantages to hard copy or digitized information over voice transmissions is that the forecasts can more easily be referred to at a later time. Occasionally it may be necessary to plot the information on a chart in order to get a better understanding of the weather patterns. An additional benefit to telex is that messages can also be sent from the vessel and converted into faxes for re-transmission at a number of coastal radio stations. Weather forecasts received on board by telex were formerly free services provided by private coastal radio stations. In some cases now, however, there is a charge for this information service, and the charges may be high when considering the actual amount of information that is relevant to the particular vessel.

Often the most convenient form of weather forecasts is a combination of both text and graphic explanation of the weather patterns and how they are expected to impact the forecast area. The more highly refined the forecast area, the more detailed and accurate the information can be.

Custom weather forecasts

Custom weather forecasts, such as those provided by Commanders' Weather, supplied to a specific vessel along a specific track and speed to a specific destination, can provide the most comprehensive level of weather information. Small area forecasts can provide the next level of detailed information. By necessity a text-only forecast covering the entire U.S. or the western half of the North Atlantic would be general in nature, providing little specific information. But a forecast for a narrowly defined area or location can be more specific in detail, providing wind speeds and directions, sea state descriptions, and approximate times for frontal passages. By combining both text and graphics, the general progression of the weather systems can be shown while they are explained in the detail that is most appropriate to the scale of the forecast.

GRIB data

GRIB (Graphics In Binary) data provides communications-efficient weather information over digital systems, including INMARSAT C. Primarily a text-based satellite communications system, Standard C has not been sitting by without further development. Originally, French racers and the competitors in the Whitbread Round the World Race used MaxSea, a French developed software, to enable offshore reception of wind field and isobaric data via Standard C. Other software systems can also now display the GRIB fields, including Raytheon's Raytech and Deckman For Windows.

The GRIB files are computer-generated forecast models created by several of the world's meteorological agencies. The data points can be created using a variety of elevations, types of information and distances between points. In other words, GRIB is available for higher altitudes besides sea level. It can provide information on weather data besides wind speed and direction, such as temperature. And data points, normally one degree on center (60 nm), can be filtered for different distances in order to make the file sizes smaller for a given geographic area.

The various software products not only display the weather forecast data – most commonly wind speed and direction, but when the forecast data is used with the boat's polars, the program will indicate the optimum route. Naturally, this all assumes both accurate polars and an accurate weather forecast. Computer generated weather forecasts have a significant role to play in providing us with a look into the future, but they also have their limitations on the microclimate scale. The tools are becoming more readily available and user friendly, but the validity of the base information still needs to be monitored. The rate of "garbage in, garbage out" can reach the speed of light, and even the best written routing software can't turn garbage into anything useful.

Weather fax

Graphically monitoring the weather while offshore is still accomplished mostly by use of the weather fax. Radiofacsimile weather charts are produced and transmitted over HF radio frequencies by numerous governments around the world. As with the voice broadcasts, publications are available that indicate the time, frequency and schedules for the charts. And, of course, there are a number of manufacturers of the weather fax receivers such as Furuno. Some of the fax machines are "stand-alone" models that have their own integral HF receivers. Some need to be interfaced with an HF radio.

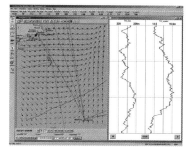

GRIB (GRaphics In Binary) based weather models generally provide data points about 1 degree on center. While they provide a very useful tool for large-scale overviews and bodies of water, the data points are relatively sparse for smaller bodies of water.

Additionally, there are computer software programs that allow the sailor to interface his on-board computer to an HF or SSB radio and receive the latest weather maps.

Some of the standalone weather fax units allow for automatic, unattended reception of the scheduled chart broadcasts. But, for some, the less expensive options provided by the computer software programs outweigh the occasional inconvenience of manually tuning in the radio, calling up the software program on the computer, and personally adhering to a schedule. When the computer has received the analyzed weather chart, the image can be zoomed, printed if that is desired, or saved to memory, thus eliminating the need for thermal paper. Once the computer has been interfaced with the SSB radio, some software programs allow telexes or faxes to be sent to and from the vessel.

Satellite communication/Internet

With the rise in popularity of the internet, Mini M satellite communications offers the ability now to call into the internet at any time and download the most recent weather fax maps, recent GOES geostationary satellite imagery, or actual weather models directly off the internet. And this can be done from anywhere on the planet. There are websites that provide near-realtime unanalyzed weather satellite pictures.

Weather satellite picture receivers

Most of the above mentioned information systems have been based on data that was collected hours earlier, analyzed by trained meteorologists and retransmitted. Real time information can be received on board vessels equipped with weather satellite picture receivers. NOAA satellites as well as Russian satellites fly in relatively low earth orbits. They continuously take visible light and infrared pictures and transmit them back to earth. Unanalyzed by meteorologists, these pictures provide up to the minute information on the location and temperature of various meteorological and oceanographic features: position of fronts, location of the greatest storm activity, the presence of a sea breeze, and the location of currents and eddies. The weather satellite picture receivers also pick up signals from geostationary satellites to rebroadcast somewhat older, analyzed photos of the earth's surface complete with geo-political borders outlined. Weather satellite picture receivers have been available to the private sector for over 15 years now. But, with continuing advances in computer technology, their capabilities are improving while their costs are decreasing. WeatherTrac, Ocens, and Qfax offer a range of models and features with a corresponding variety of prices. Some of these features include: multitasking operating system to integrate the entire navigation and communication area, automatic and unattended acquisition of data and scheduling of satellite reception, preprogrammed acquisition, simultaneous picture acquisition and processing of one or more satellites' pictures, automatic image gridding and positioning, dynamic zooming of the picture, full images stored at full resolution, pan and

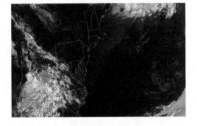

Low Earth orbiting satellites can take pictures in near real time, automatically sending them back to earth and making them immediately available to weather satellite picture receivers such as the WeatherTrac model that received this image.

scrolling the picture, color levels and editing facilities, image export to word processor or printer, overlay drawing by cursor or digital vector map, and automatic or manual animation for looping satellite images. What does all of this mean? On some units the navigator can be analyzing the last image while simultaneously receiving and processing an incoming signal. On some units the navigator can locate the range and bearing from his boat's position to his competitor's, a warm eddy in the Gulf Stream, or an approaching front. On some units the navigator can receive and process signals from NOAA satellites, Meteosat, GOES, and Russian satellites. And on some units the navigator can't. When combined with the ability to manipulate and enhance the visible light and infrared pictures, considerable information can be obtained but, ultimately, it is up to the navigator or weather analyst to provide the interpretation. Good data but poor interpretation provides relatively poor information. Someone needs to have invested the time to learn not only how to control the equipment, but also the importance of locating warm eddies or meanders. Someone needs to know how to identify a sea breeze by the band of clouds that exists 20 to 25 miles inland from the coastline, and how that sea breeze can affect the gradient wind to provide either a header or a lift as the boat approaches land. Someone needs to spend the time on the observations and analysis or it's all meaningless.

Evaluating the data

All forecasts are not created equal. Some do a better job of handling tropical storms. Others do a better job of handling extra-tropicals. Some forecasts that are available in the newspaper or on the TV don't seem to do a very good job of forecasting much of anything. They certainly don't address the issues that are of interest to us as sailors. Computer models, despite our apparent respect for all the wonders they can perform, often don't seem to give the depth of information humans can provide in the near term, and humans don't seem to have such good luck when looking out beyond more than a few days. How then can we resolve conflicts and "differences of opinion" between one forecast and another?

Resolving conflicts

Generally, forecasts will be more accurate as we get closer to real time. The variables become more refined and the chances of failure generally become more limited. For all of their marvels, computer generated models are still enhanced with human oversight and input. So, a "man-machine mix" forecast in the near term is often more relevant than a forecast that reaches out 5 or 10 days. And the man-machine mix forecast will often provide detail or insight into what can happen on a small scale – the scale in which we all live. That's assuming, of course, that the man in the "mix" is a knowledgeable synoptic or mesoscale forecaster.

Of course, some forecasters are better than others. That's not only the state of the art, it's also a human reality. That's why, when we as sailors are entrusted with coming up with the best information we think is available, we need to look beyond any one source of information. We're looking for supporting information. Does the 500 mb analysis really indicate a weather system may move as the forecaster indicates on the 48 hour surface forecast? What do the computer models suggest? Where is the supporting information? As the time draws near, we're watching the clouds, wind speed and direction and barometer. We're trying to anticipate and resolve potential conflicts in the forecast information. "Find the best forecast, and don't trust it," is perhaps a cynical view, but it's one that, taken a little tongue in cheek, can save you from surprises.

Understanding forecast limitations

Even when the forecast appears to be wrong, it may be right. There can be explanations that go beyond our immediate experience.

For example, the wind is supposed to be blowing 15 knots out of the southwest and it's supposedly going to be sunny. Instead, it's blowing 25; it's out of the west-northwest; and it's cloudy and just started to rain. Conclusion: Those weather forecasters don't even look out of their windows when they're creating this information!

Well, maybe. Another explanation might be that the cloud overhead is distorting the gradient wind pattern. As soon as the cloud passes, perhaps the wind will return to 15 out of the southwest.

Forecasts have limitations. They're not only wrong because they don't always take into account every microclimate local effect. They can also be wrong because they happen to be slightly off with the location of a small low pressure system going overhead. A difference of 50 or 60 miles can mean 180-degree different wind direction to someone located close to the center of the system. Or a system that passes north of your position rather than south of it can mean a steady header rather than a steady lift.

If you understand the limitations of the forecasts and how they can be wrong, you stand a better chance of understanding how you can act correctly despite their initial error. The way to understand those limitations is to track the systems over a period of time, using a variety of information sources and learning to trust your observations.

Predicting local conditions

Much of the apparent error in weather forecasts will be due to local conditions. The sea breeze kicks in or it doesn't. You're a little closer to a headland than previously expected. The warm current builds additional cloud cover, and the unstable air column the clouds indicate creates wind shifts and local gusting. The cold night air on top of a mountain starts to roll down the valley and creates gusting and shifts on mountain lakes or in the passages between islands in the Caribbean.

Study the causes and effects of local conditions and learn to apply them to the gradient wind pattern. There is a "system" to it all. And learning those various causes and effects will help you to make sense of it all and better understand and appreciate the general forecast.

Chapter 7
Decision Criteria

Decision making is a process. It is based on a set of criteria and our understanding of the various elements in the criteria. As such, it can be a learned process.

So far, we have been discussing how to understand weather. We've looked at various climatological, oceanographic and meteorological elements.

Routing is a process of making decisions on which way a boat should go in order to accomplish a particular goal. Understanding a weather forecast alone isn't enough to make routing decisions. Weather and oceanography are only a couple of a number of elements in the process of choosing which way to go.

Great weather forecasters don't necessarily know how to route a vessel if they don't understand the capabilities or priorities of the vessel and the people on board. Conversely, terrific technical sailors may be able to sail a boat across an ocean without knowledge of weather, but it will probably be very inefficient and could well be terribly unsafe.

Determining vessel/campaign assets and liabilities

Even if we thoroughly understand everything about the weather and how it is going to change over time, we still need to understand what we have to work with before we can make a decision and take action. We have to understand our capabilities as well as our constraints. Another way to look at it is that before we can invest our efforts in appropriate action for our sailing objective, we need to know our assets and our liabilities.

Assets

The assets that a sailing project possesses fall into several broad categories. Generally, they can be broken down into Equipment, Personnel, and Other Resources.

Those of us who are navigators may understand the concept of a boat's polars. A boat's polars are merely a graphic way of representing a boat's capability to achieve a particular boat speed in a particular wind speed and on a particular true wind angle. The polars give us an insight of how fast we can expect to get from Point A to Point B under certain weather conditions assuming we are moving at optimum efficiency. When racing keelboats, they help us to plan a strategy by telling us how fast we can expect to sail and by giving us information about when we are sailing at less than optimal efficiency.

Sailing speed and polars may not be the only or even the most important criteria, however, when considering our assets. We need to

CHAPTER HIGHLIGHTS

- Determining vessel/campaign assets and liabilities

- Assets

- Liabilities

- What factors are involved in making routing decisions?

- What are the steps involved for routing a vessel?

- The Go-No Go decisions

- Take action

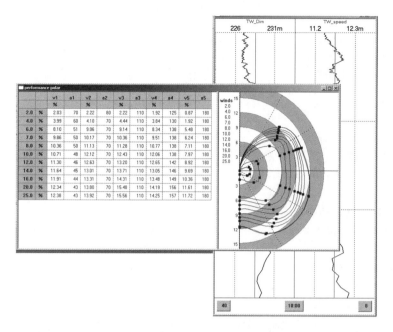

		v1	a1	v2	a2	v3	a3	v4	a4	v5	a5
			%		%		%		%		%
2.0	%	2.03	70	2.22	80	2.22	110	1.92	125	0.87	180
4.0	%	3.99	60	4.10	70	4.44	110	3.84	130	1.92	180
6.0	%	8.10	51	9.06	70	9.14	110	8.34	138	5.48	180
7.0	%	9.86	50	10.17	70	10.36	110	9.51	138	6.24	180
8.0	%	10.36	50	11.13	70	11.28	110	10.77	138	7.11	180
10.0	%	10.71	48	12.12	70	12.43	110	12.06	138	7.97	180
12.0	%	11.30	46	12.63	70	13.20	110	12.65	142	8.92	180
14.0	%	11.64	45	13.01	70	13.71	110	13.05	146	9.69	180
16.0	%	11.91	44	13.31	70	14.31	110	13.48	149	10.36	180
20.0	%	12.34	43	13.80	70	15.48	110	14.19	156	11.61	180
25.0	%	12.38	43	13.92	70	15.56	110	14.25	157	11.72	180

Polars provide us with an accurate quantifiable means of estimating our boat's sailing potential in a variety of weather conditions.

look at all of our assets in choosing a routing strategy. How are our sails? Are they up to the task? Whether that is for a transoceanic passage or putting together an Olympic campaign, we need to understand whether or not our sails will be able to perform adequately to satisfy our sailing objective.

How is the rig? Will it hold up in the expected conditions? Will we need to alter course in certain circumstances in order to insure that it stays up? What about the engine? If we're passage making or doing coastal cruising, and our water maker relies on the main engine, can we actually rely on that piece of equipment? If not, do we have sufficient tankage to take care of any eventualities? If the answer to any of these questions is no, do we want to plan for stop over points along the way if the weather becomes overly severe or winds get too light to continue sailing?

While some of the above assets may actually turn into liabilities, the difference in how critical it can become may be dependent on the crew. The human factor may well be the difference between a successful Olympic campaign or a fabulous cruise or mediocrity in one and near disaster in the other.

Are the selected crewmembers assets or liabilities? Are they assets in some conditions but when the seas pick up do they tend to seasickness? Are there others on the crew who can pick up the slack in those, hopefully, rare moments? Is there someone there to take care of the members who are sick or need attention? If not, will it become necessary to put into port or limit the number of days that can be used for sailing because of the weather?

Ultimately, anything that facilitates accomplishment of the sailing objective becomes an asset. Everything else becomes a liability. Boat speed and performance curves are only one component of the total equation. Good people, catching wind shifts that no one else sees coming and working together, can still take an average boat to an extra-ordinary finish and have a great time doing it. And that includes the cruisers who avoid the bad weather

Regardless of the type of sailing we're doing, we have assets or liabilities that help or hinder us as we try to achieve our own sailing objectives.

for the day, and the crew that goes to play miniature golf rather than going out and destroying their vessel. The route to the miniature golf course may be, in that case, the optimal choice.

Liabilities

Liabilities, once identified, can often be accommodated. In some cases, you will want to make sure that there are enough qualified people to help with eventualities. In other cases you will want to make sure that you have spares and sufficient provisions to handle some basic emergencies. In other cases you will want to have some "bail-out strategy" or series of ports you can put into in an emergency. Weather will frequently be a consideration on how you can best adapt to the changing situation.

I've sailed boats with suspect rigs across oceans and other sailboats with no means of auxiliary propulsion or electrical generation for hundreds or thousands of miles. We've had fresh water tanks leak, people get sick or injured, masts come down or other pieces of equipment fail, but always by working together we were able to adapt to the evolving situation. Frequently, that adaptation required an alteration in the route to suit the situation.

Understanding your liabilities or risks and planning for emergencies will help you to control them and how they impact on your original goal – your sailing objective. Understanding how they may interact with various weather scenarios will help you to select an appropriate route.

What factors are involved in making routing decisions?

The following are the major factors you will consider in making your routing decisions:

❶ Your specific sailing objectives or goals – what are you trying to do? (Sailing Objective)

❷ The experience of your crew and how well they are matched to your Sailing Objective (Crew Selection)

❸ The degree to which you can, or are willing, to increase risk (Safety)

❹ A realistic assessment of your equipment and sail inventory

❺ Your boat's design and performance characteristics

❻ Understanding how the evolving weather and oceanographic considerations will help or inhibit your achieving your sailing objective subject to the above criteria

Sailing objective

In order to accomplish any goal, you first have to define and understand the goal. You have to ask the question: "What is the sailing objective?" In the field of sailing, the sailing objective can be any of the following or more:

❶ I'm here to do a specific long distance race.

❷ I'm here to win a specific long distance race.

❸ I'm here to win a dinghy racing series.
❹ I'd like to go coastal cruising with my family next weekend.
❺ I'm sailing across the Atlantic with my family.
❻ I've been hired to deliver a boat from New England to the Caribbean.

Each of the above sailing objectives is different and they each have their own implications. Just looking at the first two statements: "I'm here to DO a race" or "I'm here to WIN a race" has significant implication. Everybody on the start line is there to do the race. Boil out the bravado and big talk, and the few competitors that are there to win the race are probably spending time in gyms working out, practicing their sailing, studying tactics, making sure the boat bottom is totally flawless, and the sails, rig, electronics and everything else is in prime condition and ready to go. Someone who is there to do the race may win. Someone who is there to win the race will probably win it.

Day sailing, coastal cruising and long distance passage making all use weather differently because their objectives as well as their assets and liabilities are different.

Dinghy and day sailing is different from long distance keelboat sailing. Neither one is better than the other, but they are different. Both the dinghy sailor and the keelboat sailor may be totally prepared and dedicated to winning their respective events, but their sailing objectives are different. If there is a hurricane approaching, the sailing event for the dinghies may well be re-scheduled. That may not be an option for the crew involved in a trans-oceanic event. How weather affects each as well as the options each may have are different.

Similarly, cruising across an ocean is different from coastal cruising. Both require a knowledge of weather, but the coastal cruiser may be able to put into a safe harbor if there is a storm approaching. On the other hand, the coastal cruiser who disregards the weather warnings may be subjected to higher and steeper seas because he may be in shallower water with a tide running. The routing options for each are different. Both the long-distance and the coastal cruiser may have flexible dates of departure so that they can leave in a favorable weather pattern, whereas a race may imply a particular start date and time, regardless of all but the most severe conditions.

Cruising is not the same as doing a boat delivery. The cruiser may have flexibility in both his date of departure as well as what he would like to stop and see throughout the passage. There may or may not be a time constraint. The delivery skipper has to consider overall efficiency of the delivery. He may not depart in the worst conditions, but he also can't opt to delay the departure until next season. He isn't generally hired to stop and see anything along the passage. Rather, he needs to consider costs and time rather than sightseeing. Speed and efficiency may be important, but not at the expense of safety or risking equipment.

Different strategies for different sailing objectives We know that different types of sailing objectives require different routing strategies. There are different priorities in play, so the route should reflect those priorities to the extent that it can. Even within a particular general category, such as cruising or racing, there will be subcategories such as coastal or trans-oceanic cruising, or long distance or round the cans racing and fleet or match racing. Each of those categories and subcategories has its own type of tactics and perhaps strategies.

Often the strategy can be broken down by duration. If an event or project is going to last many days or several weeks, we can be reasonably sure that the weather will change significantly within that time frame. If an event is only going to last a few hours, the weather changes may be minimal.

In the first case, it becomes increasingly important to be better positioned within the expected weather pattern. At the start of a trans-oceanic passage, as an example, we are more concerned with "racing" or cruising toward a favorable weather pattern than we are to making directly toward our ultimate goal or finish line. If we properly set ourselves up in the weather patterns, we can, hopefully, get to our ultimate goal more efficiently and in a way that is consistent with our sailing objective and priorities.

Ultimately, the point is that our tactics are constantly evolving. The longer the event, the more our tactics tend to change. In the first stage of a long distance race we're most interested in getting to the right weather pattern. In the second stage of the race we're interested in consolidating our advantage in front of our opposition, keeping in mind that we may be racing in a fleet. In the third stage of the race, we will be racing, perhaps, boat for boat with a particular competitor for line honors or the

During long distance passages our tactics will change over the course of the trip.

next boat to finish, and, in that case, we may go to a tactical approach that is more similar to match racing.

Even when cruising or doing deliveries, our tactics change because our options change throughout the course of a long distance passage. As an example, at the start of a trans-oceanic passage we have a great deal of time and distance in front of us. We can afford to "dive to the south" to get on the bottom of a Northern Hemisphere low-pressure system if that is going to be advantageous and give us following breezes as we try to go from North America to Europe.

As we get closer to Europe, we may only have a few days left before we make landfall. We can no longer afford to go a couple of hundred miles out of our way to try to position ourselves within a weather pattern. We're already committed to a final approach in the last couple of days. To radically alter our approach would incur a substantial amount of extra distance to cover, and the advantage gained may not be worth the "expense" in terms of additional miles to cover. Options effectively are closed to us as we proceed along our route and get progressively closer to our destination.

Day racing or cruising, however, covers a relatively short period of time. We may change our priorities if suddenly there is severe weather approaching, and we may decide to get back to the harbor for the rest of the afternoon. In most cases, however, we won't radically alter our tactics and change our plans based on weather. We may adapt to it differently as the wind builds or drops off, but we won't generally change our overall tactical approach.

Crew selection

Another element that goes into routing decisions is the crew selection. If you're doing an Olympic dinghy campaign, you may opt to go sailing on some pretty rough days. If you're just learning how to handle your new Laser, you may decide that you will stay in relatively protected waters on the lee side of an island or maybe even forego sailing for the day.

For longer passages, the team doing a Volvo Round the World Race may be tuned up and ready to face a wide variety of conditions in a serious attempt to win that race. A family cruising across the Atlantic with two children ages 6 and 10 at the same time of year may decide that they would prefer to have relatively moderate breezes for their passage, even if that means taking "the long way around" a weather pattern.

In some circumstances, crew that is normally an asset to a project can become a liability if, for example, they get seasick. If the seasickness or other malady becomes severe enough, it may be necessary to alter course to accommodate the waves better or to make for a port and get the sick crewmember to medical help.

The crew can either help you to achieve your desired sailing objective or they can become a serious hindrance and a liability. Depending on their capabilities, weather may have a greater or a lesser effect on them. Matching the right crew with the right sailing objective and putting that project in the most advantageous weather conditions for that mix of criteria is how weather routing takes various elements into consideration.

Safety

We may not like to think that safety is a variable. But, in reality, that is exactly how most people treat it. If safety were the primary concern in sailing to the exclusion of all other factors, no one would ever untie their dock lines. It is a major consideration, to be sure, but it is still a variable when it comes to weather routing.

The family cruising across the Atlantic should not be put in front of a tropical storm if there are other, more reasonable options. On the other hand, we have routed very competitive, seasoned long distance racers in well-tested vessels in front of tropical storms in certain conditions. They took advantage of the weather conditions and were able to successfully make substantial gains against competitors. Safety was a consideration in both cases but, in one case, the risk of failure was unacceptably high. In the other case, the skill of the crew, condition of the vessel, and sailing objective combined to suggest a route that would otherwise be considered "too risky." It wasn't an easy decision or one to be taken lightly.

Ultimately, safety is a variable that is dependent upon the qualifications of the crew, the suitability of the vessel for the given task and the conditions to which they are subjected. We may place a higher or lower value on ultimate safety depending on the above as well as what our particular sailing objective is at the time and for the project.

Equipment and sail inventory

Routing is subject to our ability to actually carry out the sailing objective. If we're attempting a long passage and the sails are susceptible to failure or the other equipment isn't up to the task, we may be forced to attempt a less rigorous route or keep options open to put in somewhere during our passage.

If we're trying to put together an Olympic campaign, and our budget doesn't allow for replacement sails, we may need to reduce the amount of sailing we do in heavy conditions in order to preserve our equipment. The equipment that we have can either help to facilitate our sailing objective, or it can force us to modify our plans and/or how we relate the boat to the stresses associated with certain kinds of weather.

One example of how equipment dictated routing to a certain extent was during the 1988 Single-handed Trans-Atlantic Race. Phil Steggall, racing aboard "Sebago" the 60' tri – foiler, had his port hydrofoil destroyed during the early part of the race. With a prevailing wind direction out of the southwest and wanting to keep his port float out of the water for most of the race so that he could sail on the "good foil/float," we decided to have him favor the southern side of the course so that his approach to Newport, RI would be on port tack. By taking his equipment limitations into consideration, he was still able to finish in the top 4 boats and set a new record for Americans in the race.

Some boats can easily handle conditions that would present a great deal of risk to other boats. As a result, how we handle weather situations will vary from boat to boat.

Boat design/layout/ performance

Similarly, the basic boat design and layout will affect the ability to execute on a particular plan or route. It's intuitively obvious that weather affects a dinghy differently than it does a keelboat. A J-24 is different from a heavy displacement Maxi or an ultralight sled. Monohulls are different from multihulls. Even power boats differ from each other. A steel-hulled converted offshore tug is different from an aluminum-hulled motor yacht. They may each be luxury yachts, but one may be able to handle heavy seas, and the other may sustain expensive damage to hull plates if subjected to the same conditions.

Most advanced sailors are aware that different boats have different performance characteristics. These can be represented by polars, a three-variable graph that illustrates how a particular boat will perform. Simply put, under varying wind speeds and true wind angles, a boat will achieve a particular boat speed.

Weather routing takes that into consideration at the very least. But there are other variables which aren't quite so easy to quantify, but may be at least as important, with safety perhaps being one of them. As a cruising couple is about to make landfall in Maine in early June, perhaps they should stand off and go in during daylight hours or at a time when the proposed anchorage is free from fog. If they're going to heave to and wait for suitable conditions they will no doubt want to know the wind direction, heading, set and drift of any currents, and boat speed while hove to.

Even while sailing in normal conditions, our performance is not always optimal. Polars and routing software assume that we will always be sailing our boat to its maximum efficiency. That may not be the case. Furthermore, if we are cruising or doing a boat delivery, there may be occasions on which we're using the engine to augment our boat speed under sail. In that case, we would exceed our polars. Routing software assumes that we will be in a certain place at a certain time in order to "catch" a weather system. Sailing too slow or too fast introduces error into the automated routing solution, and as such alters the route.

What are the steps involved for routing a vessel?

A good route for one boat may not be a good route for another. And a very efficient and effective route for the same boat may be changed by how efficiently we sail and use the boat's design to its optimum for a given task

Effective routing of a vessel takes a number of variables into consideration as it solves the problem of which way that vessel should go in order to get from Point A to Point B. Weather and oceanography are, of course, a couple of the prime variables. They aren't the only ones.

On long passages or even during short coastal cruising passages, we often don't go in a straight line to efficiently get from Point A to Point B. Rather, we have intermittent waypoints to go to in order to avoid some geographic considerations or perhaps take advantage of a weather or oceanographic feature.

The process of routing a vessel includes the following steps:

❶ Setting initial waypoints based on the best data available prior to your departure

❷ Removing or moving those waypoints as new data becomes available, or as your decision-making criteria changes

Setting waypoints

Waypoints can be thought of as guidelines or marks to approach as you go through your passage or race. Some of them are more important to honor than others. As an example, if you are going through a narrow channel, it may be important to come quite close to the waypoint. However, some of them may not be quite so important to hit squarely.

Some waypoints, such as the geographically critical marks, may be rigidly fixed. Others will be modified prior to actually getting to them.

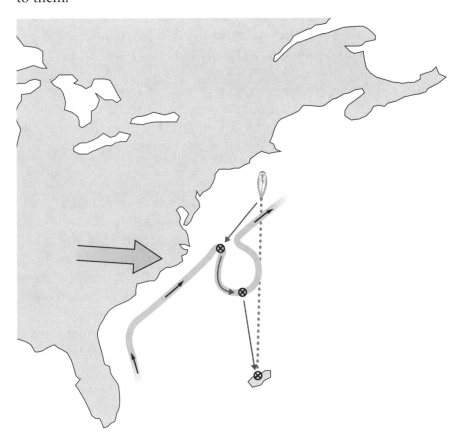

We know that our final waypoint is at our destination. In order to select intermediate waypoints, we look at factors that will help us achieve our own objectives. If that is speed, we will look for favorable current if it does not take us too far out of our way to get to the current.

Months before an event, I will often go through a proposed race or passage and look at a potential route. Based on climatology I can add waypoints to places I think I may want to select. Some waypoints may be selected based on a possibility of adverse weather conditions. If the bad weather looks like it will develop on my approach to a landfall, I will honor that waypoint. If it looks like good weather will prevail, I may elect to bypass that waypoint altogether. The adverse weather is planned for, but if it doesn't develop, I remove the waypoint.

From a practical standpoint, we already know two of the waypoints we will select. The first one is the starting point. The last one is our destination. How do we get the ones in between?

I go about it from a rather unconventional point of view. Whether I am racing or doing a boat delivery, I always look at a range of options like I am on Boat "A" competing against Boat "B." In fact they are competing ideas rather than boats. If both A and B are equidistant from the destination where would I rather be situated at a particular place along the rhumb line, to the right or left of rhumb? How far to the east or west of Boat "B" would I like to be, given a climatologically average weather pattern? If I am crossing a current, such as the Gulf Stream, I know I will have an entry point and an exit point. Without knowing the specifics of the Gulf Stream, I may just put the initial waypoints along the rhumb line, trying to minimize my distance to the destination. Later, as the actual time draws near and I've located the various features of the current, I'll pick more appropriate waypoints, taking into consideration the speed and direction of the current, how the current will affect the particular boat I am on, and how the wind speed and direction will affect the sea state, and my overall weather strategy.

Moving or removing waypoints

From a weather standpoint, waypoints are seldom rigidly fixed. A day or two before the race, I'll look at those waypoints selected using climatology and I will modify them based on more refined synoptic scale meteorology. As I later get into the race, I may look at a more near real time forecast and again modify the waypoint to reflect the higher reliability of the forecast. Plans aren't completely thrown out; rather they are refined based on more accurate information.

I will estimate where I am going to be located at a particular time, and I will look at what the weather forecast is for that time frame. I will want to be in the most advantageous position for my boat and the goals I have set for myself. The goal may be to get to my destination faster than another real or hypothetical alternative boat. Or my goal may be to be in the safest conditions possible. In either case, I will try to put my vessel in the place that suits my vessel best along a line of possible choices for that time – an isochrone.

For long distance passages, when I'm in the role of navigator, I may tell the watch captains to think of our proposed route as if we were proceeding toward a gate rather than a fixed waypoint. I may not want the helmsman to go too far to the left because that route would take us into a high pressure system, but I also may not want him to take us too far to the right because that would add too many miles to the total route. So I may tell them to steer between 160 and 165 degrees magnetic, whichever gives them the best boat speed. The actual waypoint may be located on a bearing of 161 degrees at a range of 300 miles, but the added flexibility allows the deck watch to work on maximizing boat speed and overall sailing efficiency without detracting from the overall strategy.

In short course racing we may not set intermediate waypoints, but that doesn't prevent us from having places we'd prefer to be. We might want to be inshore to catch a favorable wind shift along the beach or seek relief from the tide. But even those preferences can be changed. As an example, if the tactician perceives that we would gain a tactical advantage by standing a little further offshore and tacking in a clear lane, that may be a short term optimal solution. Keep in mind that weather is only one of several criteria for determining a route. The navigator's role is to safely and efficiently position the boat in a geographic location and/or weather pattern. The tactician's role is to safely and competitively position the boat in a fleet. The two must work together. Sometimes the priorities of one must over-ride the preferences of the other. Whose priorities prevail will change from circumstance to circumstance.

As we approach waypoints, they become progressively less and less relevant. Unless they are set to keep us in the middle of a channel or from going aground, we don't need to go right over the top of a way-point. They act as guidelines. Sometimes we should pass near to the actual waypoint but, more frequently as they get closer, we disregard them and keep our focus on an imaginary goal 50 or 100 miles away. In trans-oceanic events, the distances may be greater. In an overnight race, of course, the distances would be shorter.

Changing waypoints: keeping options open Route planning and setting waypoints is meant to help us keep our options open as long as possible. We are committing to a course of action, but that shouldn't preclude the possibility – in fact the likelihood – that we will modify our original plans based on new information. Perhaps the best way to look at this is that we will be refining our plans, not completely changing our overall strategy. Planning is meant to help us avoid randomly or completely changing our strategy in mid-passage or mid-race. In light of that, we want to have a full range of efficient choices and options available to us within our chosen strategy.

The Go-No Go decisions

Perhaps the first and most important routing decision any of us confront is whether to actually go or to remain in port. These "go – no go" decisions are the ultimate responsibility of the captain of the vessel. Weather routing services can offer suggestions, and race committees can make races available, but the decision to untie the dock lines and leave the safety of port rests with the captain of the vessel. It then becomes incumbent on the captain and the crew to do their

Whether we're racing or cruising, going for a day sail or leaving on a long passage, the decision to leave is ultimately up to us as individual sailors and decision-makers aboard our vessels.

respective jobs and get the boat safely back to port.

Regardless of the type of sailing or kind of event, the responsibility for appropriate decisions rests with the person in charge of the vessel.

Race

Whether or not a race committee decides to hold an event the captain of the vessel assumes responsibility for the safe operation of the vessel. The navigator provides input, and is responsible for the safe navigation of the vessel, of course. Each of the crew have their own respective duties to perform but, in recreational sailing, if there are inhibitions about expected conditions, they should voice those to the captain so that they are fully discussed prior to encountering heavy weather or difficult situations.

Speed record

Frequently, teams prepare for speed records and wait for the weather to achieve characteristics that seem like they will favor a successful run at the record. Depending on the type of vessel, that may imply strong winds and sizeable waves on a broad reach, or it may imply relatively flat water and moderate wind speeds at a particular wind angle or other "ideal" conditions for a particular boat. Also, during these speed records, a team will frequently work with the services of a weather routing company. The weather forecasters will advise the team when, in their estimation, the conditions seem to match the desired characteristics.

Ultimate responsibility to go or to wait for other conditions or time to depart still rests with the captain of the vessel, however. He makes that decision in conjunction with advice from the weather forecasters. Since the state of the weather forecasting art is not one of certainty but rather one of probability, weather forecasts are imperfect. It is the captain who assumes the responsibility for the decision to go or stay.

Go – No Go decision for cruisers or delivery captains

Cruisers often have a relatively flexible schedule, so the go – no go advice from a weather routing service can be very helpful in how they chose to allocate their time.

Some services will try to give a day or two of advance notice to let the cruising or delivery skipper know when the conditions will be favorable for departure. They can remain productively occupied elsewhere and mobilize for their departure when conditions seem like they will fall into place for a pleasant or efficient passage to their next destination.

Ultimately, the decision to mobilize to go or stay and whether they depart or not still falls to the skipper of the boat. Weather forecasts and routing services provide input and guidance but not final decisions. As such, it would be wise to choose the forecasters and routers with care and understand that, ultimately, it is up to the captain to assess how that information should be accepted or rejected.

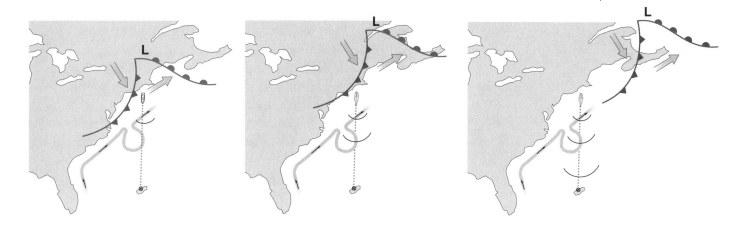

Plotting where we will be located on a weather map will help us to understand our tradeoffs in terms of weather to be expected. Using isochrones – small concentric arcs of approximate position – will help us to see where we'll be at a given time, assuming a given speed.

Take action

Armed with our understanding of our sailing objective, our assets and liabilities and how the weather is expected to change, we are almost ready to take action. First, however, we need to finish selecting our waypoints.

We looked at how to predict the weather for where we are going to be located (See: Chapter 6, "Gathering Data"). In that example we were on a theoretical passage to Bermuda. We had drawn rough isochrones on the 24 and 48 hour forecast maps. We had also collected the 96 hour surface forecast as well as some satellite imagery.

Continue to project out your position along an isochrone on the 96 hour surface pressure forecast. The wind speed and direction would probably change sometime during that 4-day period from the time you departed Newport to the valid time of the 96 hour surface forecast.

Where would you like to be along that isochrone? Ultimately the answer depends on your sailing objective. Are you trying to maximize speed to the destination? You would try to be on the point of the isochrone that is closest to Bermuda. Are you trying to maximize safety? If the point closest to Bermuda is located in extremely high winds, you may elect to divert slightly to put yourself in a more favorable weather pattern or minimize your time in heavy weather. That may be a bit further to the west, behind the heavy weather as it moves off to the east.

Although in the original example we began with an assumption that current wouldn't play an element in our routing, the reality is that current does play a role in routing. Depending on the speed of the vessel and how long it is subjected to the current, it can add more or less speed over the ground. An extremely fast multihull, doing 30 knots through the water, may be in a 90 mile meander for less than 3 hours, gaining an average of 2.5 knots for that amount of time. Very slow monohulls in light air, doing 5 knots, may be in the same current for 12 hours gaining a 50% speed boost!

It becomes obvious that, in that case, the monohulls is probably well-advised to take advantage of the current while the multihull has considerably less to gain from the current.

Wind against current, however, can pitch up a very steep and uncomfortable seaway. In reality, we are again back to our original set of questions: What is our sailing objective? What are our assets and liabilities? If we're racing a monohull, we'll try to take advantage of the current – assuming the crew isn't dangerously seasick in the process. If we're cruising we'll select a waypoint that gets us where we'd like to go, but placing a higher value on comfort than speed. If we're in a multihull, the current may be a secondary consideration to the wind angle since we'll be in the current a relatively brief period of time and the wind angle may have a more significant impact on the overall speed toward our destination.

As we continue to look for our optimal route, taking into consideration the weather, current and other priorities, we begin to see how we want to get our trip underway initially. We will continue to look out in front of us by several days, even if our event is a weeklong regatta and our only immediate consideration is what kind of weather we will be faced with today. Collecting the data days in advance will give us an insight into the reliability of the weather forecasts in the days ahead.

We're ready to take action and proceed to the first waypoint with reasonable expectations of where that will lead. The subsequent waypoints will later be moved if weather forecasts change in near real time or if problems arise with our vessel.

Chapter 8
The Role of
"Weather Routers"

The clock showed 4:00 A.M., and in the darkness the fax machine could be heard spewing forth this morning's 00 Z surface analysis. I had been semi-conscious for the last hour waiting for this information, as ALLIED BANK and DURACELL raced towards Tropical Storm Josephine. Had the storm gone to Hurricane strength? I got up, grabbed the fax, and went to fix a cup of coffee; it was going to be a long day. But at least I knew that today I wouldn't be getting wet: this time I was not the navigator on the boat; I was the router doing my analysis back in Newport, Rhode Island.

That episode in my sailing career was more than a decade ago. I've been routing boats to records, victories and around adverse weather now for more than 17 years. Sometimes we win. Sometimes we don't. But we always gain an edge through studying the information that is available. The advantage is not only competitive; it is also an improved margin of safety. Often I work with a team of meteorologists who are on shore. I may be the onboard navigator or the shoreside router. How my involvement is structured depends on what the rules for the event allow and how the other decision makers aboard would like to use my experience.

What or – perhaps more correctly - who are "routers"? Imagine a navigator/tactician/weather analyst, eliminate the pitching of the boat and the occasional wave through an open hatch, add the availability of almost unlimited computer power and observations from obscure islands, points of land, satellites, and ships at sea, and you have "a router." That perhaps is a bit of a simplified definition, but it serves as a starting point. Helping to guide Open Class boats in races such as the C-Star, Two-Star, and Around Alone, routers have provided shoreside support in the form of tactical/weather guidance for years.

Some races prohibit the use of shoreside routing, saying that it provides an unfair advantage. My view is that it is only unfair if it's not available to everyone. "Fairness" has to do with adhering to the rules, and as such is everyone's responsibility. But as global communications become ubiquitous, picking up a phone and discussing the weather becomes a rather simple task. Understanding how to best use that information is somewhat more complicated. If a race committee prohibits the use of private weather or routing information but can't enforce the rule and protect the honest competitor, who is being unfair to whom? For now, I will choose to leave that debate to someone other than myself, although I certainly have my views.

Some races allow for the use of privately purchased weather information. They may or may not allow for specific routing suggestions.

CHAPTER HIGHLIGHTS

• What's in a
"Weather Package"?

• Selecting a weather
routing company

• Discussion on weather
routing software

Routers help to understand both what the weather will be and how to best utilize the expected conditions by going the fastest or safest route as opposed to the shortest route. Routing, of course, is available to both cruisers and racers. When I was a founding principal in Weather Window, a weather routing company, about half of our business was with each of those two user groups.

Even highly experienced sailors have questions about the weather and, in fact, very often the most qualified sailors will consult with a weather routing company. Why? Because they know that poor information may ultimately cost them the most in terms of broken equipment, delayed or re-routed passages, or even injuries. Qualified information – even if there is a fee involved – often ends up being the least expensive form of education. But how do you sort the golden nuggets of information from the mud?

Weather information is everywhere, but all information isn't created equal. For decades meteorologists have improved their understanding of weather, how it works and how it's expected to behave. Most have little idea of the problems encountered by sailors. By understanding the forecast, they may understand the "solution," but, by having a limited understanding of what it's like aboard a small craft, in many cases they still have a limited understanding of the overall problems we encounter while sailing. There are ship routing companies guiding tankers and bulk carriers around the globe. But the problems encountered aboard a container ship may not exactly replicate those encountered aboard your Oyster or your J-24. Different vessels. Different problems. Different perceptions. And, therefore, there are different answers to the question, "which way do we go from here?".

What's in a "Weather Package"?

The following are items that the best weather routing companies provide for passages or events of varying lengths. First they supply a written text that explains the large-scale weather patterns that will affect you. If you are located in The U.K., the North Atlantic patterns will eventually provide an impact on you. The text should also cover the ways in which the patterns will specifically affect you. Completing that written information, there should be a listing of wind speeds and directions for at least 5 days and as many as 8 days. The speeds and directions should cover the conditions you will expect to encounter on a 12 hourly or 6 hourly basis. As you move from Point "A" to Point "B," the weather obviously also changes. Getting a text or verbal message from the Internet or VHF on the weather at Point "A," say in Newport, RI, only provides one very small piece in the puzzle. The written information that is provided by the weather routing company explains the weather that you will probably experience as you proceed along a given route at a given speed. The forecast may change or become invalid after only a few days, but you should have an idea of the best current thinking on the topic. Additionally, you should have 5 to 8 days of weather forecast maps. It is said that a picture is worth

10,000 words. If that is the case, a weather map is probably worth far more as it explains the changes to be expected in the weather.

Some of this information is free via High Frequency weather fax, VHF radio, or via the Internet (See www.WxAdvantage.com). However, the detail, time horizon, and accuracy of what it is that you specifically can expect is often worth the difference between free and the relatively small amount charged by reputable weather routing companies. Fees, of course, vary with the type and frequency of service provided.

For short courses, weather routing companies will provide information on expected hourly wind patterns and shifts. During the recent Swan Worlds, I was on site in Porto Cervo to correlate forecast data with the actual conditions that were developing prior to the start of the races. This type of monitoring has been going on for some time in America's Cup competition. Understanding the expected wind shifts and currents on a short course – any short course – will help you as you form your own tactics.

Selecting a weather routing company

When you're searching for a qualified weather routing company, there are a few things that you need to know. First and foremost you need to know yourself: your abilities, constraints and preferences. You need to formulate a sailing objective. Whether your primary goal is racing, setting speed records, cruising, delivering a sailboat from point "A" to point "B," fishing, or chartering a vessel with time constraints, you need to understand what it is that you're trying to accomplish. Each of those categories has their own sets of priorities and limitations. In one circumstance you may place a high priority on speed. In another you may hold comfort in higher regard. And, in yet another, having the flexibility to alter course and duck in for shelter or to poke around in a beautiful gunk hole may present a desirable alternative.

Similarly, it's important to understand your capabilities and constraints. Are you single-handing? Is your crew well trained and highly experienced, many of whom have tens of thousands of miles of experience? Are you sailing with your spouse and a couple of children under 10 years old? These considerations and others will help you to understand your capabilities in adverse conditions. If the weather really goes downhill, how many people can you count on to help and how many will require assistance? Knowing and accurately assessing your crew's capabilities will help you to understand how effectively you can deal with heavy weather and how much effort you will need to invest in order to avoid weather that might present a serious problem to you and your crew. If the meteorologist with whom you're dealing doesn't understand the importance of those things, then he doesn't fully understand the problem.

The human element is part of the equation, but there's still more to it. Ship routing companies base their route planning on hull forms and how a ship's speed is affected by waves. Sailboat routing companies partially base their routing suggestions on wind speeds and directions. Of course, there are other factors such as currents, fuel consumption rates during deliveries, overall safety, and so forth, but the basis for determining shipping routes has much to do with wave patterns and, for sailboats, it has to do with expected wind conditions. Your vessel has its own unique performance characteristics. Whether it's a powerboat or a sailboat, you should be able to achieve certain speed and distances over a course depending on the conditions. You will also have your own particular set of constraints. As an example, a steel-hulled fishing boat can withstand greater waves at a given high end speed than an aluminum-hulled Feadship. Even though the Feadship may have a higher top end boat speed, pushing a Feadship at top speed into an 18-foot head sea could result in very expensive hull damage. For sailors, an ultra-light sled designed for the Transpac will have radically different sailing characteristics from a Swan 56. Given your own sailing objective and priorities, what kind of distances can you expect to make in a particular set of conditions? Meteorologists may not always know or understand some of these constraints, and it may be necessary for you to help them understand your own particular situation and priorities. If you can't achieve a particular speed and aren't in the place they expect you to be when the forecast becomes valid, then you will experience different conditions from those forecast.

As you begin to more thoroughly understand your own sailing objective, assets and liabilities, you need to understand what it is that you want from your weather routing consultants. If you are racing, you may only be able to receive information from a private forecasting firm prior to your departure on the race. If you're cruising or doing a delivery, the only limitation on the information you may receive may be presented by your own communications capability. Often, boats on a speed record attempt set up 24 hour per day availability from their shoreside routers. When the wind shifts at 2:00 a.m. a call goes in to the met center and a discussion is held to determine whether or not the shift is permanent or local. Should they gybe or stand the course? A phone conference is held to help make the decision.

Although I've often used a weather routing service for a variety of inputs, one of the more typical experiences was during a passage from Stamford, CT, to the Virgin Islands in late November. We received pre-departure weather forecasts for 3 days prior to our departure. We wanted to be sure that we would be south of the Gulf Stream before the cold northerlies filled in following a frontal passage. If we were caught on the warm Gulf Stream with cold northerlies, the winds and sea state could easily exceed 45 knots and we could increase the possibility of damage to the vessel. After assessing the speed of the fronts and how fast we could get past the Stream, we departed. Later in the passage, we were about 175 nautical miles SSW of Bermuda. The weather we were experiencing seemed to indicate that we might be able to head directly toward the Virgin Islands without getting headed in the Northeast Trades. Calling into the weather routing company, they suggested that we should put into Bermuda because the cloud cover over Jamaica was beginning to show signs of circulation. Forecasts were that a hurricane would develop and be located over the Virgin Islands right at the time that we expected to arrive in those islands! It was a forecast that flew in the face of conventional thinking, moving a hurricane into the Trades rather than traveling with the direction of the Trade Winds. We put into Bermuda and avoided a possible disaster. To say that the $200 to $300 spent on the overall weather routing service during that passage was worth the expense is certainly an understatement.

Getting custom weather information and/or routing suggestions while offshore will depend to a great deal on the type of communication equipment you have on your vessel. While it's true enough that you can still call the met center using SSB radio and raising WLO in Mobile, Alabama, satellite communication is quite a bit more convenient. It is also becoming less expensive than voice radio. If you're still using your radio for communication with those on shore, be aware that it is subject to reception, and frequently reception by HF radio is somewhat sporadic during the middle of the day, especially over great distances. If you're calling or sending data over satellite such as INMARSAT Mini M, Standard C, or using Iridium, relatively easy frequent communication becomes much more convenient.

Whether you're a seasoned offshore veteran or a relative novice, getting information from a trained weather professional has substantial benefit. Not only can that information help you avoid weather-related problems and maximize your vessel's potential, you can also learn a great deal about weather in the process. Over the years, you will heighten your own awareness of weather and how to optimize routing for your own set of priorities. Even as you become more experienced, you may decide that you still prefer to consult with a meteorologist or router but, with more experience, you can add more to the discussion and continue to improve the overall decision making process.

When you hire a weather routing company, you, as the skipper and/or navigator, are still responsible for safely getting your vessel from one place to another. The routing company is there to assist you and to provide the best information that they can. While we would all like today's weather forecasts to be flawless, that's not the current state of the art. Forecasts have improved greatly over the past 10 years, but perfection is still over the horizon. As sailors, it is in our own best interest to help the meteorologists deliver the highest quality goods they can. In order to do that, they need to know not only about our priorities, capabilities and limitations, they can also use some help in understanding the current conditions we're experiencing. When working with a weather routing company, even on those days I don't expect to receive a weather forecast or routing suggestion from them, I always try to send them my daily observations.

The daily observations help the routers to place us in a particular weather pattern, give them a point of reference and spot weather patterns that are moving slower or faster than expected. These "obs" include: the time of day (in UTC), our position, True Wind Speed, True Wind Direction (in degrees True rather than magnetic), Boat Speed, Heading (in degrees True), Barometric Pressure, Sea State, Sky Conditions, and any comments or particular questions we may have.

When you're shopping for a weather routing service, they should also see the importance of the above information, priorities and limitations. If they feel that they don't need that information or it doesn't materially help them in their decision-making, perhaps they're not looking at the entire problem on your behalf.

Like doctors, there are specialist meteorologists. And, also like doctors, half of them graduated in the lower 50% of their graduating class. There are good, bad, and great ones out there. Some of the meteorologists are content with just reading the computer-generated model and issuing an opinion. Others are more proactive and more thoroughly study the situation, looking at actual observations, satellite pictures, and creating their own forecasts to get a clearer understanding.

Experience counts for a great deal. A meteorologist who has spent years doing global marine forecasts understands the differences between what a weather map implies and how local conditions such as the Gulf Stream affect the gradient weather. Just as you might be searching for a doctor, if you need an Internist, an Ophthalmologist may not do. If you are interested in securing the services of a weather routing specialist, a meteorologist who prepares weather for the 10:00 P.M. news may not be completely up to the task. He may understand the solution, but he may or may not completely understand the problem. Has he worked extensively with passage makers with a variety of goals and mindsets? Does he understand the importance of a 20 degree wind shift during the middle of a day race?

When preparing routing suggestions for a variety of projects in the past, we paid close attention to both the goals and the capabilities of the sailors with whom we were dealing.

In the early '90's when John Martin and his brother Ian were racing double handed across the North Atlantic aboard ALLIED BANK from England to Newport, RI, they were highly experienced heavy weather sailors. Both had sailed in Whitbread Round the World Races, and they grew up sailing on the edge of the Southern Ocean. They were in the process of testing their boat prior to a single-handed round the world race. And they were aggressive in their sailing – extremely aggressive. The routes that were suggested for them were considerably different from a route we would suggest for two couples and their small children on a passage.

When you're seeking out the services of a weather router, you should both be doing a bit of interviewing. They should know a bit about you, and you should certainly know about their backgrounds and experiences with passage makers. They don't need to be sailors, but they should have a thorough understanding of the problems encountered by small craft while under power or sail. That understanding can help you to avoid your own unique set of problems. And, as you become more experienced with offshore passage making and the use of a weather routing service, it is most likely that you will only increase your appreciation for the services that they offer.

Discussion on weather routing software

Options that are open to passage makers also include the use of routing software. The various routing softwares available today base their route selection on GRIB formatted weather forecasts and the vessel's polars. If either of those factors is incorrect or the boat is not sailed to its polars, the route selection may be less than optimal. GRIB formatted weather forecasts are usually computer-generated models providing data points approximately 60 nautical miles on center. The forecasts are often in 12 hourly increments. The intermediate forecast points offered by the routing software are strictly straight-line interpolated data. That fact alone provides for a certain degree of error in many cases.

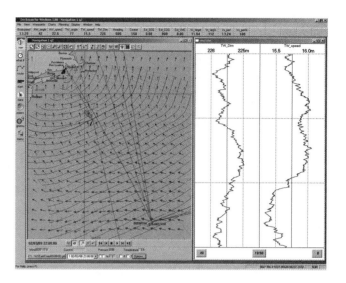

Weather – especially in areas of low-pressure systems and frontal passages – doesn't work as a consistently smooth transition over those distances and time frames.

That, however, is not to say that routing software doesn't have its value. It does provide a useful tool to the navigator who is able to understand its limitations and use the tool as part of an overall routing strategy. I use routing software to offer suggested routes based on a general set of criteria. I then look at other options, given a more refined set of criteria or my own subjective perspective. Routing software does not tell me which way to proceed. It's just another "opinion," but having another perspective – especially if it's an idea that hasn't been previously explored – can have a significant value. As such, Deckman for Windows, MaxSea, and Raytech all provide useful information. Some are more convenient to use than others, and they each offer some different features.

The art/science of weather routing has come a long way in the last 15 years. Global communications make it convenient. Safety considerations and overall efficiency make it an option whose time has come.

Plotting where we will be located on a weather map will help us to understand our tradeoffs in terms of weather to be expected. Using isochrones – small concentric arcs of approximate position – will help us to see where we'll be at a given time, assuming a given speed.

Summary

The concepts and knowledge you gained from this book should immediately improve your skills as a sailor. Specifically, you should be able to get closer to your sailing objective whether that objective is to improve your performance in round-the-buoy races or round-the-world races, or increase your safety factor in weekend cruising or world cruising. We are confident that, with practice, the information here will be a great benefit, adding to your safety, enjoyment and competitive inclinations.

We have brought the subject of weather progressively closer to the moment of decision and action by progressively moving from the theoretical to the practical. Starting with principles of global climatology, we narrowed the focus to synoptic-scale meteorology, and concluded with the effects of local weather. We then covered the process of locating and gathering data appropriate for a particular sailing objective. We discussed techniques for validating the data through cross-referencing various weather sources and factoring in your shipboard observations. Finally, we provided examples of how to apply these concepts and techniques to your particular situation by including your assets and liabilities in the decision-making process.

At this moment, perhaps you're experiencing a feeling of information overload. Perhaps the question in your mind is, "How do I apply this information to my particular circumstances?" "How do I get started on my next sailing project?"

For example, if you have ever tried to use the Internet to gather weather-related data, the sheer number of sites undoubtedly frustrated you. Which sites offer the best information? What site has distilled the information appropriate for your particular need? What happens when one weather service changes its web address – who keeps track of those changes? The Internet can be a magnificent source of information, but too much unfiltered information can be as dangerous as too little information. If you find yourself spending most of the time searching for information with little or no success, or if you are missing a hot new Internet resource, you aren't leveraging this resource to its maximum potential and are probably wasting much of your time.

From reading this book you should recognize the fact that you can start preparing for any sailing event weeks, even months, before the day of departure. Starting with an understanding of the general weather and oceanographic patterns for a particular location and time of year (global climatology), you can make high-level decisions on routing, crew, equipment, etc. Then, starting 7 – 10 days prior to departure, you can begin to track the development of actual weather activity affecting your event (synoptic-scale meteorology) in order to refine the set of decisions you have made. Finally, understanding the effects of local conditions and factoring in your own shipboard observations will allow you to make real-time routing decisions.

The process of leveraging your new understanding of weather can, therefore, take many weeks or months. Ideally, there would be a tool that walks you through the process step-by-step, similar to the way a professional weather router or a sailing 'coach' would tackle the project. The tool would lead you through the questions that the weather router or coach would ask about your sailing objective, your assets and liabilities, the time of year, sailing area, etc. It would suggest the appropriate data to collect, provide references to those sources and help you gather the information. It would then help you analyze the data to help make pre-trip routing decisions, or real-time, onboard decisions.

Although such a tool may be just beyond the capabilities of current communications and computing technologies, we have, in fact, created an Online Weather Toolkit designed to walk you through the process to prepare you for your next sailing adventure. The Online Weather Toolkit is designed to complement this book, or any of our Weather Seminars or CDs. It assumes you have a basic understanding of meteorology, climatology, oceanography, and the ability to read weather maps. Once you've acquired these fundamental skills, you can use the Online Weather Toolkit as a step-by-step coach to walk you through the process, and will also serve as a reference tool, and as a refresher on any of the background concepts or principles. The Online Weather Toolkit has filtered through the vast resources of the Internet to bring you the best it has to offer.

Weather Routing Toolkit homepage
http://weather.northu.com/

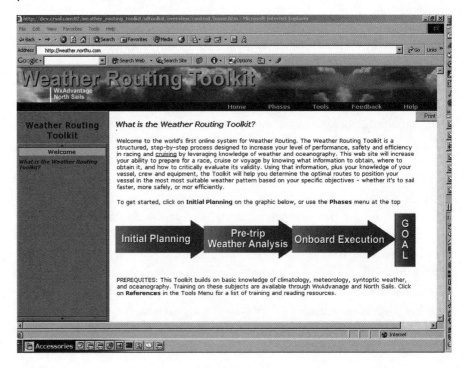

The Weather Routing Toolkit organizes the process into three distinct phases:
- Phase 1: Initial Planning
- Phase 2: Pre-Trip Weather Analysis and Routing
- Phase 3: Onboard Execution

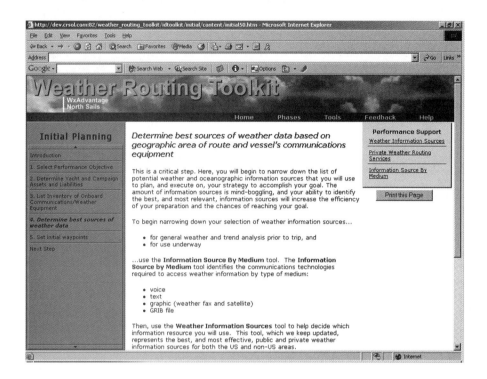

Sample screen in Phase 1: Initial Planning.
This step discusses the process of narrowing down the types of weather data based on your sailing objective and available communications technologies. Note the Performance Support Box that provides links to tools, references, resources and further information for this step.

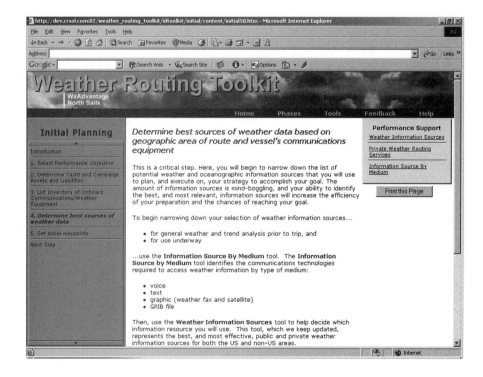

Sample screen in Phase 2: Pre-trip Weather Analysis and Routing.
This step discusses the process of collecting synoptic weather information and provides links to specific weather information sites.

Sample screen in Phase 3:
Onboard Execution
This step discusses the process of making real-time routing corrections based on onboard observations, and provides links to helpful tools and resources.

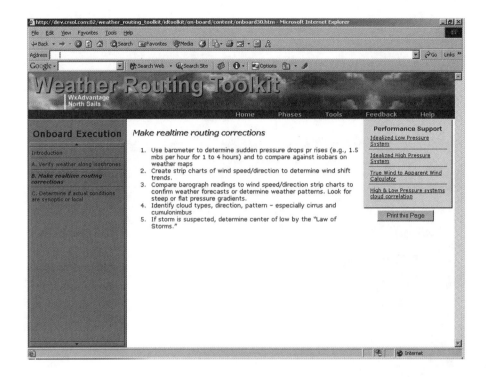

Thank you

I hope that the information contained within this book helps you to successfully realize your own sailing objectives. From my own experience, I know that the information will go a long way to improve your approach to sailing. But I also know that your improvement will be a direct result of the time and effort you put into the endeavor. Acquiring the weather information, interpreting it and actually using it to make decisions and take action will help to sharpen your skills. Most of us learn through mistakes – either vicariously through someone else's errors or through our own. Maybe that's the price paid for the lessons we learn. Don't get discouraged if weather doesn't always behave like you think it's "supposed to." It will provide a never-ending series of events to ponder. But, ultimately, you will discover that there is a cause and effect relationship to it all.

Good luck with your sailing, and keep putting the effort into the learning process. We will continue to offer introductory weather tools and resources to help you in that process. We wish you every success in your continued sailing.

Cheers,

Bill Biewenga
www.WxAdvantage.com
www.weather.northu.com
Email: BillBiewenga@compuserve.com

Appendix A
Key West

FROM: COMMANDERS' WEATHER CORP
154 BROAD ST, SUITE 1517
NASHUA, NH 03062
TEL: 603-882-6789, FAX: 603-882-6661

✳✳

Please hold for the PRIVATE and EXCLUSIVE use of:
North U. Sailing Team.

✳✳

Location: Key West
Forecast for: Saturday, January 18, 2003
Outlook for: Sunday January 19-Friday January 24, 2003
Prepared: 0700edt Saturday, January 18, 2003

Summary... A gusty breeze and unseasonably cool this weekend. Then lighter winds first half of week followed by stronger winds again end of week as next cold front moves thru.
a) Weather map this morning shows a mid winter weather pattern across the US.
b) Strong cold front which moved thru yesterday is now moving east of the Turks and Caicos.
c) High pressure is building in behind it across the SE states and the Gulf of Mexico.
d) Result is a moderately strong northerly wind across the keys this morning.
e) Latest observations at 6am.
   a. Key West 350 at 11 kts
   b. Navy Key West 010 at 12 kts
   c. Buoy offshore Key West 360 at 20-23 kts
   d. Buoy Dry Tortugas 350 at 17-24 kts.
f) So lots of wind early this morning especially over the water as fairly strong wind gradient exits between the higher pressure in the Gulf of Mexico and the front near the Turks and Caicos.
g) Also it is very cool this morning with temperatures down into the lower 50s and as the cool air passes over the warm waters (water temps mid 70s) it is causing unstable conditions and adding to the breeze over the water.

a. This is one reason why the buoys have more wind.
h) Computer models are showing that this breeze will persist this morning and perhaps drop off a few kts this afternoon .
i) Direction is forecast to change very little during the day although there will be some slight oscillations of 10 degrees or so either side of 360 today.
j) Speeds this morning likely 17-22 kts over the water tending to ease off to 15-20 kts this afternoon.
Wind Forecast
Wind directions are TRUE, wind speed in kts, time is EST

0900: 350-010/ 17-22
1000: 350-010/ 17-22
1100: 360-020/ 17-22
1200: 360-020/ 16-21
1300: 010-030/ 15-20
1400: 360-020/ 15-20
1500: 360-020/ 15-20
1600: 360-020/ 15-20
1700: 360-020/ 14-18
Weather...Intervals of clouds and sun and very cool. Highs only around 60.

Error factor...

a) Do not expect any permanent shifts today with the breeze holding in not too far from 360.

b) Some oscillations either way could make winds as far right as 020 and as far left as 340 with primary breeze at 360.

c) Vertical profiles do not show much stronger wind at 1-2 thousand feet and also show a similar direction.

d) Peak winds likely 20-25 kts this morning and down near 20 kts this afternoon with the peak winds

coming during the sunny periods and lulls in the breeze as low as 15 kts during cloudy periods.

Sunday, Jan 19

a) High pressure will be centered just south of Louisiana and tending to expand eastward toward Florida.

b) Frontal boundary will be weakening not too far east of Turks and Caicos.

c) Computer models still showing a decent wind gradient across the race course of 14-18 kts.

d) Air will be cool so air will be unstable again and this could result in some wind gusts into low 20s especially in the morning.

e) Direction will favor a N-NNE(360-030) direction with some oscillations likely within that range but but a large permanent shift not likely during the day.

0900: 360-020/17-22
1100: 360-020/17-22
1300: 360-020/15-20
1500: 360-020/15-19
1700: 360-020/14-18
Weather... Sunny to partly cloudy, breezy, and cool. Highs in the mid 60s

Monday, Jan 20

a) High pressure continues to shift slowly eastward in the Gulf of Mexico.

b) It should also be expanding eastward across central Florida keeping any fronts
 Further north from affecting the race course.

c) Models show lighter wind gradient across the Keys with speeds in the 10-15 kts range.

d) Could see breeze a little higher earlier in the day but would expect it to diminish down to 10-12 kts by mid to late pm.

e) Direction may favor a slight right shift with breeze more N early then sliding right to 040 by mid pm.

0900: 360-020/14-18
1100: 010-030/13-17
1300: 010-030/12-16
1500: 020-040/11-15
1700: 020-040/10-14
Weather...Mostly .   High temps upper 60s

Tuesday, Jan 21

a) Center of the high will be north of the Keys just south of Tampa.

b) Frontal system will be further north across southern Georgia but will no impact on the race course.

c) With the high nearby this looks to be a light wind day with speeds probably no higher than 8-12 kts.

d) Still enough breeze though to support a consistent direction from the NE with a slight right shift during the day.

0900: 010-030/ 6-10
1100: 020-040/ 8-12
1300: 030-050/ 8-12
1500: 040-060/ 7-11
1700: 040-060/ 6-10
Weather... Mostly sunny with highs around 70.

Wed, Jan 22

a) What is left of the high will be dissipating over South Florida during the day.

b) This will make for the lightest wind day of the weak and directions likely a little more shifty.

c) Initially the breeze may be NE early but tend to shift to E then SE in the afternoon as what is left of the high tends to shift eastward into central Bahamas.

d) Winds speeds likely under 10 kts.

0900: 040-060/ 6-10
1100: 070-090/ 6-10
1300: 080-100/ 5-9

1500: 120-140/ 5-9
1700: 130-160/ 5-9
Weather…Sunny. Highs in the low 70s

Thurs, Jan 23
a) Changing conditions expected as next low pressure system tracks rapidly eastward off the SE US coast.
b) Frontal system will be pushing southward in the Gulf of Mexico and will bring an increasing SW-W breeze that may reach 18-25 kts in the afternoon.
c) Expect that this front could push thru late in the day perhaps with a brief fast moving shower or thunderstorm and a wind gust over 30 kts.
d) Winds likely to shift right in the afternoon to WNW by evening.

0900: 220-240/12-16
1100: 230-250/15-20
1300: 240-260/17-22
1500: 260-280/18-25
1700: 280-300/18-25

Weather…Partly sunny with chance brief shower/thundershower in the afternoon. Highs in the mid 70s

Fri, Jan 24
a) Strong front continues rapidly eastward and high pressure follows into the eastern US.
b) This should set up a strong northerly wind gradient of unseasonably cold air into the Keys.
c) Wind speeds likely in the 18-25 range

0900: 340-360/ 17-22
1100: 350-010/ 18-25
1300: 350-010/ 18-25
1500: 360-020/ 18-25
1700: 360-020/ 17-22
Weather…Variable clouds and sun windy and cool. Highs in the low 60s

Regards, Tom Mattus

FROM: COMMANDERS' WEATHER CORP
154 BROAD ST, SUITE 1517
NASHUA, NH 03062
TEL: 603-882-6789, FAX: 603-882-6661

****

Please hold for the PRIVATE and EXCLUSIVE use of:
North U. Sailing Team.

****

Location: Key West
Forecast for: Sunday, January 19, 2003
Outlook for: Monday, Jan 20, 2003
Prepared: 0600edt Sunday, January 19, 2003

Summary…

1) High pressure sprawled out from Louisiana eastward towards the Florida Panhandle this morning with the actual main center over Louisiana
2) Frontal system is well east of the area and extends across the central and eastern Bahamas
3) The high will tend to organize into one main high during the day just to the NW of Tampa
4) Very cool air dominates the eastern US but temps will moderate to the mid 60s with a decent amount of sunshine today
5) Overall gradient is from the N and NNE and this will be the dominant wind direction today
6) Currently, seeing buoy reports averaging 350-020 around 15-20 kts with a few gusts to 22 kts while land obs much lighter, mainly 7-11 kts
  a) should have wind speeds of 15-20 kts this morning and into early afternoon, then maybe a shade less, (12-18 kts) mid and late afternoon
7) Airmass is cool and still somewhat unstable, so could see a few puffs to 20-22 kts with best chance of this occurring this morning
8) Expect primary wind direction from 360-030

Wind Forecast

Wind directions are TRUE, wind speed in kts, time is EST

0900: 360-020/14-19
1000: 360-020/15-20
1100: 010-030/15-20
1200: 010-030/15-20
1300: 360-020/14-19
1400: 360-020/14-19
1500: 360-020/14-19
1600: 360-020/13-18
1700: 010-030/13-18
Weather… Sunny to partly cloudy and cool. Highs in the mid 60s

Error factor…

a) max left of 340 and max right of 050
b) think majority of the time, 360-030
c) stronger puffs from the left
d) most left also closer in towards land
e) some peak winds to 20-22 kts and this most likely during this morning
f) wind further left with more clouds around, a little more right with bright sun

Monday, Jan 20

1) High pressure will be over Florida (close to Tampa) and will slowly drift east during the day
2) Will have another strong cold front from NY state to the Ohio Valley and then to the south-central Plains
  a) the front will be heading ESE with a more easterly component than south
3) It will be another very cool start, but temps should moderate fairly quickly during the morning and should be pleasant late morning and afternoon
  a) should have mainly sunny skies
4) Will have less breeze and direction should trend right, more to the NE
5) Expect wind speeds of 12-17 kts early morning then easing to 10-14 kts midday and afternoon

0900: 010-030/13-18
1100: 030-050/12-17
1300: 030-050/12-16
1500: 040-060/11-15
1700: 040-060/10-14
Weather…Mostly sunny.   High temps 66-70

Regards
George Caras

FROM: COMMANDERS' WEATHER CORP
154 BROAD ST, SUITE 1517
NASHUA, NH 03062
TEL: 603-882-6789, FAX: 603-882-6661

****

Please hold for the PRIVATE and EXCLUSIVE use of:
North U. Sailing Team.

****

Location: Key West
Forecast for: Monday, January 20, 2003
Outlook for: Tuesday January 21, 2003
Prepared: 0600edt Monday, January 20, 2003

Summary…
1) High pressure this morning is sitting just to
the SE of Tampa
   a) the high covers much of the east-central
   Gulf and extends east to NE of the Bahamas
2) Low pressure passing across northern New
England with a cold front from western NY
state and then down across Kentucky
3) The high will stay in control of the weather
across the area today and should provide sunshine with some passing clouds
4) It will be a bit milder this afternoon after
another chilly start this morning
5) With the high closer to the area today, expect
the breeze to be a bit lighter than yesterday
6) Forecast will call for a NE to ENE breeze
today, generally 11-15 kts this morning and 9-14
kts this afternoon
   a) the breeze will likely edge right during the
   day, especially closer to the shore
7) Look for the breeze to be most left when
patchy clouds around and edging right with
more sunshine

Wind Forecast
Wind directions are TRUE, wind speed in kts,
time is EST
0900: 040-060/11-15
1000: 040-060/11-15
1100: 040-060/10-14
1200: 040-060/10-14
1300: 050-070/10-14
1400: 050-070/10-14
1500: 060-080/10-14
1600: 060-080/ 9-13
1700: 060-080/ 9-13
Weather…Partly to mostly sunny.   High temps
66-70

Error factor…
a) max left of 020 and max right of 090
b) main range likely around 040-070
c) breeze may be a bit further left closer to land
d) more clouds will favor the breeze staying a
little more to the left and should see strongest
puffs on the edges of the clouds
e) think, if anything, breeze may be on the right
side of ranges

Tuesday, Jan 21

1) High pressure will remain across the area with one center near Tampa and another likely just to the north of the Bahamas

2) Cold front will lie across North-South Carolina and extend west-southwest to eastern Texas

3) The high will tend to edge very slowly east during the day

4) With the high essentially over the area, look for a very light wind day

5) Expect lots of sun over the region with light E flow

  a) will be cool once again early in the morning

6) Wind speeds may struggle to make 10 kts

0900: 060-080/ 8-12
1100: 070-090/ 7-11
1300: 080-100/ 6-10
1500: 080-100/ 6-10
1700: 070-090/ 6-10

Weather… Mostly sunny with highs 70-72.

Regards
George Caras

FROM: COMMANDERS' WEATHER CORP
154 BROAD ST, SUITE 1517
NASHUA, NH 03062
TEL: 603-882-6789, FAX: 603-882-6661

****

Please hold for the PRIVATE and EXCLUSIVE use of:
North U. Sailing Team.

****

Location: Key West Race Week – Key West, FL
Forecast for: Tuesday, January 21, 2003
Outlook for: Wednesday, January 24, 2003
Prepared: 0600edt Tuesday, January 21, 2003

Summary…
Tuesday, Jan 21

1) Low pressure near Little Rock, Arkansas will move E-SE over the next 24 hrs, but will not be a factor today

2) High pressure over southern-most Florida will be the key weather player today

  a) the high is centered over the southern peninsula and will be slow to move east this morning, but will be just east of Miami by this evening

  b) the high will extend southward thru the Keys today bringing light winds to the race courses

3) Gradient wind is currently light NE, 050-060/ 8-10 kts, but will move right during late morn-ing/mid-day with a slow decrease in wind strength

  a) conditions would be favorable for a sea breeze, but there is not much land to generate a significant sea breeze around the Keys

  b) the most important question will be how fast will the winds move into the east – once they are east, they will tend to stick in the east

  c) the Dry Tortugas, west of Key West, has gradually shifted into the east during the early morning hrs

4) There is a band of clouds moving thru the Keys early this morning, but skies should become sunny and temps will warm to 66-69 this afternoon

5) Forecast will call for the right shift to occur as

temps warm significantly between 1000 and noon
6) Winds will shift from an average direction of 050 to an average direction of 070-080 by 1000-1200

    a) wind speeds will become a soft 6-10 kts during that time period

7) Winds will oscillate around 080-090 this afternoon

    a) if wind speeds are 7+ kts then the oscillation will be around 20 degrees, but

    b) if wind speeds fall under 7 kts then the oscillations could be as large as 40 degrees and swing from 060-120

8) Wind speeds will likely hold 6-10 kts or slowly diminish – not looking for a lot of wind speed today!

Wind Forecast

Wind directions are TRUE, wind speed in kts, time is EST

0900: 060-080/ 7-10
1000: 060-080/ 7-10
1100: 070-090/ 6-10
1200: 070-090/ 6-10
1300: 070-090/ 6-10
1400: 070-090/ 6-9
1500: 080-100/ 6-9
1600: 070-100/ 6-9
1700: 060-100/ 4-8

Weather…Some early clouds otherwise mostly sunny with highs 66-69.

High tide in Key West is 1134 and low tide is 1810

Error factor…

1) Primary concern is how fast will the wind directions rotate right

a) this may be a function of wind speed – as wind speeds fall, the winds will move right

2) Once wind directions reach 080-090, they may not move much further right, unless wind speeds are under 7 kts

    a) max right with wind speeds 7+ kts will be 100-110

    b) max right if wind speeds are 4 kts or less could be 120-140

3) Max left should be early in the day, but if wind speeds are under 7 kts, ALWAYS watch out for a significant left oscillation, especially if there are cumulus or stratocumulus clouds passing over the N side of the race course

    a) max left should be 040-050

4) Wind speeds should peak this morning and should not exceed 10-12 kts

    a) concerned about too little wind speed for racing this afternoon!

Wednesday, January 22, 2003

1) Low pressure will be over Georgia during the morning and moving east

    a) attached cold front will be quite strong and moving into the NW Gulf of Mexico

2) It will be another clear, cool morning in the Keys as the high pressure area will be near Miami to start the day

    a) high will move slowly E-SE during the day

3) Another light wind day and there will be a large struggle for significant wind speed today

4) Winds will move right and become S-SE to S-SW by late in the day

5) Strongest wind speeds at the start of the morning, 6-10 kts, but

a) wind speeds will fall to 4-8 kts mid-morning and generally stay in the 2-8 kt range all day

0900: 050-080/ 6-10
1100: 060-100/ 4-8
1300: 080-120/ 2-6
1500: 100-140/ 2-6
1700: 140-200/ 4-8

Weather…Sunny. High temps in the low 70s

Regards, Ken Campbell

FROM: COMMANDERS' WEATHER CORP
154 BROAD ST, SUITE 1517
NASHUA, NH 03062
TEL: 603-882-6789, FAX: 603-882-6661
****

Please hold for the PRIVATE and EXCLUSIVE use of:
North U. Sailing Team.

****

Location: Key West Race Week – Key West, FL
Forecast for: Wednesday, January 22, 2003
Outlook for: Thursday January 23, 2003
Prepared: 0600edt Wednesday, January 22, 2003

Summary...
Wednesday, January 22
1) Low pressure in southern Alabama/Georgia will move east today
   a) this low will have no impact on the weather in the Keys today, but will intensify into a major Atlantic Ocean storm tomorrow afternoon into Friday
2) Same old high pressure area will be the forecast key today
   a) highest pressures are over the Everglades into Miami
   b) big questions are; will the high move east, south, or remain over south Florida today and if it moves, how fast will it move
3) If the high moves slowly east today, the present NE winds will diminish and clock into the east and finish the day in a light SE-S wind
   a) am favoring this scenario - if this scenario plays out, the speed of the right rotation will depend on how fast the wind speeds fall
   b) in other words, wind directions will remain 020-050 as long as wind speeds are 8-12+ kts
   c) once wind speeds fall under 8 kts, then the wind directions will move quickly into the east
   d) in this scenario, winds will be very light this afternoon
   e) this scenario is only slightly more likely than the scenario in 6)
4) There are some clouds over the Gulf Stream – if these clouds approach the race course then look for a wind shift into the SE and S
5) The most unlikely scenario is for the high to hang around south Florida for another day
   a) low pressure over Alabama/Georgia will/should force this high S or SE today
   b) once again, winds will hold NE, 020-050, as long as wind speeds are 8-12+ kts
6) There is a small chance the high will move overhead during mid-day/afternoon
   a) winds will hold NE this morning and may edge a touch left, 030-050 moving to 010-040
   b) wind speeds will hold 8-12 kts for much of the morning, but start to drop as the winds edge left
   c) winds will become very light during the afternoon, wind speeds under 5/6 kts
   d) new wind will develop from the SW late in the day or at night
   e) the cumulus clouds over the Gulf Stream will remain there and may actually be pushed a little S
   this morning – in this scenario
7) Bottom-line, favoring NE winds diminishing and moving right late morning/early afternoon
   a) possible late afternoon SE-S wind with a few clouds returning
8) Winds at 1000-3000 ft aloft are very light and tend to the SW and W this afternoon
a) lots of wind shear between 500 and 1000 ft today

Wind Forecast
Wind directions are TRUE, wind speed in kts, time is EST

0900: 030-050/ 8-12
1000: 040-060/ 7-11
1100: 050-080/ 6-10
1200: 060-090/ 5-9
1300: 060-100/ 4-8
1400: 060-100/ 2-6
1500: 070-110/ 2-6
1600: 100-160/ 3-7
1700: 140-180/ 4-8
Weather…Sunshine may mix with a few clouds this afternoon. Highs in the low 70's.

Error factor…
1) Must wipe out the last 2 days – wind speeds will diminish this afternoon and hopefully not too quickly this morning
   a) wind speeds will be slow to increase again, once they diminish
   b) peak wind speeds will be 1st thing this morning and should not exceed 12 kts by 1000
2) Max right with wind speeds 8+ kts will be 070-080
   a) further right, wind speeds will be lighter than 8 kts
   b) new wind will form from 140-180 with a few clouds moving into the area during the 2nd half of the afternoon
   c) small chance we could get a left rotation, so watch out for that this morning
3) Max left with wind speeds 8+ kts will be 010-020

   a) new wind will form from the SW and no cumulus clouds from the Gulf Stream in this scenario

Thursday, January 23, 2003
1) We will have some good wind speeds today!
2) Low pressure will be intensifying rapidly between the Carolinas and Bermuda
   a) attached cold front will be quite strong and moving thru Key West between 1300 and 1500
   b) a few clouds and showers, but no squall line is expected at this time
3) Wind directions will be W and W-NW ahead of the cold front, but shift to a strong, cold NW to N-NW wind once the cold front passes
4) Wind speeds will start the morning 8-14 kts, but build to 14-20 kts just before the front passes
   a) wind speeds will be a cool, heavy, 20-30 kts, once the cold front passes
   b) seas will build quickly during the afternoon on the race courses exposed to a NW swell

0900: 260-280/ 8-14
1100: 270-300/12-18
1300: 280-310/14-20 and a bit squally
1500: bcmg 320-340/18-24, gusts 30
1700: 330-350/20-30
Weather…Partly to mostly cloudy, chance of a few showers during the afternoon. Highs in the low 70's, but falling to the low 60's by evening.

Regards, Ken Campbell

FROM: COMMANDERS' WEATHER CORP
154 BROAD ST, SUITE 1517
NASHUA, NH 03062
TEL: 603-882-6789, FAX: 603-882-6661
****

Please hold for the PRIVATE and EXCLUSIVE use of:
North U. Sailing Team.
****

Location: Key West Race Week – Key West, FL
Forecast for: Thursday, January 23, 2003
Outlook for: Friday January 24, 2003
Prepared: 0600edt Thursday, January 23, 2003

Summary…
Thursday, January 23
1) Low offshore South Carolina will be heading for Newfoundland and deepen to under 965mbs during the next 24-36 hrs
2) Strong cold front is approaching Tampa at 0400 and will reach the race courses between 1400-1600
3) Satellite animation shows patches of clouds approaching from the NW, but there is a solid area of lower clouds along and just after the cold front passes
   a) expecting only a spot shower or 2 mid-day/afternoon, no squall line
4) Prior to the cold front, winds aloft at 2000+ ft, are right of the surface winds
   a) clouds will be approaching from the W-NW and NW
   b) as a lower cloud approaches, there will be puff wind coming out of the cloud. This puff will most often come with a right turn
   c) less wind speed underneath the lower clouds
   d) prior the cold front, winds will not stick to the right, but will oscillate back to the left
   e) overall there will be a gradual right turn as the cold front approaches, but the breeze will be oscillating and puffy prior to the cold front's passage
5) Winds are currently a soft 240-280/ 4-8, but will slowly increase this morning, reaching a puffy, shifty 10-16 kts mid morning and up to 12-18 kts early afternoon
   a) overall trend in wind direction will be to the right, but remember there will be left oscillations prior to the cold front's passage
   b) will call for 250-280 to start the morning and 260-290 by mid-day. Clouds approaching from the NW will most frequently pull the winds right with a bit of pressure on the sides of the lower clouds
6) Winds will shift to 310-330 when the cold front passes. Temps will start to fall and the breeze will become a solid, cool, heavy breeze after the cold front passage
   a) band of solid, lower cloud cover should signal the cold front – no earlier than 1400
   b) wind speeds will increase quickly to 16-22 kts and by late afternoon it will be 22-26 kts and gusts to 30-32 – temps will fall to the low 60's by evening
7) NW swell may start to increase mid-day/early afternoon, prior to the cold front's arrival

Wind Forecast
Wind directions are TRUE, wind speed in kts, time is EST

0900: 250-280/ 9-14
1000: 250-280/10-16
1100: 260-290/10-16
1200: 260-290/11-17
1300: 270-300/12-18
1400: 270-300/12-18
1500: 270-300/14-20
1600: bcmg 310-330/18-24
1700: 320-340/22-26, gusts 30-32
General weather…Partly to mostly cloudy,

maybe a shower or 2 this afternoon. Highs 72-74, but falling to the low 60's by evening.

Error factor…
1) Oscillating, puffy breeze prior to the cold front
  a) lower clouds could pull the wind as far right as 300-310 prior to the cold front
  b) winds could be as far left as 240, especially when there is a lot of sunshine
2) Breeze will be soft this morning, but a much different, heavier wind, once the cold front passes
  a) wind speeds should not exceed 16-20 kts prior to the cold front's passage and could be as low as 8 kts or so this morning
3) Cloud signature is not good on early satellite picture, but I would be looking for a solid, low, grayish cloud area approaching from the NW this afternoon – this should be the cold front

Friday, January 24, 2003
1) Intense low pressure will be heading for Newfoundland while the cold front will be moving SE thru the NW Caribbean
2) Arctic high pressure will be over Arkansas during the morning and head for the Gulf coast Friday night
3) A cool N-NE wind will affect the Keys
a) winds mainly 20-30 kts during the morning, but will slowly diminish during the afternoon
  b) the strong, cool wind will bring a significant NW swell/sea state into the western Keys

0900: 350-010/20-25, g 30
1100: 360-020/20-25, g 30
1300: 010-030/18-24
1500: 010-030/16-22
1700: 020-040/14-20
Weather…Partly to mostly sunny with highs near 60.

Regards, Ken Campbell

FROM: COMMANDERS' WEATHER CORP
154 BROAD ST, SUITE 1517
NASHUA, NH 03062
TEL: 603-882-6789, FAX: 603-882-6661

****

Please hold for the PRIVATE and EXCLUSIVE use of:
North U. Sailing Team.

****

Location: Key West Race Week – Key West, FL
Forecast for: Friday, January 24, 2003
Prepared: 0600edt Friday, January 24, 2003

Summary…
Friday, January 24
1) Strong cold front is now in the NW Caribbean and moving SE
2) Arctic high pressure is over Arkansas this morning and will reach N Mississippi this evening
  a) high will be over Alabama/Georgia by this time tomorrow morning
3) Very windy and cool to start the morning
  a) sustained wind speeds are near 25 kts and many gusts to 30-32 kts
  b) wind directions are fairly steady near 360
  c) temps are in the 40's and will only warm to near 60, so this will be a heavy, cool breeze today
4) Many stratocumulus clouds in the Gulf of Mexico, just west of Key West
  a) if winds edge a little left, then the clouds will move into the Keys with the strongest winds in the blue skies in-between the clouds
  b) I don't think we will see a left rotation, but a slow right rotation, especially this afternoon
  c) however, winds at 1000-3000 ft will always

be a little left(5-10 degrees), and stronger than the surface winds, until the 2nd half of the afternoon. This means the puffs/gusts will tend to favor wind directions a little left of average until the 2nd half of the afternoon when the winds start to settle down

   d) watch the clouds, if they move onto the race course, then expect a left shift to 345-350

5) Wind speeds will be slow to diminish this morning

   a) still looking at sustained wind speeds of 20-25 kts thru 1200 and gusts to 30-32 thru 1000

   b) wind speeds will ease down to 16-22 kts by 1500 and 14-18 kts by evening

6) Wind directions will favor 360-010 this morning and mid-day, but remember the puffs will favor a little left of this range

   a) as wind speeds diminish, wind directions will edge right, but 020-030 will be max right by evening

7) Wind directions are coming off the Florida Peninsula, but there will be some swell from the Gulf of Mexico, especially on the courses west of Key West

Wind Forecast
Wind directions are TRUE, wind speed in kts, time is EST

0900: 355-010/22-26, gust 30-32
1000: 355-010/20-26, gust 30-32
1100: 355-010/20-26
1200: 360-015/20-25
1300: 360-015/18-24
1400: 360-015/17-23
1500: 005-020/16-22
1600: 005-020/15-20
1700: 010-030/14-18

General weather…Maybe a few clouds this morning otherwise sunny and cool with high near 60 this afternoon.

Error factor…
1) Strongest winds will be 1st thing this morning – question is, how fast will winds diminish

   a) don't think wind speeds will ever get lower than 12-14 kts today, even by dark

   b) conversely, wind speeds may stay 20 kts or higher thru mid-afternoon

2) It will be a slow process for wind speeds to diminish today

   a) the rate of right rotation will be linked to how fast wind speeds diminish – if wind speeds fall faster than forecast (unlikely), then winds could move right 1-2 hrs faster than forecast

   b) max right today will be 030 regardless of the rate of rotation

3) Winds aloft are 5-10 degrees left of surface – puffs will favor lefties this morning thru early afternoon

   a) if clouds move onto the race course then wind directions could set up 5-10 degrees left of forecast

   b) max left will be 340-350 – if it occurs, it will occur during the morning

Regards, Ken Campbell

Appendix B
Block Island

FROM: COMMANDERS' WEATHER CORP
154 BROAD ST, SUITE 1517
NASHUA, NH 03062
TEL: 603-882-6789, FAX: 603-882-6661

****

Please hold for the PRIVATE and EXCLUSIVE use of:
North U. Sailing Team.

****

Race area:	**Vicinity Block Island**
Forecast for:	**Sunday, June 22, 2003**
Outlook for:	**Monday, June 23, 2003**
Forecast prepared:	**0630EDT Sunday, June 22, 2003**

Summary…

a) Another lousy weekend in Southern New England as low pressure surface and aloft is located south of Cape Cod this morning.

b) This system will show only a slow movement to the east today so do not look for much improvement.

c) Winds around this low are running NNE –NE across the race course with observations at 6am showing :

    a. Block Island 040 at 8kt

    b. Newport 020 at 13 kts

    c. Westerly RI 020 at 8 kts.

    d. Buzzards Bay Buoy – 020 at 17 kts g 19

d) Expect the strongest breeze this morning with tendency for the breeze to drop off some this afternoon.

e) If the low shifts eastward the gradient wind may tend to shift left to more northerly midday and this afternoon and likely drop off some to 8-14 kts.

f) But if the low makes a loop westward which is also a possibility winds may drop to less than 8 kts and direction then becomes a little more uncertain and could see it remain NE or possibly shift right some.

g) Forecast will call for 020-040 breeze this morning tending to shift left to more northerly by early afternoon but again confidence not as high this afternoon.

    a. Speeds may come down a few kts this afternoon.

8) Clouds, drizzle and a few showers around today will prevent any thermal influence on the breeze

Time

0900   020-040/ 12-17

Could see some gusts to 20 kts at times this am

1000   020-040/ 12-17

1100   020-040/ 12-17

1200   010-030/ 11-15

Winds begin to drop off but how much a little uncertain.

1300   010-030/ 10-14

Could see winds drop off to less than 10 kts if low loops westward – then direction could shift right instead of left.

1400   360-020/ 9-13

1500   360-020/ 8-12

1600   360-020/ 8-12

1700   350-010/ 8-12

General weather…Cloudy with some drizzle and a few showers today. Highs 65-70

Error factor...
a) Lots of wind this morning but uncertain what wind does this pm.
b) Fell most likely it will shift left some and diminish with max right 040 this morning and max left this afternoon at 340 with speeds above 10 kts.
c) But if low loops westward then could see breeze shift right possibly as far as 090 but will get light likely < 8 kts if it does that.
d) Peak winds this morning 20 kts but tending to diminish some this afternoon.

Monday, June 23, 2003
a) Expect low to be not far from Cape Cod at sunrise tending to drift eastward and weaken further during the day.
b) Associated upper low will be just to west of surface low .
c) This likely will mean not much gradient wind for racing tomorrow .
d) Direction will favor light NW in the morning with speeds under 10 kts.
e) Expect cloudy skies to continue and can not rule out a brief shower early in the day but tendency during the day will be for brightening

skies and perhaps some sunshine in the afternoon.
f) Amount of sunshine will determine what wind does.
g) If decent sun develops winds will shift into the W then SW with speeds likely in the 6-10 kt range in the afternoon.
h) If skies remain cloudy could see breeze remain NW-W with speeds more in the 5 kt range midday and afternoon.
i) Either way do not expect strong winds and could see a light and shifty day unless skies show definite clearing trend by late am.

0900: 320-340/ 4-8
1100: 300-320/ 4-8
1300: 230-260/ 4-8
1500: 220-240/ 6-10
1700: 220-240/ 6-10
General weather...Cloudy with a brief shower possible early then brightening midday with skies becoming partly sunny in the afternoon. Highs around 70.

regards, Tom Mattus

FROM: COMMANDERS' WEATHER CORP
154 BROAD ST, SUITE 1517
NASHUA, NH 03062
TEL: 603-882-6789, FAX: 603-882-6661
✱✱✱

Please hold for the PRIVATE and EXCLUSIVE use of:
North U. Sailing Team.
✱✱✱

Race area:	**Vicinity Block Island**
Forecast for:	**Monday, June 23, 2003**
Outlook for:	**Tuesday, June 24, 2003**
Forecast prepared:	**0630EDT Monday, June 23, 2003**

Summary…Going to be a tough day to get sailing breeze today.
a) Pesky low pressure still centered not far from Nantucket this morning.
  a. Wind at Nantucket 2306 kts at 6am
  b. Marthas Vineyard 360 at 5 kts
  c. Block Island 280 at 7 kts
  d. Newport 330 at 4 kt
  e. Buzzards Bay Buioy 360 11-14 kts.
b) So the weak and weakening low is just NW of Nantucket but circulation is weaker than yesterday.
c) Expect the surface low may take a loop southward this morning then drift eastward this afternoon as the associated upper low tracks eastward as well.
  a) Breeze may tend to shift right to more northerly by midday as this happens
d) But then as the low shifts eastward this afternoon this is going to leave behind very little gradient wind to work with across the race course as high pressure now near West Virginia remains nearly stationary.
e) Models are showing strongest gradient wind now (6-10 kts) with tendency to drop to less than 5 kts midday.
  a. Direction is W-NW early today then shifts right to more N by noon but as the gradient diminishes direction becomes very uncertain this afternoon ranging from NE to SE
  b. Could even see light S-SW develop if there is some sunshine.
f) But speeds are going to be light and confidence in direction this afternoon is below avg as wind speeds likely will be < 6 kts.

g) Radar shows band of rain interior Southern New England drying up but cloudiness with the upper low will be slow to move out today.
  a. There may be some breaks at times this am and midday but real good clearing may not arrive until late pm or eve.
h) This with limited sunshine any thermal will be slow to get going.
i) In addition it may get quite warm this pm interior Southern New England 80 or better and this air
 as it moves out aloft over the colder water will add a stabilizing affect to the atmosphere which would be another negative on developing a significant thermal this afternoon.
j) So not optimistic about sailing breeze this afternoon with most consistent breeze likely this morning and winds this afternoon possibly light and flukey.

Time
0900   280-300/ 6-10
1000   300-320/ 6-10
Expect a slow shift right as low makes loop southward
1100   320-340/ 6-10
1200   340-360/ 5-9
1300   360-020/ 4-8
Confidence in direction this pm below avg
1400   020-080/ 3-6 Winds may get light and flukey
1500   080-140/ 3-6
1600   140-200/ 4-8
1700   220-240/ 6-10

General weather…Cloudy to partly cloudy today, clearing this evening. High around 70

Error factor…
a) Most uncertainty this afternoon with best hope for breeze in the 6-10 kt range will be if quality sunshine develops midday.
b) This may help to develop some thermal breeze from S-SW but do not count on it as with warmer aloft atmosphere will be quite stable.
c) So tough to give limits this afternoon.
d) This morning max left likely early at 270 with tendency to shift right with max right by noon 360.
e) Peak wind this morning at 10 kts but likely less than 8 and possibly < 6 this afternonn

Tuesday, June 24, 2003
a) High pressure remains anchored in West Virginia with low now moving out into central Atlantic.
b) Little gradient wind expected between the 2 systems across the race course.
c) Will likely have to rely on thermal influence to develop significant wind midday and pm hours.
d) Breeze could be light and variable in the morning then becoming light S-SW around noon freshening some to 6-10 kts in the afternoon.
e) Will need good sunshine for this to happen though but expect any low clouds and fog to burn off by mid morning.

0900: Variable 3-6
1100: Variable/ 0-5
1300: 180-200/ 4-8
1500: 200-220/ 6-10
1700: 200-220/ 6-10
General weather…Any areas of low clouds and fog burning off then hazy sunshine warm with highs in the 70s. (Near 90 over the mainland)

regards, Tom Mattus

FROM: COMMANDERS' WEATHER CORP
154 BROAD ST, SUITE 1517
NASHUA, NH 03062
TEL: 603-882-6789, FAX: 603-882-6661
✳✳

Please hold for the PRIVATE and EXCLUSIVE use of:
North U. Sailing Team.
✳✳

Race area:	**Vicinity Block Island**
Forecast for:	**Tuesday, June 24, 2003**
Outlook for:	**Wednesday, June 25, 2003**
Forecast prepared:	**0630EDT Tuesday, June 24, 2003**

Summary…Summer finally arrives next few days with typical onshore SW expected.

a) Weak back door front that moved thru yesterday midday(late am NE of the Island and early pm SW of the Island) and shifted winds into the NE-E has dissipated this morning.
b) Not much gradient wind left behind across Southern New England.
c) Low pressure now well off the E and high pressure still anchored over the lower Ohio Valley will not have much influence on the breeze across the race course today.
d) So will need the thermal influence to generate the wind.
e) Satellite pictures show some patchy middle cloud cover nearby mainly to the E and there is some thin ground fog over the mainland.
f) But expect skies to be mainly sunny today and this should generate thermal breeze beginning midday.
g) Block Island showing light W drift at 5am and calm at 6am but expect not much breeze until 11-12am when onshore should become better established.
h) Thermal should develop first near the mainland beaches and work its way out to Block Island around noon.
i) Direction will favor initially a 180-200 direction then perhaps a right shift to 200-220 early afternoon.
j) Speeds likely only 4-8 kts by noon but should build to 8-10 kts by early afternoon.

Time
0900	variable/	0-5
1000	230-250/	2-5
1100	200-220/	3-6

Onshore develops near the mainland beaches
1200	190-210/	5-9

Sea breeze works its way out toward Block Island
1300	200-220/	6-10
1400	200-220/	7-11
1500	200-220/	7-11
1600	200-220/	6-10
1700	200-220/	6-10

General weather…Partly to mostly sunny today. Hot over the Mainland with temps 85-90 inland but cooler 70s offshore

Error factor…
a) Looks like mainly a thermal influence to the breeze today and feel once it develops direction should be mainly 200-220.
b) Max left 190 and max right 230.
c) Until the breeze develops not much wind favoring W-WSW but could be variable as well thru 10 am.
d) Could see breeze shift slowly left from 260 to 200-220 this morning but do not think speeds get above 6 kts until direction is in the 200-220 range.
e) Best breeze likely toward the mainland beaches where it could get briefly above 10 kts at times this pm.

Wednesday, June 25, 2003

a) Models showing more gradient wind .

b) Low pressure strengthens out in the central Atlantic and combined with high pressure now near eastern Tennessee/western NC there is more wind gradient from the NW-W across Southern New England.

c) So likely a W-WNW gradient breeze early possibly as high as 6-10 kts.

d) Then with sunshine expect the breeze to shift left to WSW-SW(220-240) onshore second half of the morning.

e) Speeds likely in the 8-12 kt range midday and afternoon and could be puffy and shifty near shore With the very hot temps inland and cooler temps over the water.

0900: 260-280 6-10
1100: 240-260/ 7-11
1300: 230-250/ 8-12
1500: 220-240/ 8-12
1700: 220-240/ 8-12

General weather…Mostly sunny. highs in the 70s over the water . (Near 90 over the mainland)

regards, Tom Mattus

FROM: COMMANDERS' WEATHER CORP
154 BROAD ST, SUITE 1517
NASHUA, NH 03062
TEL: 603-882-6789, FAX: 603-882-6661

****

Please hold for the PRIVATE and EXCLUSIVE use of:
North U. Sailing Team.

****

Race area:	**Vicinity Block Island**
Forecast for:	**Wednesday, June 25, 2003**
Outlook for:	**Thursday, June 26, 2003**
Forecast prepared:	**0630EDT Wednesday, June 25, 2003**

Summary…

1) High pressure over western North Carolina this morning will not move much during the today

2) A weak upper level disturbance over western NY state continues to weaken as it heads ESE

   a) this has some patchy cloudiness with it, but that should be about it as it comes across this afternoon

   b) slight chance it may kick off an isolated tstm interior areas this afternoon, but doubtful for you to have any over the water

3) Winds still look to be on the light side today, but hopefully a little more than yesterday

4) Current observations show light air around with breeze mainly W around 5-6 kts

5) Very warm air aloft again today (around 2000-3000 ft) and this will tend to keep the atmosphere stable with not a great deal of mixing

   a) consequently, light winds expected again today

6) That weakening trough coming across may tend to want to bring the breeze a little more right today

Time
0900	270-290/ 4-8
1000	260-280/ 5-9
1100	250-270/ 5-9

Thicker haze will favor breeze lighter and more right

1200	240-260/ 5-9
1300	230-250/ 6-10
1400	220-240/ 7-11
1500	220-240/ 7-11

Patchy cloudiness or a tstm to north will favor wind more right

1600	220-240/ 8-12
1700	220-240/ 9-13

General weather…Partly to mostly sunny today. Hot over the land with temps in the 90s but upper 70s offshore

Error factor…

a) winds still on the light side and more clouds and haze will keep then lighter and further right
b) max right of 300 – this most likely mid to late morning while max left of 200 and this most likely after 3-4pm
c) stronger puffs from the left
d) breeze may edge right for a time this morning due to the weak trough coming thru then back this afternoon
e) lightest flow mid morning to midday
f) watch for occasional right turns (240-260) this afternoon, especially close in to shore

Thursday, June 26, 2003

1) High pressure continues over the SE US
2) Front will be far to the west, across Lake Michigan to central Illinois and then to Oklahoma
3) Will have another summery day with hazy sun, hot and humid conditions
4) Winds light WNW early in the morning then becoming SW and SSW later morning and afternoon
5) Think better chance of a little stronger breeze during the course of the afternoon

0900: 280-300/ 6-10
1100: 240-260/ 6-10
1300: 220-240/ 8-12
1500: 210-230/ 9-13
1700: 210-230/ 9-13
General weather…Mostly sunny. Highs 90s over land, upper 70s over the water

regards, George Caras

FROM: COMMANDERS' WEATHER CORP
154 BROAD ST, SUITE 1517
NASHUA, NH 03062
TEL: 603-882-6789, FAX: 603-882-6661

****

Please hold for the PRIVATE and EXCLUSIVE use of:
North U. Sailing Team.

****

Race area:	**Vicinity Block Island**
Forecast for:	**Thursday, June 26, 2003**
Outlook for:	**Friday, June 27, 2003**
Forecast prepared:	**0630EDT Thursday, June 26, 2003**

Summary…

1) Another summery day today
2) High pressure from north of the Bahamas extending west to another high over Georgia
3) Cold front well to the west of the area, from Lake Michigan to Missouri and to northern Texas
4) The front will be moving east, but will remain well west of the area thru the day
5) Big upper ridge continues over the eastern

US from Alabama north into central NY state
6) This is bringing a light NW gradient and stable conditions over the region
7) Some patchy cloudiness is moving across early this morning, but this should pass east of the area next couple of hours and will have hazy sunshine, very warm (hot inland) conditions
8) Very light air observed at this time (Block Island reporting calm)
9) With ridge of high pressure at all levels,

expect a light air day

10) Look for a light WNW flow early to mid morning with the breeze tending to back slowly during the late morning and afternoon

    a) wind speeds of 5-10 kts mid morning thru midday and hopefully 7-13 kts afternoon with a more WSW flow during the afternoon

11) More haze the more right the breeze

Time

0900	280-300/ 4-8

any patchy clouds exiting

1000	270-290/ 6-10
1100	270-290/ 5-9

Thicker haze will favor breeze lighter and more right

1200	250-270/ 5-9
1300	240-260/ 6-10
1400	240-260/ 7-11
1500	220-240/ 9-13

Thicker haze will keep wind more right and lighter

1600	220-240/ 9-13
1700	220-240/ 9-13

General weather…A few early clouds then hazy sunshine today. Highs in the 80s (90s over the mainland)

Error factor…

1) thick haze will favor the breeze light, low end of range, and also further right

2) max right of 320 this morning, especially early, max right of 270 this afternoon

3) max left of 210 and this most likely late day

4) stronger puffs from the right this morning, from the left mid aftn on

Friday, June 27, 2003

1) Cold front will be across central NY state to PA and then to the western Carolinas

2) Front will be coming east during the day

3) It will be another warm and humid day

4) Tighter gradient and atmosphere becoming more unstable

5) Expect more in the way of wind with SW flow of 8-12 kts morning, 12-16 kts aftn

6) May have some scattered showers and tstms developing in the afternoon – most likely after mid afternoon

0900: 240-260/ 7-11
1100: 220-240/ 9-13
1300: 210-230/11-16
1500: 200-220/12-16
1700: 210-230/11-15

General weather…Variable cloudiness, hazy, and humid with a chance of scattered showers and tstms aftn and evening. Highs around 80, warmer over the mainland

regards, George Caras

**FROM: COMMANDERS' WEATHER CORP
154 BROAD ST, SUITE 1517
NASHUA, NH 03062
TEL: 603-882-6789, FAX: 603-882-6661**
✳✳

Please hold for the PRIVATE and EXCLUSIVE use of:
North U. Sailing Team.
✳✳

Race area:	**Vicinity Block Island**
Forecast for:	**Friday, June 27, 2003**
Forecast prepared:	**0630EDT Friday, June 27, 2003**

Summary...

1) Cold front now across west-central NY state and extends south to the western Carolinas and then to northern Louisiana
2) The front will be coming east during the day, likely reaching the area very late this afternoon/early evening (5-8pm)
3) Should be able to do a little better on the breeze today, still pretty light this morning, though as we continue with some very warm air aloft
   a) however, we should get some better mixing ahead of the front and the airmass should be getting more unstable during the day – notice the "shoulds"
4) Radar shows some scattered showers along and ahead of the front, but nothing very impressive with echoes widely scattered and no tstms noted
5) With the daytime heating, however, the airmass will become more unstable, and this should generate some more showers and some tstms this afternoon and evening
   a) strongest activity likely to be N and W of you
6) Forecast will call for a SW to SSW flow around 6-11 kts this morning, 11-16 kts this afternoon

Time

0900	200-220/ 5-9
1000	210-230/ 6-10

Wind as far left as 190

1100	210-240/ 7-11
1200	210-230/ 9-13

More sun, wind may be a little higher

1300	210-230/10-15
1400	220-240/11-16
1500	220-240/11-16

Watch for the chance of a few showers/tstm –wind may move hard right ahead of a shower or tstm

1600	220-240/11-16
1700	220-250/10-15

General weather...Hazy sun with increasing clouds this afternoon. Some pockets of fog early this morning as well. Chance of a few scattered showers or a tstm after mid afternoon into the evening. Most likely after 3-4pm. Highs in the upper 70s (low 90s over land)

Error factor...

1) max left of 180 and max right of 250 – max right excludes near any tstm in which case could see a brief hard right shift to 300 then backing as the cell moves past
2) highest wind speeds this afternoon
3) more sun this morning, then breeze more likely to be a little further left
4) more clouds/thick haze/patchy fog will favor the wind being right and also keep the breeze lighter

regards, George Caras

Appendix C
Chicago Verve Cup

FROM: COMMANDERS' WEATHER CORP
154 BROAD ST, SUITE 1517
NASHUA, NH 03062
TEL: 603-882-6789, FAX: 603-882-6661

****

Please hold for the PRIVATE and EXCLUSIVE use of:
North U. Sailing Team.

****

Event: Chicago Verve Cup
Forecast for: Friday, August 15, 2003
Outlook for: Saturday, August 16, 2003
Prepared: 0630CDT Friday, August 15, 2003

Summary…Looks to be a light air day
1) Lots of high pressure around today, mainly south of the area
2) General high pressure over southern West Virginia extends west to another high over Arkansas then to another over NW Texas
3) Cold front up over Hudson Bay to Lake Winnipeg and then west from there
  a) weak trough out ahead of the main front from near NW Minnesota extending to NW South Dakota
4) This will remain well west of the area today
5) At upper levels, big ridge of high pressure is also the dominant weather feature
6) May have some pockets of low clouds/patchy fog around early this morning then a mix of clouds and sun thru the day
  a) it will be very warm and humid and will likely have a lot of haze around
  b) should pop some puffy cumulus clouds around noon and during the afternoon
  c) some will build a fair amount, but do not think they will produce a shower, although can't rule it out 100%
7) Gradient is westerly, not particularly strong, so main question is whether it will be strong enough to preclude a seabreeze
8) Forecast will call for a light W flow to develop early this morning, speeds 5-8 kts
9) Flow likely to become light and variable late morning midday and may flop between a WNW breeze and occasionally an ESE breeze
  a) the most likely onshore will come with lots of sun and in close to the shore – haze may be a limiting factor here
  b) better chance of staying with a WNW to WSW flow more than 2-3 miles out with light and variable in between
10) Wind speeds mainly 5-9 kts much of the day, may become more SW and tend to come to 7-11 kts after 3pm

Wind forecast
Wind directions are TRUE, wind speed in kts, and time is CDT

Friday, August 15, 2003
Time
0900   260-290/ 5-9
1000   270-290/ 6-10
Patchy low clouds/fog lift
1100   280-300/ 5-9
1200   290-310/ 5-8   Hazy
1300   Var 4-7
1400   270-290/ 5-8
Variable clouds –haze –more haze, less chance

of onshore flow
1500   270-290/ 5-9
1600   230-250/ 6-10
1700   220-240/ 7-11

Weather…Patchy low clouds and some fog early to mid morning then variable amounts of clouds and sun, hazy, very warm, and humid. Highs 87-90.

Error factor…
1) more sunshine will favor the breeze trying to become onshore, at least for a time, late morning thru mid afternoon
   a) direction may be 140-160 at times and this most likely would be close in to shore and not extend out more than 2 miles
2) may have a zone of light and variable wind between the trying to develop onshore and the gradient west flow more than 2-3 miles out – again, will need decent sun to get any onshore and haze may help prevent this – more haze, better chance of a W flow
3) more clouds/haze favor breeze of 250-310 – furthest right mid morning thru early afternoon
4) stronger puffs will be from the right
5) May be able to tell by watching if any clouds linger near shore (onshore developing) or move from a general W to E direction – west gradient holding

Saturday, August 16, 2003
1) Expect the cold front to be from Lake Huron to north-central Lake Michigan then west to southern Minnesota
2) The front will be heading SE
3) Expect the front to move across the area during the late afternoon
4) There could be a few showers or tstms along and ahead of the front – most likely occurring after mid afternoon
5) Winds mainly W much of the day, shifting to the N late day – may have a brief wind shift to the N ahead of a shower, prior to the real front

0900: 250-270/ 6-10
1100: 240-260/ 8-12
1300: 270-290/ 6-10
1500: 300-320/ 8-12
1700: 340-360/10-15
Weather…Variable clouds with a few showers and tstms possible afternoon/evening. Highs near 90

Regards, George Caras

FROM: COMMANDERS' WEATHER CORP
154 BROAD ST, SUITE 1517
NASHUA, NH 03062
TEL: 603-882-6789, FAX: 603-882-6661
✳✳

Please hold for the PRIVATE and EXCLUSIVE use of:
North U. Sailing Team.
✳✳

Event: **Chicago Verve Cup**
Forecast for: **Saturday, August 16, 2003**
Outlook for: **Sunday, August 17, 2003**
Prepared: **0630CDT Saturday, August 16, 2003**

Summary...

1) Cold front in northern Lake Michigan is moving steadily south and should arrive between1600-1900LT today

   a) there is a band of clouds preceding and accompanying the cold front, along with a few scattered showers/thunderstorms

   b) the showers/t-showers will be moving from NW to SE, but the cold front will be moving N to S, down the Lake

2) Currently, the winds are W and NW, 260-300 with wind speeds of 8-14 kts

   a) the higher wind speeds favor further right

3) These winds will likely continue thru mid-morning with a slight right trend, so

   a) will call for 270-300/ 8-14 to start the morning

   b) 290-320/ 8-14 late morning. Wind speeds may peak at 10-16 kts this morning, but

   c) the best puffs by late morning will be coming off the shoreline with lighter winds the further offshore you go

4) NW gradient wind will become lighter during the afternoon and this may set the stage for a weak sea breeze again today

   a) will call for 290-330 at 4-8 kts by 1300/1400 and this may lead to wind holes 1-4 miles offshore

5) Will call for a soft 060-100 sea breeze to develop offshore by 1400/1500 – wind speeds only a few kts, 4-7 kts

   a) sea breeze will be weak and tend to flop around between 060 and 120, maybe 130

   b) always keep in mind the potential for a shower/thunderstorm arriving from the NW

this afternoon – this will kill the sea breeze and turn the winds back into the NW

   c) if there are low and middle clouds over the Lake, then the winds will be light and shifty NW

6) Finally, late afternoon, the cold front will pass. It could be after 1700, but this forecast will show a wind shift into the NE, 020-050 and wind speeds increasing to 10-16 kts

   a) there may not be a shower or thunderstorm preceding this front, but there will be some lower clouds arriving from the N, which will herald the arrival of the cold front and the NE winds

   b) remember, the cold front could arrive after 1700cdt

Wind forecast
Wind directions are TRUE, wind speed in kts, and time is CDT

Saturday, August 16, 2003
Time
0900   270-300/ 8-14
1000   280-310/10-16
1100   290-320/ 8-14
Highest wind speeds will be coming off the shoreline and lighter winds further offshore
1200   290-320/12-6
1300   290-330/ 8-4
If skies are sunny over the Lake then watch out for wind holes and then a NE-E sea breeze
1400   060-100/ 4-7
1500   080-120/ 4-7
1600   090-130/ 4-7

1700   Bcmg 020-050/10-16   The cold front will be accompanied by some lower clouds coming in from the N

Weather…Partly sunny, chance of a shower or thunderstorm during the afternoon. Hot with highs 90-94. Turning cooler late day or evening with a band of clouds and a NE change arriving.

Error factor…
1) Could see wind speeds as high as 16 kts this morning with the W-NW wind
  a) wind speeds could reach as high as 16/17 kts with the cold front passage late today or this evening, but
  b) on the low end, noon to 1600+, could be a near repeat of yesterday
2) Max left this morning will be 260
  a) max left with the sea breeze will be 040-050
  b) max left with the cold front passage will be 010
3) Winds max with the wind speeds 8-10+ kts this morning will be 330-340
  a) max right with the sea breeze and wind speeds 6+ kts will be 120-130
  b) cold front could have winds as far right as 050-060
4) Exact timing of all the weather features is far from certain, but
  a) hanging with 280-320 wind until wind

speeds fall under 8 kts – remember, the best puffs will be coming off the shoreline mid and late morning
  b) watch out for wind holes/weak NE-E sea breeze as soon as wind speeds fall under 8 kts, but any
shower/thunderstorm moving into the area from the NW could kill off the sea breeze and return the winds to NW before the NE change/cold front arrives

Sunday, August 17, 2003
1) Cold front will be in the Ohio Valley and tending to sag southward
2) High pressure over Ontario will be moving slowly SE
3) NE gradient wind could be as high as 16-18 kts at times during Sunday
  a) this breeze will also produce a 3-4 ft sea
4) Lots of sunshine and cooler temps with highs along the Lake front, 75-80

0900: 030-050/10-16
1100: 040-060/14-18
1300: 040-060/14-18
1500: 040-060/13-17
1700: 030-050/12-16
Weather…Sunny with highs 75-80.

Regards, Ken Campbell

FROM: COMMANDERS' WEATHER CORP
154 BROAD ST, SUITE 1517
NASHUA, NH 03062
TEL: 603-882-6789, FAX: 603-882-6661

****

Please hold for the PRIVATE and EXCLUSIVE use of:
North U. Sailing Team.

****

Event: **Chicago Verve Cup**
Forecast for: **Sunday, August 17, 2003**
Prepared: **0630CDT Sunday, August 17, 2003**

Summary…
1) Cold front is now in southern Illinois and it will continue to sag slowly SE
2) High pressure is centered in eastern Ontario and will drift S over the next 24 hrs
3) A few patchy clouds early this morning, but it should trend to mostly sunny later this morning
   a) a few cumulus clouds will develop over the land later this morning and afternoon
4) Winds are currently 110-140/ 8-16 with the highest wind speeds found offshore 1-2+ miles
   a) this wind is pretty far right for where the high is located, so I expect it to drift left, especially
   when the thermal/sea breeze influence develops
5) Forecast will call for 100-130/ 8-14 kts to start the morning – on average, the top mark will see the higher wind speeds early this morning
6) Will drift the winds a little left late morning/mid-day, with winds becoming 070-100/ 8-12 kts by mid-day. The offshore wind speeds will be similar to the inshore wind speed
7) Will hold the winds 070-100 for much of the remainder of the day except for a slight rightie late in the day – not certain about the rightie, just keep an on eye out for it
   a) wind speeds may freshen a kt or 2 later during the 1st half of the afternoon and if wind speeds
   stay in the 9-14 kt range then the right turn is less likely
   b) if wind speeds fade a little bit, then look for the right turn
   c) wind speeds may actually average a little

higher at the bottom mark versus the top mark during the afternoon

Wind forecast
Wind directions are TRUE, wind speed in kts, and time is CDT

Sunday, August 17, 2003
Time

Time	Wind
0900	100-130/ 8-14
1000	090-120/ 8-13
1100	080-110/ 8-12
1200	070-100/ 8-12
1300	070-100/ 8-12
1400	070-100/ 9-13
1500	070-100/10-14
1600	070-100/ 9-13
1700	080-110/ 8-12

Weather…Mostly sunny with highs 75-80.

Error factor…
1) I could see wind speeds 1-2 kts higher than forecast, but wind speeds should not exceed 15/16 kts
   a) this should be a fairly solid wind, once it fills in at the shoreline later this morning
2) Max right should be 140-150 and that will occur early this morning
   a) overall winds should shift left during the morning/mid-day
3) Max left should be 060-070, but would not be surprised to see the whole wind package set-up 10-20 degrees right of forecast

Regards, Ken Campbell

Appendix D
Big Boat Series - San Francisco Bay

FROM: COMMANDERS' WEATHER CORP
154 BROAD ST, SUITE 1517
NASHUA, NH 03062
TEL: 603-882-6789, FAX: 603-882-6661

✳✳

Please hold for the PRIVATE and EXCLUSIVE use of:
North U. Sailing Team.

✳✳

Race area: **Big Boat Series- San Francisco Bay**
Forecast for: **Thursday, Sept 11, 2003**
Outlook for: **Friday - Sunday, Sept 12-14, 2003**
Prepared: **0700PDT Thursday, Sept 11, 2003**

Summary...

1) High pressure along the Oregon/Nevada border will build and move SE today

2) This will force the thermal trough, now over the central Valleys, to move westward – it may touch the eastern Bay for a time late morning thru early afternoon

    a) winds will be light NE-E on the side of the thermal trough and it is possible for some of this breeze to touch the eastern-most Bay

    b) it is unlikely that the thermal trough will move further west today since its' arrival on the Bay will be about the same time the sea breeze will be starting to get cranked up

3) Currently, the winds are very light S-SW and SW, 200-240/ 3-6

    a) over the eastern Bay, winds are basically calm

4) Despite the sunshine and quickly warming temps – high temps will reach 82-86, there will be little wind this morning and early afternoon

    a) there may be puffs from the W-SW and W from 1000-1300, but these will most likely fade out before ever reaching east Bay

    b) the lightest winds will see the winds back into the S, but over east Bay, east of Treasure Island, there could be a few puffs from 040-100 thru 1300

5) Around 1300-1400, there will be more an effort for the sea breeze to fill in

    a) the sea breeze will come from the Golden Gate into the Bay and for the 1st hour or so, this breeze will have a tough time penetrating east Bay

    b) will call for 220-250/ 8-14 kts by 1500 and 230-260/10-18 kts by late afternoon

    c) East Bay will see the lightest winds and the wind direction will be further left

Wind forecast

Wind directions are TRUE, wind speed in kts, and time is LT

Thursday, Sept 11, 2003
Time
0900   200-240/ 3-6
1000   Light/variable
Could be a few westerly puffs near City Front and a few NE-E puffs east of Treasure Island. This light/variable battle will likely continue thru early afternoon
1100   Light/variable
1200   Light/variale
1300   Light/variable
1400   210-250/ 5-10
Best breeze will be from the City Front westward. Sea breeze will tend to fade and back further east

1500   220-250/ 8-14
1600   220-250/ 9-15
1700   230-260/10-18

General weather...Sunny with highs in the mid 80's.

Error factor...
1) Think it will be a real struggle to get a reliable wind thru early afternoon – could be puffs from both the SW and NE-E
   a) don't think we will see a hot, strong NE-E wind, but it could briefly touch 6-8 kts 1100-1300. Strongest winds will be coming off the eastern shoreline
   b) sea breeze may come in strong this afternoon, but it may take until 1600/1700 for it to cover the Bay with 10-12+ winds
   c) could see a sea breeze up to 18-20 kts for a while late afternoon/early evening
2) Max left with wind speeds 8+ kts will be 200-210
   a) lighter winds could fade out completely and back into the NE
3) Max right with wind speeds 8+ kts will be 260
   a) any NE-E wind will range from 040-100 if wind speeds exceed 6 kts

Friday, Sept 12, 2003
1) Cold front moving thru eastern Washington and Idaho will move more east than SE
2) Morning high pressure will be over Nevada/Utah, but strong high pressure will build into Oregon/ Washington during the afternoon
3) Thermal trough will be in the area again – probably right over the Bay during the morning
a) once again, a struggle for wind, especially 1000-1400edt
4) Will play a light NE-E wind to start the morning then light/variable conditions until the 2nd half of the afternoon.
   a) sea breeze probably won't exceed 16 kts during the afternoon

0900: 040-100/ 4-8
1100: light/variable
1300: light/variable
1500: 200-240/ 5-10
1700: 230-260/ 8-16

Weather...Hazy sunshine and warm with highs near 85.

Saturday, Sept 13, 2003
1) Strong high pressure will move more E than SE – it is heading for Idaho/eastern Montana
   a) if the high were to move into northern Nevada then strong, hot easterlies could occur, but that is unlikely at this time
2) Thermal trough will be right over the Bay during the morning and early afternoon
   a) will play a gentle easterly to start the morning
   b) sea breeze will be slow developing, probably not arriving until the 2nd half of the afternoon
3) Sea breeze could touch 16-20 kts, but that won't occur until 1700/1800
   a) overall, another tough day waiting for wind
0900: 040-100/ 5-10
1100: Light/variable
1300: Light/variable
1500: 200-230/ 4-8
1700: 230-260/14-20
Weather...Patchy low clouds early otherwise hazy sunshine and warm again, highs 80-85.

Sunday, Sept 14, 2003
1) High pressure now well established in Wyoming
2) Low pressure trough a little further west and may be offshore.
3) Could be weak low just west of the Bay.
4) This favors weak wind gradient across the Bay with breeze light SE-S in the am.
5) With decent sunshine will see SW take over again in the afternoon.
6) Some concern that marine layer may be thicker and slower to break up – if this occurs wind speeds will be 10-12 kts or less all day
0900: 140-180/ 3-6
1100: 160-190/ 2-5
1300: 190-210/ 4-8
1500: 200-220/ 7-11
1700: 210-240/10-14

Weather...Low overcast with some fog early morning then partly sunny afternoon. Highs in the low 70's.
Regards, Ken Campbell

FROM: COMMANDERS' WEATHER CORP
154 BROAD ST, SUITE 1517
NASHUA, NH 03062
TEL: 603-882-6789, FAX: 603-882-6661
****

Please hold for the PRIVATE and EXCLUSIVE use of:
North U. Sailing Team.

****

Race area:	**Big Boat Series- San Francisco Bay**
Forecast for:	**Friday, Sept 12, 2003**
Outlook for:	**Saturday, Sept 13, 2003**
Prepared:	**0700PDT Friday, Sept 12, 2003**

Summary…

a) Weather map shows high pressure west of Washington State with extension SE into the Great Basin(Utah)

b) Thermal trough once again is located along the coast from San Francisco southward.

c) This again is resulting in very light winds across the Bay tending to favor offshore NE-E in spots.

   a. Golden Gate 050 at 3 kt at 6am

   b. Angel Island 020 at 5 kt at 6am

   4) Expect the thermal trough will hold across the Bay this morning and this means very light winds likely variable in direction and probably not enough for racing.

d) So will have to wait for onshore thermal to become established and this likely will not be until early afternoon.

e) Satellite pictures and surface observations show clear skies so expect a good deal of sunshine and temps will be warm again like yesterday well into the 80s.

f) Look for light NE-E breeze for a time early this am then likely uncertain winds <6 kts late am to around noon.

g) Then look for onshore to develop 1-2 pm

h) Initial direction may start from S-SSW(180-220) in the Bay then may have a tendency to shift right as onshore from the Bridge works its way into the Bay from west to east late pm(3-5pm)

   a. As this more westerly breeze comes in it may have more speed with it perhaps to 12-15 kts.

   b. Otherwise initial thermal breeze may only be in the 6-12 kt range.

Wind forecast

Wind directions are TRUE, wind speed in kts, and time is LT

Thursday, Sept 11, 2003

Time
0900   040-080/ 3-6
No consistent breeze expected this am.
1000   040-080/ 0-5
1100   Light/variable
1200   Light/variale
1300   Bcmg 180-220/ 4-8
Thermal begins to develop in the Bay
1400   200-220/ 6-10
1500   220-240/ 8-12
More westerly breeze begins to works its way into the Bay from west to east along with some increase in strength. Strongest breeze likely closer to City Front with lighter winds to the east second half of afternoon.
1600   230-250/ 10-14
1700   230-260/12-18

General weather…Sunny with highs in the mid 80's.

Error factor…

a) Once thermal becomes established feel max left will be 180 at the start then a gradual shift right 1-3pm possibly as far as 240 with peak wind likely 12 kts thru 3pm.

b) After 3pm watch for a further shift right perhaps as far as 260 as westerly comes in from Golden Gate Bridge.

   a) Peak wind with this surge likely 15-18 kts but not until 4-6pm

Friday, Sept 12, 2003

a) Looks to be a similar situation as Thursday.

b) Thermal trough holds tough along the coast with strong Pacific high pressure well to the NW.

c) Strong NW-N to 30 kts well offshore but with thermal trough near the Bay look for light E-NE drift early am.

d) Then variable winds late am before thermal gets established again early afternoon.

e) Look for gradually increasing thermal and slight shift right second half of afternoon.

0900: 040-090/ 3-6
1100: light/variable
1300: becoming 180-220/ 4-8
1500: 210-240/ 6-10
1700: 230-260/ 12-18
Weather…Hazy sunshine and warm with highs mid 80s

Regards, Tom Mattus

FROM: COMMANDERS' WEATHER CORP
154 BROAD ST, SUITE 1517
NASHUA, NH 03062
TEL: 603-882-6789, FAX: 603-882-6661

****

Please hold for the PRIVATE and EXCLUSIVE use of:
North U. Sailing Team.

****

Race area: Big Boat Series- San Francisco Bay
Forecast for: Saturday, Sept 13, 2003
Outlook for: Sunday, Sept 14, 2003
Prepared: 0700PDT Saturday, Sept 13, 2003

Summary…

1) Weather map shows Pacific high pressure centered out near 40n 140w this morning with another high pressure cell in northern Washington State

2) Thermal trough continues well established along the California coast from San Francisco southward

3) But there is a light westerly breeze at Golden Gate and Angel Island this morning as opposed to light   NE at this time yesterday so the trough may be a little further east this morning than yesterday.

  a) But much stronger NW breeze though is still well offshore beyond 100 miles again to the W and N.

4) Models are showing the thermal trough hanging tough much of the day and with another hot day expected (temps near 90) likely will expand out over the Bay by midday today.

5) So do not look for much wind this morning with direction likely becoming lt/variable mid to late am.

6) Watch for the thermal breeze to develop noon-1pm initially from SW at 6-8 kt then freshen to 10-15 kt by mid afternoon.

7) Because of the hot air over the colder water this will be a very stable situation and may lead to considerable puffiness to the breeze and also some wind shear from top of mast down.

8) Direction could also oscillate with these fluctuations in speed from 230-240 in lighter air to 250-260 in stronger puffs.

Wind forecast
Wind directions are TRUE, wind speed in kts, and time is LT

Saturday, Sept 13, 2003
Time
0900   250-270/ 3-6

No consistent breeze expected again this am.

1000   Light/variable
1100   Light/variable
1200   Light/variale

Thermal begins to develop in the Bay noon-1pm

1300   Bcmg 220-240/ 4-8
1400   230-250/ 6-10
1500   240-260/ 8-12

Winds may be quite puffy and shifty mid to late pm

1600   240-260/ 10-14
1700   240-260/11-15

General weather…Sunny and very warm with highs 85-90.

Error factor…
1) Main concern is that westerly breeze now holds this am and freshens midday quicker than shown.
2) Do not think that will happen but it could.
3) However with the air hot and stable over the water still do not favor winds above 15 kt
4) Also with the stable air watch for considerable puffiness to the breeze with lulls as low as 8 kts.
5) Winds likely again mostly in the 230-260 range this afternoon but directions may shift left toward 230 in the lulls and favor further right toward 250-260 in the stronger puffs.

6) One of these days the thermal will struggle to get above 8-10 kt and that could be today but more likely it will be tomorrow.

Sunday, Sept 14, 2003
1) Thermal trough actually expands westward out over the ocean.
2) So again looks quite light with uncertain direction in the morning.
3) Thermal breeze will kick in again early afternoon.
4) But with hot/stable air over the water again the strength of breeze will be limited and this could be a day when the breeze struggles to get above 10 kt

0900: 040-090/ 3-6
1100: light/variable
1300: becoming 220-260/ 4-8
1500: 220-260/ 6-10
1700: 220-260/ 8-12

Weather…Mostly sunny and very warm with highs 85-90.

Regards, Tom Mattus

FROM: COMMANDERS' WEATHER CORP
154 BROAD ST, SUITE 1517
NASHUA, NH 03062
TEL: 603-882-6789, FAX: 603-882-6661
****

Please hold for the PRIVATE and EXCLUSIVE use of:
North U. Sailing Team.
****

Race area: Big Boat Series- San Francisco Bay
Forecast for: Sunday, Sept 14, 2003
Prepared: 0630PDT Sunday, Sept 14, 2003

Summary…

1) Big Pacific high pressure west of 140w this morning with another good sized high now over Colorado
2) The 2nd high has been heading SE and will continue to do so today
3) Weak upper trough over the Pacific Northwest to west of the area is edging east
4) Thermal low over the northern Baja and extending north along western California to northern California
   a) the trough will edge east today as the big high over Colorado moves SE
5) Will not be as warm today as we have had a influx of some low clouds very close by and seeing the marine layer developing up to around 1000 ft
6) Satellite imagery shows low clouds and some fog patches very close to the area and may see some in and out of the region this morning
   a) latest sounding data also shows the NE flow of yesterday thru much of the column now has been replaced with NW flow up to almost 3000 ft
7) With the high moving east and having less influence, looking for a return to a more pronounced onshore flow, especially this afternoon
8) Currently, seeing light WSW flow which will drop off for a few hours this morning, then fill in late morning-midday and pick up this afternoon
9) If the high is a little stronger or slower moving, then winds will be lighter and WSW flow will be slower getting going
10) Will go with light winds much of the morning then increasing WSW winds to 13-18 kts by 1pm and maybe 15-19 kts by 4-5pm

Wind forecast

Wind directions are TRUE, wind speed in kts, and time is LT

Sunday, Sept 14, 2003

Time	
0900	240-260/ 5-9
1000	220-240/ 6-10
1100	220-240/ 7-11 Some chance winds light and variable
1200	230-250/ 9-13
1300	230-250/12-17 Patchy clouds keeps wind further left
1400	230-250/12-17
1500	230-250/13-18
1600	240-260/14-19
1700	240-260/15-20

General weather…There could be some patches of low clouds at times thru mid morning then, partly to mostly sunny and much cooler.   Highs in the low 70s

Error factor…

1) Will go with the high continuing east and allowing the onshore flow to fill in
2) max left of 220 and max right of 270
   a) favor 230-250 late morning on
3) may see some oscillations in the wind early this morning, but sounding data shows onshore flow should take over
4) highest winds after 2pm
5) more low clouds will tend to keep the breeze down and more left, while brighter sunshine will bring winds further right
Regards, George Caras
